The Scudamores

THREE OF A KIND

The Scudamores

THREE OF A KIND

Michael, Peter and Tom Scudamore
with Chris Cook

RACING POST

First published in Great Britain in 2018 by
Racing Post Books
27 Kingfisher Court, Hambridge Road, Newbury, Berkshire, RG14 5SJ

10 9 8 7 6 5 4 3 2 1

A catalogue record for this book is available from the British Library.

ISBN 978-1-910497-72-2

Designed by J Schwartz & Co.
Cover designed by Samantha Creedon

Printed and bound in the UK by CPI Group (UK) Ltd, Croydon, CR0 4YY

www.racingpost.com/shop

I remember my father once saying that the worst thing that could happen to any young farmer was to get a broken-down racehorse on his property. If he got him right and he won once, it would ruin him for life, so Father said – *Geoffrey Scudamore 1906–82, Founder of a racing dynasty*

To Oxo and Arthur without whom this book would not have been written

CONTENTS

FOREWORD

There can never be another book quite like this one. For while families often pass interests from generation to generation, no clan has ever, or will ever, match the Grand National role of the Scudamores. Between 1952 and 2018 (the year of this book), father Michael, son Peter and grandson Tom have logged up 44 rides in what remains the most watched annual sporting event in the calendar.

Michael's victory on Oxo in 1959 meant that to his dying day he was introduced as 'Grand National winning jockey'. But, as you will read, alongside this headline tale comes the deeper one of how three generations handled the challenge, fulfilment and traumas that come with the life of a professional steeplechase jockey in a changing world where risk is becoming a fearful word.

It's much more than seeking a test for youthful daring, although that is wrapped in there at the beginning. With the Scudamores, it's a call from the heartland. They hail from Herefordshire where sending half a ton of thoroughbred at a five-foot fence has been a root sport for two centuries now. It's what Michael's father Geoffrey returned to from a German prison camp, what Michael was destined for all the way to Grand National and Gold Cup glory, what drove Peter to his eight mould-breaking jockeys' championships and what has now inspired Tom to become one of the most accomplished and articulate jockeys to ever sling a leg across a saddle.

They are indeed three of a kind. As a jockey I revered Michael for his skill and unflustered mindset. As a man I cherished his avuncular friendship and treasure a photo of jumping the second last alongside him on my first ride at the Cheltenham Festival – he won, and I faded to fourth! As a writer I chronicled Peter's career from long-haired teenager to hard-eyed veteran, and as a TV presenter it was a personal thrill to do an interview with a 16-year-old Tom after he had ridden his first winner at Cheltenham.

He was in a hurry as he was already late for his English A-Level class at Cheltenham College. By happy chance Chris Haslam, the English teacher, was an eager punter and the hour was spent not on Thomas Hardy but in reliving the winning moments on the video. As Peter relates in his introduction, it was that same enthusiasm which got Chris to sit Michael down and put his memories on to tape and so keep them for posterity when Michael left us in 2014.

The importance of doing that should not be lost on any family in the land. For its perspective links us with a world that is lost and whose details are quite unimaginable today. In the Scudamores case it was in many ways a simpler, slower, stricter deal, but there was still fun aplenty and glory to be sought. Best of all, horses were at the heart of it, and these pages glow with the warmth of the relationship that jockeys will always have with the four-legged athletes whose efforts they share and whose dangers they face.

The jump jockey's changing room is a very special place. For while no-quarter given is the rule on the track, off it you have the camaraderie of knowing that you are just one ride away from calamity. It means that the old hands envy the young their youth but worry at the agonies the game will soon most certainly inflict upon them. The young smile at the struggles of age but envy the achievements and experience. This book takes you right to the heart of this, but it also links to something else very touching in these often-intemperate times – the love and admiration the family members all share.

In 1988 Mike Rutherford captivated the nation with his hit record 'The Living Years' and its haunting opening lines: 'Every generation blames the one before.' Thirty years on, three generations of heroic and independent minded Scudamores respectfully disagree.

BROUGH SCOTT MBE

INTRODUCTION

Work began on this book six years ago, in the autumn of 2012, when my father sat down for a series of interviews with Chris Haslam, a friend of the family who had taught English at Tom's school. They chatted for hours on end, kicked around a lot of subjects and Chris taped it all. I'm so grateful to him for the idea and for having the initiative to make it happen.

Two years later, my father and mother died within days of each other. Anyone who has lost much-loved parents will understand what I went through then and the loss I've felt since. It was a long time before I felt able to return to this project and look it in the face.

But now, thanks to Brough Scott, Liz Ampairee and others at Racing Post Books, my family and I have been able to finish the job that my father and Chris Haslam started. Chris Cook, who writes about racing for the *Guardian*, joined in to do interviews with me and Tom and some others. He's taken all our stories and jokes and passionate arguments and set them out in a way that hopefully any reader can enjoy. If you'd turned up for Sunday lunch at our stable in Herefordshire, this is the sort of thing you'd have heard.

Like me, Chris had a famous father who is no longer with us. His dad was Robin Cook, a Labour MP whose love of horse racing became well known. I was a bit taken aback, as we walked round before the start of a race at Newton Abbot in the late 1980s, to see Robin standing on the other side of the rails with his two young sons. Our politics were not the same, but Robin and I met a few times after that and found we had a lot in common; he showed me round Parliament and I gave him lunch at Hereford races. I'm delighted Chris has been working with us on this book, and we've both had a lot of fun, talking about races that happened 30 years ago.

On behalf of my sons, Michael and Tom, I'd like to thank everyone who has helped, including Jane Clarke, a historian of Aintree, and Ben Cox at Racenews, who kept us right about historical details. Edward Gillespie, who ran Cheltenham so well for so long, also gave up time for us, as did Sophia Dale, who still works there. Stan and Elain Mellor gave Chris a warm welcome. Ivor Herbert reminisced about Linwell over a long lunch. Many thanks to Martin Pipe and Lesley Gillies, who gave their time generously, and to Bruce Dowling and Joe Rendall at the BHA for answering our questions.

Thanks also to many old friends and colleagues who, like me, used to frequent the weighing room but are no longer allowed in, who shared memories of riding in jump races: John Francome, Hywel Davies, Jonjo O'Neill, Steve Smith Eccles, Neale Doughty, AP McCoy, Richard Dunwoody, Ron Barry, Bob Davies, Eddie Harty, Stan Hayhurst, David Mould, Brendan Powell and Gerry Scott.

I'm so lucky to be sharing my life with Luce, who has been supportive and interested all the way through. I think she 'gets' the Scudamores. My father used to repeat a lot of his stories by the time she knew him, but she always loved hearing them, because she loves horses and steeplechasing and she wants to know more about how it used to be. This book has been a labour of love that she's embraced as much as I have.

Finally, I'd like to thank you and anyone else who has ever shown an interest in jump racing, especially if you've ever stood by the rail and cheered on a wet, wintry Wednesday at Wetherby. It is, of course, the greatest game there is, and I hope it will continue to prosper.

PETER SCUDAMORE
Arlary, Perth and Kinross, June 2018

1

OXO TO ARTHUR

Saturday March 21, 1959. Grand National day. Michael Scudamore wakes in a Southport hotel where much of the jump racing community is based for the races at Aintree. The jockeys like Southport for its old Turkish baths on the promenade, where many of them spend the morning, trying to boil themselves down to the weights specified for their mounts that day.

MICHAEL SCUDAMORE

I wasn't doing light, but it was something to do in the morning, take your mind off it, and all the others were there as well and taking the mickey out of each other. We came back to the hotel and Mary said, 'Willie wants to see you in his room.'

'Willie' is the trainer Willie Stephenson, who has booked the 26-year-old Scudamore to ride Oxo in the National. Stephenson is known as a hard man, easily angered, and his jockey is uneasy about being summoned just three hours before the big race.

MICHAEL

I said, 'What does he want?'

She said, 'I don't know.'

I thought, 'Oh, bloody hell. I bet he's going to tell me this horse doesn't run.' Well, he was up there with a bottle of bloody champagne. I couldn't believe it. 'Have a drink of this,' he said.

Saturday April 8, 2017. Grand National day again. Peter Scudamore, son of Michael, is taking a more abstemious approach to the preparation of One For Arthur, trained by his partner, Lucinda Russell. Scudamore and Russell wake in a camper van at the racecourse, the better to supervise care of the horse and to keep tabs on the state of the racing surface, which is drier than they had hoped.

PETER

The trouble is, Aintree's fantastic, but you get carried away with the partying. Everybody else is up there to have a good time. We were there to welcome the horse on the Friday night, and Luce was able to see him in the morning and have a pick of grass with him. You feel you're concentrating on the horse instead of humans, if you're there. If you're out in Liverpool, you're concentrating on owners. So I felt good about that.

More than half a century apart, both Scudamores have good reason to fancy their chances. Michael first made Oxo's acquaintance earlier that season when Stephenson called him up for a ride at short notice.

MICHAEL

I'm lying in bed, half past six in the morning. I'm not going racing anyway, day off. Phone rings. Willie Stephenson. I'd only had one or two rides for him.

'What you doing?'

I said, 'I'm in bed.'

'Bloody get down to Lingfield and ride one for me.'

I said, 'All right, thank you very much,' because I thought the world of him – he was a big trainer.

'I won't be there. Shooting.'

So I got down to Lingfield and I won on him. And I can always remember coming in; I chucked the saddle on the table and I said to one of the valets and the jockeys round me, 'I wouldn't mind riding that round Liverpool.'

Fifty-eight years later, One For Arthur has revealed himself to be a Grand National contender by slogging through the Warwick mud ahead of 19 rivals. Since that midwinter afternoon, Peter and Lucinda have been determined to do anything that might improve his chance at Aintree three months later.

PETER

After Warwick, we said to each other, 'Right, we've got a Grand National horse. We've got this one chance, let's do everything, leave no stone unturned. Let's get the security, get the right stable lads riding it.' Luce has mapped out the plan, from January to April, what work he's going to do, with a spare week in it, in case something happens. We're milking this. We're going to get to the Grand National, we'll get a lot of publicity, we'll get another horse out of it. People were asking: 'Is he going to win?'

All I could say was, 'I've never had this horse in better condition. He's never worked better, his blood's right, his trachea wash is right and he's 100 per cent sound.'

For both Scudamores, the Aintree race has a resonance beyond the obvious appeal of its fame and prize money. Michael, taking part for the ninth time, is on his way to setting a record by riding in 16 consecutive Nationals, a record that will last into the following century.

MICHAEL

When I was a kid, the great legend locally was a man called EWW Bailey, Eric Bailey. He'd been in the 1937 National on a mare called Pucka Belle. We were brought up on Pucka Belle and EWW Bailey, and they were only third.

I always remember the first National I rode in, I was so overcome by it all. Well, not overcome, so proud to be there. And I looked up in the stand, and it was packed, and I said to myself, 'I hope I don't stand up there for 20 years!'

It doesn't last for seconds, but when you jump out of that gate and go down that old Melling Road, 40 of you, and the thunder of hooves, it's something out of history. You think: 'Oh, what a thing this is!'

Peter has a more complex relationship with the National, having failed to win it during his time as a jockey, with a couple of notable disappointments along the way. He is keenly aware of what victory would mean for everyone at Russell's yard, bearing in mind there has been just one Scottish winner in the National's 180 years. But One For Arthur is not Peter's only interest in the 2017 race. His son, Tom, is to ride Vieux Lion Rouge, an impressive winner at Haydock in February.

PETER

It's a funny feeling. The owners said to me beforehand, 'If you cheer Tom before Arthur, we'll take Arthur away . . .' – jokingly. But blood is thicker than water, isn't it? It's your son, you can't help wanting him to win. But then your professional thing kicks in.

Oxo and One For Arthur are both eight, not too young for National glory, but younger than 80 per cent of post-war winners. Both are obviously built for Aintree, being big, robust-looking animals. Even in a time when most steeplechasers are sturdy types, Oxo stands out, dwarfing some of his rivals as they circle in the paddock. Both are to be ridden by jockeys who have only just recovered from broken bones. Michael rarely spoke of his injuries in public, but often told Tom of how he nearly missed the ride on Oxo.

TOM

He broke his collarbone and had to go and see Mr Tucker, a doctor in London who specialised in patching up sportsmen. It was touch and go until about a week before. I think he wore a figure-of-eight brace for a while. Jockeys used to wear those after collarbone injuries, hoping it would help you to not break it again, but the trouble was, if you had another fall, you could end up breaking something else instead, like your wrist.

One For Arthur seems sure to be without his regular jockey when Derek Fox breaks a collarbone and *a wrist four weeks before Aintree. Incredibly, he recovers from both injuries with days to spare, helped by the Injured Jockeys Fund's rehab team at Jack Berry House in Malton. Pensively, Peter eyes Fox's ride on an outsider in a 16-runner race an hour before the National.*

PETER

I was watching to make sure he finished in one piece. You can't help but look to see who's available if something goes wrong. Richard Johnson was on standby, so we knew that, if Derek did have a fall, I would have rushed in to try and get him before anybody else.

But all is well and the National is next. At this late stage, tactical discussions are brief. Fox knows his mount well and Peter trusts him. Michael's chance to chew over his plan with Oxo's trainer is cut short when Stephenson rushes away to have another bet on the horse. In any case, the pre-race plotting proves of little use when the tape goes up. Stephenson's plainly expressed desire is for Oxo to be restrained in rear to preserve his unproven stamina, but the big horse travels and jumps so well that he is soon among the leaders.

MICHAEL

Willie said, 'Hold him up, wait with him,' worrying about him getting the trip. So we're in mid-division going to Becher's the first time. Four or five fell there and interfered with others, and I came out second or third.

Decades later, One For Arthur is supposed to hold a prominent early position but just isn't quick enough and soon finds his comfort zone behind most of his 39 rivals. Peter watches the race with the horse's owners, Fraser and Belinda McClung, Colin Dempster and Deborah Thomson. He wears a dark blue racehorse-themed tie that belonged to his father.

PETER

I definitely told Derek to be handier, but I knew they'd go fast, and on that ground he'd struggle to lay up. I'm standing there, hoping two things: that he doesn't get hurt, and that he doesn't make a fool of you. Of course, you have this northern mentality, your horse is three points longer in the betting than if you were a southern trainer. We know we're no worse than anybody else.

The 1959 race is the last National before TV cameras arrive at Aintree. For Fifties jockeys, there are just two ways of seeing themselves on a horse: looking at their reflection in a shop window or watching the Pathé newsreel at the cinema when it shows highlights of the National. It's a consoling thought for Michael Scudamore as he and Oxo continue to be much further forward than planned.

MICHAEL

Gerry Scott was in front on Surprise Packet. Tim Brookshaw was near me on Wyndburgh, and we three were bowling along. We jumped the water and we're going out into the country. Brookshaw looks across to me: 'Hey, mate! We'll be in the bloody pictures, anyway!'

At the same stage, Peter is beginning to wonder if anyone will notice One For Arthur is in the race.

PETER

Oh Christ, I wish he was a bit closer. The only thing giving me hope was that Derek wasn't pushing him. You thought, there's a couple behind him.

Every National winner needs their share of luck. The decisive moment in 1959 comes with about a mile to run, when Tim Brookshaw's right stirrup shatters.

MICHAEL

We landed over Becher's and Gerry fell, which left Tim and me upsides. Going to the next one, he said, 'I've bust me fucking iron.' I didn't say anything. It just went through my mind, 'Thank God for that, because I don't mind if you fall off.' He was a good friend of mine, but still . . .

Brookshaw kicks his other foot out of its stirrup and keeps a precarious balance on Wyndburgh over the remaining eight fences.

TOM

Grandad looked across and he saw that Tim had no leathers. He thought, 'That's a bloody slice of good luck – I'd better kick on here. He didn't think, 'Oh, poor Tim. Good effort.' And he never talked about: 'Oh, that was bad luck on Tim' – no mention of that. But he did always put a lot of importance on having good gear, making sure you'd checked your leathers and everything else. He always made a point of that.

MICHAEL

Anyway, it left me in front. Funnily enough, I just went about my business. I never thought about, 'What if something goes wrong?' I was just riding the race and jumping and going. I never thought it was any other race.

While Becher's tips the scales in Oxo's favour, it nearly marks the end of One For Arthur's challenge. As he lands over the fence, the big horse displaces his soft palate and is suddenly short of breath. The moment of drama is invisible to any spectator, but Fox knows something is amiss by the disconcerting noises coming from his partner's mouth.

LUCINDA RUSSELL

Derek said later, he was thinking, 'What am I going to do?' And the horse jumped the next fence and righted himself again. He suddenly came back on the bridle.

PETER

They do sometimes put themselves back like that. Carvill's Hill did it in the Welsh National.

Peter has, by this stage, lost track of One For Arthur and is admiring the ride given by his son to Vieux Lion Rouge, fourth over the Canal Turn on the final circuit, travelling powerfully.

PETER

I love the way Thomas sets off on the outer and gradually gets across. I don't think if you put John Francome or AP McCoy on this horse, it would have finished an inch closer. That's all you can ask, is do the best you can.

But all Tom's efforts are in vain as Vieux Lion Rouge begins to run out of gas at the turn for home. Meanwhile, One For Arthur has made relentless progress. Most spectators notice him for the first time, fully eight minutes into the race, as he looms up on the outside of the leading pack with two fences to take.

PETER

From the Canal Turn onwards, I'm watching Thomas – Thomas is there with a right chance. And then I see him drop back, and as he drops back, Arthur comes up. I think to myself, 'Arthur's going to be second to Blaklion!'

By the home turn in 1959, Michael has no thought of finishing second. Just a handful of rivals are still chasing him and the closest rider has no stirrups. All Oxo has to do is keep jumping.

MICHAEL

Going to the last, I thought, 'I hope he meets this right.' He met it all bloody wrong.

A famous photograph shows Oxo landing after the final fence, his hind legs thrown in the air by the collision with its take-off side. His significant heft is pitching onto his forelegs, and his jockey is a vertical line, clutching the buckle of his reins, grimacing at the prospect of the pair tumbling forward onto the turf. But somehow Oxo finds a leg and keeps running, his momentum seemingly unchecked.

MICHAEL

I could hear Brookshaw coming at me all the way up the straight, shouting. He was a great man for shouting. There was one race we could hear him at Valentine's when we were in the stands.

Brookshaw is gallant but defeated as Oxo prevails by a length and a half. It is a cosy margin, but not as comfortable as One For Arthur's.

PETER

From the second-last, it was obvious he was going to win. It was the most extraordinary feeling, that you could actually take the moment in from there. I know things can go wrong, but as long as it wasn't a Devon Loch or something disastrous, you could take it all in. I'd never really done that in racing before, not at such a high level. It was a great ride. John Francome said Derek would have won on any of the first four, riding as coolly as that.

MICHAEL

You see all these footballers nowadays, they throw their arms around each other and kiss each other. This was just a great relief. You've done a job, and it's the biggest job you've ever done. It's relief, and you didn't feel like throwing your arms round anybody.

Seeking a good view of the race, Peter has smuggled himself and two owners of One For Arthur into a hospitality box belonging to backers of Nicky Henderson's powerful Lambourn stable.

PETER

So the race goes off and who falls at the first? Nicky Henderson's. Such is racing: he goes at the first and we win. You felt quite conscious that you were in someone else's box who's had a terrible experience, and yet you're celebrating so much. Not that it damps it in any way.

TOM

I wasn't aware of it until I crossed the line, and then I've looked across and realised that One For Arthur's gone and done it. I think he might have gone past me as we turned into the straight, going down to the second-last. I was so pleased for Dad and Luce. They'd lost some horses. They weren't meeting expectations that they'd set themselves. Dad was getting fed up with not being able to compete at that level, that it was getting harder racing in the north. That's what gave them so much pleasure as well – they felt they were doing it for the north and Scotland. It was just phenomenal. You forget what an incredible race it is, and to be part of all that, and to see them do that first-hand, you're just so proud for them.

While Derek Fox got nothing but praise for his ride on One For Arthur, Michael Scudamore was told off by Stephenson in the winner's enclosure for supposedly having hit the front too soon.

MICHAEL

I found him about three o'clock in the morning at the Adelphi, sitting at a table. I went and sat with him. 'Did you mean what you said?'

'Of course I did. I had a lot of money on him!'

PETER

Luce went to the horse; I went to the winner's enclosure – I had no idea what was going on. My little granddaughters were there and I wanted them to be part of it. I really wanted to make sure they remembered, and that's why I took them up to the ceremony when we got the cup. Then we went to the owner's room and had a drink out of it. It was midnight by the time we got home.

MICHAEL

Did winning the National change my life? I often wonder about that. Kept the bank manager a bit happier. I don't think it did, really. I'd won a Gold Cup, I was pretty well known. The only thing, I think people knew me on the street. Even now, only yesterday or the day before, I was introduced to somebody as a Grand National-winning jockey.

PETER

Before the National, I was the most famous person in the yard, by a long way. And now . . . We went the other day to a Randox thing – they sponsor the National. Nobody wanted to speak to me. They wanted to speak to Lucinda, they wanted Arthur and there was Derek. I'm now fourth in line in the yard, and you treat Arthur almost as a celebrity! Before, he was just an ordinary horse, just a slow, old steeplechaser that was giving somebody a dream. Now he really is the dream.

I'm so grateful to him for what he's done. How do you say thank you? There's something about that horse that is so attractive to humanity, that sees the bravery of that horse. So many of these horses have traits that we want to see in humanity, and the National takes that to another level, because of the history. There's still people coming up to us and saying well done. We went to France the other day, and the lady at the ticket queue said: 'Lucinda! Well done on winning the Grand National!'

TOM

Grandad never mentioned either the National or the Gold Cup, what it meant to him to win it. You know he's immensely proud of it, and it was a big thing for people locally that he won the Grand National. There was a big sportsman's dinner put on for him in Hereford. That gave him a real sense of achievement. I remember we had a National winners' evening and Dad compered it. They had Hywel Davies, Neale Doughty and Grandad. He was so good at those sorts of things. That's where you'd see the pride – just the way he'd stick his little chest out. Michael Scudamore: Grand National-winning jockey – that's what he was, and it's quite an epitaph to have, isn't it?

MICHAEL

We went home and we had to go to a little racecourse the next day called Wye. It was a mile round, and I know which I was more frightened of, riding in a novice chase round there with 21 runners. So you couldn't really do too much partying. I fell in that novice chase, I remember that.

From Oxo to Arthur, from Aintree to Wye, the Scudamores have been a constant presence in jump racing for more than 70 years. They have won its greatest prizes, shared in its joys and its tragedies, ridden some of its best horses and ridden against the others. They have lived the sport, and the hardy, cheerful spirit of steeplechasing is in their bones.

2

BEING A SCUDAMORE: GEOFFREY AND MICHAEL

'I prayed to God, hard, and he looked after me' – *Geoffrey*

Those who take part in races over fences are liable, common sense tells us, to take other risks and make decisions that would not appeal to everyone. So Richard Dunwoody undertakes a 48-day trek to the South Pole along a route that defeated Shackleton, John Oaksey does a 200-foot bungee jump at the age of 63 and, after the outbreak of the Second World War, a point-to-point rider called Geoffrey Scudamore quits farming, in which line of work he had been protected from conscription, and signs up for the Royal Air Force Volunteer Reserve.

On the night of July 9, 1943, Geoffrey took part in his first bombing mission, as a wireless operator on a Halifax plane that flew out of RAF Lissett in East Yorkshire, heading for Gelsenkirchen. As it returned over Belgium, the plane was hit by flak and crash-landed at Mont Rigi, close to the German border. Geoffrey was 37. His son, Michael, back home in a sleepy Herefordshire village, was a week short of his 11th birthday.

MICHAEL

The pilot said, 'We've been hit. We'd better bail out.' He probably didn't put it quite like that . . . Anyway, a few minutes later, he said: 'Don't bail out!' He'd got them all round the hatch to bail out. He said, 'We're too low.' And he put it down in a wood. And they all survived.

It is a tale to make anyone shiver, a moment when sudden death must have seemed probable, any joy at survival being quickly overtaken by the grimness of being an enemy combatant in Nazi-controlled land. Separated by time and distance, Scudamore chattily relays the details of the crash, which he must first have heard more than 60 years earlier.

MICHAEL

When you come to think of it, hitting the top of the trees would slow it down a lot. If you're coming in like that [steep], you've got no chance. But if you're losing height gradually . . .

Apparently the pilot said afterwards he could have got away, but he said the crew were so badly hurt that he stayed with them until the Germans came and picked them up. And he did write a letter to Mother, saying how proud he was that he had someone like Father on the crew, or words to that effect.

An extract from Flight Lieutenant Bridger's letter was sent to the families of crew members. 'Those who were conscious showed courage and fortitude of the first order,' he wrote, 'particularly in the case of Sgt Scudamore, who received facial injuries and lost a lot of blood.' Geoffrey had acted 'in a way that made me proud to be a fellow Englishman'. A son of gunner Gilbert Kendrick, whose legs were broken in the crash, credits Geoffrey with pulling his father clear of the wreckage.

MICHAEL

I often wonder what would have happened if he'd never come back and Mother would have been left with two children. Anyway, he survived the crash and was a prisoner for two years.

He was a hard man, a tough man, and I always remember he once said to me, 'The most frightened I was, we were lost in the fog and all the bloody works had gone, couldn't get it back, navigation and so on.' And he said, 'I prayed to God, hard, and he looked after me.' And they got back. That was a training mission.

When he was taken prisoner, he was missing for six weeks. You didn't know, didn't have a clue, until a woman rang up, a complete stranger, said she'd been listening to German radio and thought she'd heard his name mentioned as a prisoner. And that was the first thought we'd ever got that he might be all right. So it was six weeks of hell, really, for Mother. Anyway, the air people confirmed it soon after.

You're a kid of ten. I remember going to school and wanting to tell somebody. I wasn't taking any notice of lessons; I never did anyway. Then a couple of years later, the headmaster was taking us at school: he said, 'I've had bad news. My son Jack has been reported killed.' He said, 'Don't worry, I can take it. I'll carry on teaching.' He went on for 20 minutes, then he said: 'I can't go on.' And he went home to his house. I always remember that. It sank in then.

Geoffrey spent the last two years of the war in Stalag IV-B, one of the larger POW camps in Germany, about 30 miles north of Dresden. The year after his arrival, he was joined by Johnny Bullock, who would eventually ride Nickel Coin to win the 1951 Grand National.

MICHAEL

Johnny was taken prisoner at Arnhem. We rode together quite a bit after the war, Johnny and I. Father knew him before. Johnny always said Father saved his life – he gave him a piece of soap and some toothpaste and a bit of chocolate. He was a funny little man, he used to get very down.

Eventually, Stalag IV-B was liberated by the Soviet army, though the British and American prisoners were not freed for another month. A general food shortage meant they were, however, allowed out on day release to forage for supplies in the area. Geoffrey had clearly not forgotten the life he had left behind and planned to resume.

MICHAEL

He went to a farmhouse one day and found a brand new saddle. So he said, 'I'll take that home!' He put it in a bag and, of course, when he got back to camp, they all thought he'd got a ham in there. Anyway, this saddle, I used it quite a lot – I can't remember what winners I rode on it, but it was about 7lbs made up, with the girths and the stirrups on. I don't where it is now, it got broken up so many times. By the time I'd finished with it, it wasn't the same saddle.

Geoffrey was among those who escaped the camp after the Russians arrived, and made his way on foot to the American troops at Leipzig, a journey that included crossing the girders of a broken railway bridge. Eventually, he found his way back to Llangarron, between Ross-on-Wye and the Welsh border, with his new racing saddle under his arm.

MICHAEL

He came back and started up a small point-to-point stable. He rode quite a lot of point-to-point winners. I always used to think he was a bit of a legend, locally. Everybody seemed to know him. So we farmed and he had a few point-to-pointers and worked hard.

Michael turned 14 in July 1946, a year after the war had ended. It was a landmark that proved to be the end of his schooling and the start of some very long days, digging up and storing potatoes, while also enjoying a kind of village life that might now sound ideal to many.

MICHAEL

I remember coming home for summer holidays. We'd bought this farm at Much Dewchurch. When the time came to go back, nobody ever said, 'Get ready, go on . . .' October, after the hay-making, I stayed on the farm; I never went back. Nobody said a word. It was the end of the war – things were tough. Father just bought this farm, and I would tell him I was cheap labour.

He was very strict, but most of the time he was like another brother. When we'd finished in the summer, when we weren't potato-bashing, we used to go and play cricket up in the orchard. There were three of us, maybe four. Father used to come back on Wednesday; he'd had a few at market. 'Come on, boys, I'll give you some leather-hunting,' he called it. And he'd be three-parts pissed and he could knock spots off us. He'd loft a ball and say, 'When you've found it, come down the pub and fetch me.' He loved it.

I remember coming back from racing somewhere, midnight, I don't know where we'd been. We'd had a few, or Father had, anyway. And the Black Swan, there was a light on. 'We'd better see if Jack's all right,' he said. So we'd go and have another session. They used to drink after time there. Time didn't matter. And the neighbours used to get a bit upset about it, so they'd ring Ross police up and say, 'Look, we're being kept awake.' As soon as they put the phone down, the police used to ring Jack and say: 'Chuck 'em out, Jack – we're on the way . . .' I think the latest I went in was twenty to seven one morning.

My daughter said the other day how lucky we were, looking back, to be brought up like we were. She was brought up on a farm with ponies, and I look back, I'm in the same boat. We were lucky to be brought up amongst horses and on farms. I mean, we worked hard. It wasn't all thrown on a plate for you. Father used to make us work.

As an example of what was expected, Michael remembers a holiday to Ireland he took with his brother, Handley, and a friend. They returned overnight, reaching home at 6.30 a.m. after a two-mile walk from a country station.

MICHAEL

We were just going upstairs to bed and Father said, 'Where are you going?'

We said, 'To bed.'

He said, 'You're not bloody going to bed!' He said, 'Get out! Errands! Do some work! You've been away for three days.' Oh, he was tough. Tough and fair.

When he'd been back about a year, I had my first ride in a point-to-point. And he rode in the same race. There were about 24 runners. Anyway, I never gave mine a ride. That's the only time in my life I didn't! He came back and said he didn't give his a ride either because he was looking for me!

The first ride I had under rules was in a hunter chase when Father came and got me off the stands at Hereford and said, 'Tim Hamey's looking for a jockey in the hunter chase and I've told him you'll ride it.' That was a horse called Tipton Lad. He was the start of it. I was 15.

I didn't have a boot or a helmet or anything, you see. Father took me and introduced me to Arthur Lord [a valet] who said, 'That's all right, I'll fix you up.' Some of it fitted and some didn't, but that's how it went. Nowadays, you couldn't do that, because you'd have to have a permit or a licence and a doctor's certificate. Even as an amateur. Make sure you're sane and clean and sober.

Now in his 40s, Geoffrey soon turned to training, and provided his son with his first winner under rules, Wild Honey at Chepstow in February 1950. Three weeks later, they combined for Cheltenham Festival success with the 25-1 shot Sir Charles in a division of the Gloucestershire Hurdle, now known as the Supreme Novices' Hurdle.

MICHAEL

He trained quite a few winners and then got some bad horses. He said, 'I'm going to stick to the farming. I've got you going,' and he got my brother and said, 'We'll go farming,' which they did do and were quite successful.

Geoffrey can have had no inkling of what he had started in launching his son as the first of the Scudamore jockeys. He was present when Michael won the Cheltenham Gold Cup in 1957, and for his Grand National two years later, though he did not join in the celebrations afterwards at one of Liverpool's grander hotels.

MICHAEL

When you do something like that, your feet don't touch the ground. I never saw him till I got home two days later. First, the press want you here and somebody else wants you there. Owners want to see you. He always kept in the background anyway. But I often wish he'd come to the Adelphi.

Geoffrey lived to 1982, just long enough to see his grandson crowned champion jockey. He is remembered by the family, not just as the founder of a dynasty but as part of that heroic generation who risked everything to help protect a way of life.

PETER

We were immensely lucky to have this idyllic upbringing. I always felt my grandfather fought for this. He fought for lots of reasons, but it was their bravery that allowed us to have this upbringing.

His level of bravery was on a different level to what we're talking about. When people say National Hunt jockeys are brave, this puts that into context. Maybe there's something that runs through the family because of his example. If you said, 'I've hurt myself,' in our family it didn't necessarily get a lot of sympathy.

MICHAEL

During the war, when Father crashed in Belgium, the navigator was an Australian. Anyway, Peter goes to ride in New Zealand 40 years later. And a chap comes knocking on the weighing room door, asking to see 'Scudamore'. And he said, 'Was your father in the Air Force?'

Peter said, 'No, but my grandfather was.'

This man says, 'I was his navigator.'

PETER

It was a very emotional moment for me. It was almost a full circle of my life, because Grandfather was dead by then, and there was the realisation that this wasn't just a cartoon thing, it happened. I'd never met any of the crew. To meet somebody who was so brave and allowed us to do all these things . . .

In 1957, firmly established as a high-profile jump jockey, and on his way to setting a Grand National record for the number of consecutive years he took part, Michael married Mary Duffield. The following year their son Peter was born.

PETER

I wasn't dreadfully conscious of him as a jockey. I thought everybody's dad was a jockey, because you do as a young kid, don't you? The only thing I was very conscious of was that he'd won the Grand National. Whenever I walked into a room, I was the son of Michael Scudamore, who'd won the Grand National. I suppose as a kid we all crave identity, don't we? I think I did, at any rate, and my identity was Dad winning the Grand National.

He was brought up with a pony and a couple of point-to-pointers on a farm. His father trained, but it would have been much more of an amateur set-up. He thought he was stronger than any other jockey, because he went back in the summer and carried a cow around and pulled a sheep and hauled bales. It's a bit like you read about the old New Zealand rugby players; they used to put a sheep on their back and carry it up a hill.

He was a remarkable man because he commanded respect. He didn't have money, he didn't wear jewellery, the flash watch or the flash suit. Terry Biddlecombe and those would tease him. But Biddlecombe could have written about all those people in his book, and he's named Dad as his hero.

This is a reference to Winner's Disclosure, *the 1982 autobiography of three-time champion jockey Biddlecombe, whose admiration for Michael pre-dated his own career. Recalling a trip to Hereford races as a boy, Biddlecombe wrote, 'Michael Scudamore was riding a close finish on the rails, and he nearly sliced off my head with his whip. I remember telling Dad that I now had a hero to follow.'*

The two soon became friends during their shared years in the weighing room, indulging in regular bickering during long car journeys to the track. Once on horseback, Biddlecombe was known for his hold-up tactics, while his friend preferred to be close to the pace, prompting Biddlecombe to write, 'It was one of my chief delights to know that if he had fallen in front of me, he would be curled up waiting for the rest of the field to pass, and if I happened to be the last to jump the fence, which was often the case, I could shout at him as I sailed overhead: "It's all right, Scu, you can get up now!" which used to infuriate him.'

Peter also remembers high praise for his father from Gerry Scott, a fellow Grand National-winning jockey, and from Captain Ryan Price, five times champion jumps trainer and a famously hard man to impress.

PETER

It really is something special to us, who admire people jumping. Why one man is carted over a fence better than another man, I don't know, but it's a sort of mythical hero-worship of which I was immensely proud. To those great people, Dad was really somebody and I noticed it.

But all great people, once you close the door, they're just your dad. And your dad repeats so many stories . . . I never rebelled, but I'd say things like, 'Oh, Dad! Why aren't you champion jockey?' I don't think I openly respected him, but I always did absolutely adore him.

Dad told me his faults, so I was determined not to have his faults. It was never a, 'Sit down here, young man, and listen to me.' But he had a propensity to repeat himself, especially the story of how 'One of my biggest problems was, I think I got them jumping too well early on . . .'

And that's when it hits me – when Ryan Price comes up to me and says, 'I think your father's the finest man I've ever seen over a steeplechase fence.' It's a huge compliment, but also, he didn't say he was the finest jockey. He didn't say he was the strongest finisher. He said he's the finest *man* I've ever seen over a fence, and I think that's defining. I know it's defining.

When I first rode, I didn't want to ride like Dad, because it would be like Stanley Matthews' son playing in Stanley Matthews' boots. I wanted the flash boots. I thought they were old-timers and we were better. Dad used to tell me his way of riding, but it wasn't until I got more confidence in myself that I listened to him more. Look, we never argued, but I probably put him down a little bit and didn't pay him enough respect, because familiarity breeds contempt.

What does the Bible say? 'The prophet is never respected in his own land?' I knew Father was immensely strong, mentally and physically, so I took it for granted. He never rode from his hands: he rode from his vice-like legs that even a horse of the strongest calibre respected: 'I'm beaten here – I'm not going to take this man on.'

While his legs were an asset, Michael's feet were a liability, a constant source of trouble to him. He was born with high arches, a condition which puts excessive weight on the ball of the foot, meaning that most types of exercise become more difficult or more painful.

MICHAEL

All I'm walking on is air. I mean, they've given me hell. I had them operated on just after the war – Mother wouldn't have it done when Father wasn't there. They put me in plaster, each leg for six weeks, and then apologised when they took the plasters off. They were wasting their bloody time. So they said, 'Will you come back and we'll do one leg at a time and take your foot apart?' And I said, 'Not bloody likely. I'll stick with them.' They are hell some mornings. I've had shoes made and different things.

PETER

They were a lot of pain to him. He couldn't wear fashionable shoes. His toes were right clawed up. It's funny, as a kid, he's my hero, so I thought, 'When I grow up I'll have feet like that. That's what all men have.'

He played cricket, but I never saw him play golf or rugby or football, or anything like that. He was never a hiker or a walker. He was always walking round the farm doing farm things – that was his way of exercise and fitness. I knew he had corns and blisters. It was almost a joke. Biddlecombe and those used to tease him about his feet. But it never affected his riding at all. The only thing you could say about it is, they rode with the full foot in the iron. He had a deformity, but the one athletic event that was not going to affect him was riding.

And on one occasion, Michael's bad feet gave him exactly the support he needed: when he was taken into the army on National Service in 1952. As an established jockey who had already been placed in a Grand National, Michael feared that spending any length of time away from the sport would lead him to put on weight that he might struggle to shed.

MICHAEL

I went to Worcester for a medical, and people kept telling me, 'With your feet, you'll be great.' But I think, between you and me, people were getting a bit niggly, because I was still riding and their children were in the army. Anyway, the day I had to go I went to Wincanton. I've never given horses such a ride in my life. I had about five rides and I murdered them all, I think, trying to get a fall so I didn't have to go in the army.

No such fall came to save him, and Michael was briefly absorbed into the services. But it lasted only until the right army doctor had a good look at his feet.

MICHAEL

He said, 'What the bloody hell are you doing in the army?' I was gone the next day. I had 28 days in there, but I wasn't doing anything because I wasn't really fit, as a soldier. [My feet] were all right for riding. The only time they might have been hell is walking back from a fall.

PETER

He definitely thought, if he had gone into the army, that would have been the end of his riding career, because he wouldn't have been able to keep his weight down. He was thickset, heavy. It shows how lucky we were. It's on little things that life turns. That would have ended his riding career and all our dynasty, if he had gone into the army.

In 2007, At The Races screened a Meet The Scudamores *feature: a round-table chat with Michael, Peter, Tom and Michael Jnr. It features much ribbing of Grandad's 'elbows-out' riding style, parodied by his grandchildren. 'When they want a laugh, they look at my old National films,' Michael says.*

TOM

They were showing the Grand Nationals of the 1960s one day when the racing was off, so my brother and I were watching it, and you could pick out Grandad because he had a unique style, shall we say. So we decided to get Grandad in for a running commentary on what he thought about all these horses. It was Oxo's second year, two years after he won it, and Grandad told us, 'Oh, he was getting a bit tired going to Becher's, so I decided to pull him up.'

Did he hell! Oxo refused! He's gone down to it, Grandad's fired him into it, and Oxo's said, 'I've done this before, not likely.' Grandad says, 'I pulled him up.' He didn't want to go round again, poor old boy. Selective memory!

Peter now says he is 'a bit embarrassed' about the ATR feature with his father, 'because we don't allow him to talk'.

PETER

But on the other hand, you do see how we cope as three boys, my two boys and me, with living with a legend from a time we couldn't possibly have survived. We tease him about the way he rode at his fences. I suppose that's our way of coping with living with somebody like that. Those days, we couldn't have coped with the toughness. So rather than say, 'Gosh, you're fantastic, Dad,' we go to humour to cope with it.

Peter still treasures a profile of his father clipped from a Herefordshire paper, with an introduction that he feels perfectly describes the man during his riding career:

> *He lives in a half-timbered farmhouse with a brass fox-head knocker, which could serve as a model for a 'typical Herefordshire home'. (Even the little birdhouse on the front lawn is half-timbered.) He bears one of the best-known names in Herefordshire and has made it famous the length and breadth of Britain, but sometimes when he is lying in pain on a stretcher and spitting teeth, he wonders whether there aren't easier ways of doing it. The moments of doubt are, happily for the racing fraternity, incredibly short-lived, and Michael Scudamore rode at Chepstow this week, perfectly happily, with a cracked leg bone, 17-stitch chin wound still healing and minus three front teeth.*

TOM

One thing with Grandad, you watch him round Aintree and what a horseman! He'd have ridden like a Neale Doughty, someone like that. Just that strong, not necessarily pretty, but I remember David Mould saying to me, Grandad was as good as anyone he rode with. He said, 'If Mike came to you between the last two, you knew you were in trouble, because he could galvanise one, wrap himself around him and just get him up and running.' For a squat man, he was phenomenal. You watch him basically wrestling Oxo around there. And his National record was amazing, because he was such a fine horseman. But it was a very different way of riding to now because it had to be. The fences were different and the horses, they're great big carthorses, aren't they? To have to get Oxo to dance his way round Liverpool, wrestle him round. And sometimes it's not pretty, but it's decisive.

A treasured time for the younger Scudamores came in the mid-to-late 90s, when the newly retired Peter threw in his lot with Nigel Twiston-Davies' training operation near Guiting Power in Gloucestershire. Michael Sr, by then in his 60s and retired from training, came along to help, and spent years living next door to his teenage grandkids.

TOM

He was such a kind man, and he had such an understated way of explaining things. I was always phenomenally proud of him. He was one of those people that everyone just became in awe of, and he didn't show off. He always seemed to me very happy in his own skin, very content with what he'd done and what he'd achieved.

I'd rather go and speak to him than Dad about some things. Dad was always so intense, and you'd get a different point of view from Grandad. He'd tell you what you needed to hear. He was a very, very kind man, but by Christ he was tough. I mean physically tough, strong and fearless, utterly fearless. Probably borderline stupid – that fearless.

You'd go off with him and just have fun, just laugh all the time. His idea of feeding the horses in the field, he'd knock his Land Rover into gear, so it wouldn't stall but wouldn't run away with him. He'd have no one in front, and he'd hang out the back feeding the horses. It went down the hill, save him walking back up again. He was in his 60s doing this. He'd be doing things like that all day long.

You could talk to him for hours and hours and hours and hours – anything from Bryan Marshall to the state of the England cricket team. He'd always be fascinating. Don't get me wrong: I adored Dad, and he's done amazing, but Grandad was just from an era that – there's not many of them about, they've all gone – they just got on with things. But they were also conscious that there were better ways to do things. That generation was going to push the boundaries of change and make things better, from the NHS to the Injured Jockeys Fund – and Grandad was like that: so balanced. He was hard but very, very fair. He was an amazing bloke.

You never heard him say, 'It was better in my day.' You never heard him say, 'God, I don't know why they're training them like this.' He was never afraid of change; it never bothered him. He accepted things, right up to the very end, and never became bitter about anything.

I'd follow Grandad around all morning then go and have lunch. Grandad would sit down with his cup of tea or soup and we'd just talk about racing. Hours and hours and hours. I'd just ask him about Lester, or horses, or jockeys, trainers . . . I must have driven him mad, just constantly asking, 'What was this like? What was that like?' It was marvellous, those five years. I just followed him around everywhere, and Michael did the same. 'Grandad this, Grandad, Grandad . . .'

Going racing, you'd bump into Jeff King, Josh Gifford. I can never remember him having too much to do with Fred Winter, but I do remember him saying Fred was always very uptight on the way to the races and then, as soon as he'd had a gin and tonic on the way back, he was a different man. I think Fred used to struggle with his nerves quite a lot. And that's another reason why they admired him so much: that they were aware he had a fear, but was able to control it and still be such a great jockey. Grandad used to say he wasn't great company until he'd loosened up a bit. They were great pals, but I can never remember meeting Fred at the races, not in the same way as Grandad would go and speak to Josh and have a bit of craic with Josh and Kingy.

He'd go, binoculars in hand, trilby on, and I'd just go and follow him around as he'd go and eat these whelks or something disgusting. He used to love Barrie Cope, get some seafood from him – that'd always be the start, then off he'd go.

Grandad would like a drink, and he'd have a whisky at night. But I can never remember him drinking at the races. Not like Josh and those, who'd be drinking gin or whisky – you'd always meet them in the bar. They wouldn't be getting drunk or anything; it's just the way they were, much more hard-living.

Grandad would always talk to them and chat away and it was a very sociable thing.

He told me the worst injury he had was when he was told by Gran to go shopping and he fell down a manhole and dislocated his shoulder. That's what I mean about him – he'd go and do things like that. 'And she was bloody furious. Said I couldn't even go shopping without getting hurt.'

Michael and I would be rolling around. 'You stupid old sod, what the hell do you think . . .? Bloody hopeless old git.'

'Who are you calling a hopeless old git? What are you on about?'

'Well, look at you. Granny's right – you can't even go to the bloody shop without getting hurt . . .'

We'd wind each other up relentlessly, just in jest. We had a lovely relationship. I remember taking the mick out of him because he'd gone to get his eyes tested. 'Can you see, you old git?' or something like that.

'Of course I can see – I can see all the blackheads around your nose!' Which, to a body-conscious adolescent . . .

Tom mimics a dismayed intake of breath at the memory.

MICHAEL JNR

He was just a wonderful man, really. I remember we used to take the mickey out of him when he started telling these stories, because you'd heard them so many times. But now all you wish is that you could hear them one more time.

The one about his first ride, when he was in the stands and he was told to go and change to ride in the race . . . You just couldn't imagine something like that happening now. If a young lad was having his first ride today, he'd be told weeks in advance and school the horse ten times, build up to it – it'd be a real occasion: you'd try and do everything to get him right, walk the course with him. None of that. 'You'd better get changed: you're riding in the next.'

TOM

Grandad could mix with everyone; it made no difference whatsoever. The most critical he'd get, he might say, 'Lord X was a pompous old git,' or he'd say someone was too hard on the horses.

He met some bloody dodgy characters in the early 60s in the London scene. He'd see on the news that somebody had died, and it would be some East End gangster. He'd have trouble believing that's what this man had been. His thing was, if you said, 'Hello, Michael,' you were a nice man. 'He always said, "Hello, Michael" . . .'

PETER

I don't think he ever broke a limb, riding in races. In one of the big races he won he rode with a broken leg, but it's only the outside bone, not a supporting bone . . . I used to think to myself, 'Dad was tough,' but he wasn't, really – he was just one of many jockeys from that time who were like that.

There was a macho-ness that he was brought up with. You didn't wear a helmet; health and safety would never have crossed his mind. He believed the horse would not hurt him, therefore he was never tense round a horse, and that was one of his great skills. Horses were perfectly relaxed with him, because he moved slowly, he rode anything, and his attitude was that he wasn't going to get hurt. When he'd retired, I can remember seeing him ride horses that nobody else could ride. And yet it was never an issue to him. If I did it, I would tell somebody; he would never tell anybody.

TOM

He never would complain. He must have had lots of injuries, but he was so flippin' tough. I'd feel pathetic talking to him about when I'd been hurt or done something, 'cos he just wouldn't feel any pain. So numb to all that. He'd talk about splitting a kidney and pissing blood like I'd talk about tripping over and cutting my foot.

'It's all right. I didn't really notice. Peed blood and went to see the doctor, had a night in hospital. They said, 'When d'you do it?'

'About three weeks ago.'

'Well, it's probably healed by now. Send him out.'

That's how he was.

PETER

I remember as a kid, you wanted to break something, you wanted a bad fall. Because that's what jump jockeys do, and I wanted to be a jump jockey. So one time, somebody had a pony that was stopping, and I'd only be 12 or 13 but I was a competent rider even in those days, and fearless because I was stupid. Anyway, I get on this pony, give it two smacks, drive it into a fence, turn it over. They take me off to hospital in Hereford, bandage my ankle up. It's not broken, but they've got me in a wheelchair. So the nurse is pushing me round the corner and Dad comes round and he looks at me and says, 'I was never in a wheelchair.'

So I thought: 'Oh. I'd better get out of the wheelchair.' I was so proud to be in the wheelchair, thinking I was a jockey! And all I've got is a twisted ankle.

Michael's career as a jockey came to an end on November 1, 1966, when he rode Snakestone in a handicap hurdle at Wolverhampton. Terry Biddlecombe was due to take the ride but couldn't do the weight. Either Snakestone clipped heels or slipped while rounding a bend, but the result was that he fell and brought down three others. The thrashing legs of four horses did so much collective damage to Michael's head that he eventually felt compelled to give up the game he had loved. He was 34. Peter, eight years old at the time, was on his way home from Hereford Cathedral Prep School when he was told.

PETER

I had to wait outside the post office for the bus. My uncle came down instead, picked me up and said: 'Your father's had a bad fall.' It was on the radio that evening that he'd been badly injured. I remember thinking, my Dad must be quite famous.

We didn't see him for a time – let's say three weeks, four weeks. And I remember my sister, Nicky, and I coming into the lounge and he'd come home. He'd got plaster of Paris round his head like a bandage the rugby players used to wear. He'd got a construction of parallel wires that was keeping his jaw in place, so he couldn't move it. All he could have was soup. We wouldn't speak to him because it was like a Martian had come into the room. You're too young to take it all in. Somebody says, that's your dad. We were frightened of him.

Michael's roll call of injuries from that one fall included broken ribs, a collapsed lung, six or seven jaw fractures, two cracked cheekbones, a broken nose, a split palate and several nasty cuts to the head. Worst of all, he lost 90 per cent of the sight in his left eye.

MICHAEL

I think I was a bit lucky: I got into very good hands. They patched me up. When I was recuperating, the doctor came and said, 'You'll probably lose most of that eye . . .' 'Cos it's a nerve, and when the blood runs out of the nerve, it's white along there, it should be red.

I remember when he went, I thought, 'Bloody hell. I won't be able to jump Becher's again.'

But it could all have been a lot worse, and the surgeon came and operated a week or two later and made a wonderful job of putting it back together again. It was quite funny, really, because when I went back to hospital the last time, Mary took me up to Wolverhampton, and it was still a bit of a mess, but he put his hand up there [inside Michael's mouth] with some pincers, and he got hold of a piece of cotton wool. And he started to pull like that, and it was a long thing.

I said, 'What are you doing?'

He said, that's been holding your cheek out for the past fortnight. And then he did it the other side.

Michael felt he might still be able to recover his licence, if he were sufficiently determined. But the limitations of his vision gave him pause.

MICHAEL

A week or two before, I'd gone down the backside at Kempton and some mud exploded in my face. And I couldn't see where I was going. This was before the fall. It made me think, 'If this happened again in the good eye . . .'

In those days, we were very afraid of goggles. We used them, but I was always very worried that I'd get a kick in the face and break them. I think they're better now than they were then. And funnily enough, all the bad falls I had were kicks in the face. I used to be good-looking at one time.

I was enjoying it as much as I ever enjoyed it. I wasn't going to be champion jockey, and I'd won a National and a Gold Cup and I was really loving it. And that was it. I could have struggled on, but I thought, 'I am 34, I've got a wife and two kids. I'd better take note.'

PETER

He kept going to the eye specialist, and I remember coming home one day and he wasn't going to ride again. I couldn't quite – 'Dad, you can see a bit out of your eye, for fuck's sake. Why do you need two eyes to ride?' Your Dad was your hero. He was becoming more and more your hero because he's been on the radio – TV cameras are turning up to see when he's going to ride again – and there's the realisation of what I want to do now, so he's becoming a bigger hero to me. And then he says, 'I'm training.'

I'm looking at this fantastic horseman: although he's been smashed up, he's still a better rider than anyone else who comes into the yard. And he never moaned about it. He came from that generation that never complained.

We got closer to him than we had been, because he'd always been away and now he's always home. He's riding and doing things. And it really got me riding more than anything else. On one hand, it was a terrible thing for him, but it was a marvellous thing for me because it just opened up my life even more. Before, we had a pony stuck in a shed. Now, I've got wonderful stables, lots of horses, everybody coming in, I'm riding gallops, I'm schooling, riding in shows. When Dad turns up with these racehorses, all I want to do is ride racehorses.

But, while Mary Scudamore had married a jockey, she had no desire to raise more jockeys, particularly after bearing such close witness to the grisly way in which a jockey's career can end.

PETER

She never wanted me to ride. I think that was one of the things that drove me on more than anything, was to prove her wrong. She was much posher than us. She was upper-middle class of the Fifties. Supposedly, she had a chauffeur when she was younger. I just think there was that element . . . I wasn't that intelligent, but I was sent to public school, and I think that was probably to placate her. Even when I'd been champion jockey, she would say to me, 'I wish you'd pack up and get a proper job.' Slightly tongue-in-cheek, but there was a great deal of meaning to it. She wanted me to be somebody who lived in a smart part of Cheltenham and was a lawyer, a doctor, an accountant: a professional.

TOM

Granny used to really struggle watching me ride. She didn't used to like Dad riding either. She was delighted when he gave up, absolutely over the moon. She always used to say to him, 'When are you going to get a proper job?' She loved her racing, don't get me wrong, but she hated the fact that me and Dad did it. And I think that's part of the reason why we both, and especially Dad, had a good education – just in the hope that we'd do something else.

When we'd go and stay with her, she'd feed us up. We'd have breakfast, lunch, afternoon tea, supper – and I'm sure a lot of that was to stop me and Michael from being jockeys. Whatever we wanted to eat, food was never an issue there: it was as much as you could eat. It was absolutely mad, the amount she used to constantly try and feed me and my brother. She was trying to push us towards a desk job, I think. She'd have loved it if we were accountants or lawyers.

Michael and Mary Scudamore lived long enough to see the various careers forged by their children and grandchildren. They died within three days of one another in July 2014, and were remembered at a joint funeral at St David's, Much Dewchurch. Tom read Kipling's poem 'The Glory of the Garden':

> *Our England is a garden and such gardens are not made,*
> *By singing: 'Oh, how beautiful,' and sitting in the shade.*

Peter was among those who carried his father's coffin. Tom and Michael Jnr carried their grandmother.

Michael had been receiving treatment for cancer for some months.

NICKY (PETER'S SISTER)

Most of the time he was in the hospice he was compos mentis – he didn't go funny with the medication and stuff. But one day he said, 'When did I win the Grand National?'

I said, 'Nineteen fifty-nine, Dad.'

'I thought it was today,' he said. 'I was worried where I'd left the car. I was wondering how I was gonna get home.'

PETER

It was all coming back to him in a way that he had never really told us things. I found it rather lovely that in his later days he was still so proud of it and living it again.

3

BEING A SCUDAMORE: PETER

'My thing was, try to be more professional, try to be more driven'

P*eter learned the skills that would eventually make him an eight-times champion jockey while helping out at his father's yard at Prothither, Hoarwithy, nine miles south of Hereford.*

PETER

I had two lives, because I went to boarding school and I'd come back to this racing world in the holidays. I went to a Catholic school, and I'm coming back into a stable lad's environment. I was still a spoilt little bastard, 'cos I'm the trainer's son. But I'm friends with all the staff because we're a very close-knit thing. But they still accuse me of being gay 'cos I was educated by monks.

It was a funny thing, being brought up in a Catholic place, where rugby was the religion, and then coming back for holidays, where you've got to be up at seven o'clock in the morning, picking shit up with a shovel, working with people who weren't good with pens in their hands but were brilliant around horses.

But I learned, riding out with Dad. You learned all the old-fashioned ways. Horses had cider vinegar, they had bran mash, we gave them oats, we made hay, the horses were bedded on straw, they were given Epsom salts, we walked round the roads for ages, we galloped over a mile and a half – we did things because his grandfather had done them and his grandfather's grandfather had done them. It was the end of the era before science really came in. I think we were still using the cattle vet. You didn't have a specialist horse vet. These were old boys with potions. They had potions to stop the horses breaking blood vessels, they had potions that they put on their legs.

I was brought up in this fabulous environment in the countryside. If you'd said, 'Health and safety', or 'Animal welfare', we wouldn't have had a blind understanding of the terminology. Yet I would say the horses were fantastically treated. There was no money, but I think the closeness of it . . . You got up in the morning, you rode your lovely horse that was your favourite. You'd go to sleep in the afternoons in the same box – you'd just lie down because you loved the horse and you were with him all the time. You treated them as humans: you spoke to them, you trusted them. Rod Stewart was number one: you'd muck out and the top of your pitchfork would be a microphone and you'd sing, 'You Wear It Well'.

I'd never be able to have a happier childhood.

It wasn't a big yard: 25 horses, eight or ten people riding out. We had horses like Fortina's Palace, who won the Grand Annual, horses like Bruslee. We were trying to take on Fred Rimell, Fulke Walwyn, Fred Winter, and you had this dream . . . Bruslee won a Mackeson. And you think, 'This is going to be a Gold Cup horse!' The joy of touching these great horses that were as good as what Winter and Thomson Jones had . . . Especially as we felt very rural. They were doing an hour and a half's roadwork in the autumn – you'd trot round and you might stop at the pub, have a pint of cider and hack on.

I was immensely proud of being from Herefordshire. But you also realised that it was a backwater. We were isolated. There was one motorway in to Hereford, and then nothing. Very few people came to Hereford. You were Hereford United in some ways, taking on the big boys.

Rimell, Walwyn, Winter, to us, were gods. And Jonjo O'Neill and John Francome and Bob Davies, Jeff King, Graham Thorner – these were my heroes. And if Jeff or Graham or Andy Turnell rode one of the horses, there was tremendous pride and excitement. That's the passion of it.

These days were the happiest of my life, with no cares, riding ponies around. There were very few cars on our country lanes. I could trot up the road to a wood and gallop around all day with a mate and not come back until dusk. Those were idyllic days, and they made me.

You'd be around for the King George, and then January came and you'd go back to school. I had one teacher who used to bet – I used to give him tips, not a clue what I was talking about. He was the chemistry teacher, but I was no good at chemistry. After a while, your luck runs out, and the bets start getting beaten and your marks in chemistry drop . . .

Peter's more important education was learning to ride racehorses at home. Michael also wanted to impress upon him something about what it meant to be a man.

PETER

I remember when I was 12 or 13 coming home in a pair of flared trousers. It was one of the only times I saw my father really cross. Because he thought it was feminine. It was more than a telling-off. It was the nearest I came to having to leave the house: it was a real, real issue.

It got worse. In the end, I had my hair long, parallel trousers – that's rebellion, isn't it? I may have backed off at that stage. I probably wouldn't rub his face in it too much. Definitely by the time I came out of school and went to the racing, I knew then that you had to have your hair cut, get rid of all those things.

When Peter persisted in his ambition to be a jockey, his parents decided to send him for experience across the country to Royston in Hertfordshire, and the base of the trainer Willie Stephenson, who'd handled Oxo as well as the Derby winner Arctic Prince. Stephenson was aggressive, demanding, unpredictable and impossible to please.

PETER

I think they thought, 'Send him to Willie Stephenson's – that'll cure him.' And typical Willie, he controlled you; he just did. I was a sort of chauffeur, gopher. . . I used to get up in the morning and drive down to the yard, 5 a.m. or 6 a.m., then I would ride out, and at lunchtime we'd go and do the farm. Evening time, we'd come back and do the horses. Then at night I would drive him to Newmarket, where he'd do something at Gibson's saddlery, or they'd have nomination sales. I'd come home at 11 o'clock at night, and he made me chop logs. I was so tired sometimes, I'd fall asleep sitting on the logs. For years after that, I could fall asleep anywhere. It was like he'd trained me.

I remember he was ill and in bed, and he said to me, 'There's a white pheasant in the garden. Go and get my gun and shoot it!' Now, clearly there wasn't a white pheasant in the garden. But I had to get the gun and go walk round the garden in this pretence. It just shows you the control that he had. He wouldn't have done depression. You just got on with it, with Willie.

After weeks of trying to impress this odd man, Peter's reward was to find that Stephenson had lined him up with a job at the estate agents, Bernard Thorpe.

PETER

He said to me, 'You'll never make a jockey. Never make a jockey. Too soft. Not hard enough. This is what you should do: you should be an estate agent.'

You didn't question him. I can't explain why. He was an old man – he wasn't going to hit you or anything. He was just one of those characters. I was so thick and stupid, it never deflated me, really. I think it's probably another thing to drive you on. I didn't analyse it deeply or take offence, and I suppose I had enough confidence in myself to know. But I also thought, by his standards, I didn't want to be seen as hard anyway. Even at 16 or 17, I'm conscious that the world is changing, and what is acceptable to him isn't acceptable to me.

And so in the autumn of 1978, aged 20, Peter entered estate agency, at the Stow-on-the-Wold branch of Bernard Thorpe. It was a line of work in which he did not shine. 'For Sale' signs were forgotten, clients were asked for the wrong amount in rent, the petty cash was raided for petrol money, and after six months the job finally came to an end when the senior partner in the firm found Peter alone in the shop with his feet on the desk, reading The Sporting Life.

But the upside to the job had been its proximity to the Condicote yard of David Nicholson, where Peter had begun riding out every day before 'work'. He rode for the yard as an amateur, and managed nine winners in that first season riding under rules. He was off to the races.

Eventually, Peter became known for great strength in the saddle, and for a thoroughly professional attitude, in or out of it. He brought an intense focus to the job, and is regarded by members of the family as the most driven of the Scudamore jockeys.

PETER

That's not something I see. I take it as a compliment. I can only see myself through my own eyes. I get angry, but I don't think I'm totally unreasonable. Some driven people can't live a normal life. Luce is very, very good for me on that.

But I half feel, because I had a famous father, I was gonna be a failure if I didn't match up to him. I was affected by his winning the Grand National and the Gold Cup. When I was a young man it was my reason for being. I just wanted a certain amount of recognition, so mine was, 'I am the son of someone who's won the Gold Cup.' But when you're 17, 18, you can't live on that for the rest of your life.

My thing was, try to be more professional, try to be more driven, try to shut down as many doors to mistakes as possible. That's what I try to pass on to my children and the people who work for us now: the need to be professional.

MICHAEL JNR

Grandad was very quiet, very laid-back; I don't think I ever saw him say a cross word or a bad word about anybody. Always very chilled, whether it was good news or bad news.

Whereas Dad is like a coiled spring 90 per cent of the time. I could probably count on one hand all the times I've seen Dad switch off. Tom and I often ring each other and joke about Dad, how he's always: 'Fucking hell!' – shouting at the dog, or shouting at somebody going up the gallops because they're not going fast enough. Dad has always been, whether we were playing rugby or cricket, 'Practise harder, train harder', but not in a bad way – just, if you're going to do it, do it properly. You give it everything, you don't go out the night before. Grandad was always the first person up, the first person in the yard and you learn from them to do it properly or not bother. The professionalism of it, we've learned from them.

Peter's professionalism also showed in the ordering of his ambitions. He favoured consistency, dependability, delivering six excellent rides on a card, then getting up the next day and doing it again.

PETER

The thing I think is the greatest challenge is to turn up at Plumpton and have three winners, go to Folkestone the next day, have a fall at Hereford, get up and ride in the next. That's what champion jockeyship is all about. I think once Piggott stopped being champion, and Pat Eddery perhaps, the Flat champion jockey's title lost a little bit of stuff. Whereas to us in jump racing, it was the only thing. When you look back, all your great heroes, Bryan Marshall, Fred Winter, Tim Molony, they were champion jockey.

I remember pushing it. Jonjo O'Neill's record was 149 winners in a season. When I rode 200 winners, I couldn't quite believe it because no one had done it. But it doesn't make me a better jockey. There was more racing, there were more opportunities.

But I would like to think that Martin Pipe and I probably took it to as professional a level as we possibly could at the time. Whether I could have done it in Fred Winter's era, whether I could have done it in McCoy's era, I have no idea, and I don't care. You can only ride in your own.

I never won a National. I wanted to win it, but I wanted to be champion jockey even more. You've got to remember, in my day there were times when it looked as though the National might not survive. I look back . . . does it matter? I always think, ordinary jockeys have won particular races, but you've got to go back to 1919 for the last time an amateur was champion jockey.

There are exceptionally talented riders. I think Francome was one, and obviously people like Jonjo, but, basically, a lot of people could win on the horses that we win on. That's probably what I like about being champion jockey. It is a skill to an extent, but let's not get carried away. Still, the mentality is: you don't drink that night, you get up at six o'clock, you drive somewhere, you school and you go off to the races. It's great fun, but it's hard work. Whereas the amateur can come in and ride the winner of the Gold Cup; to be champion jockey, you have to do it every day of the week, ten months of the year.

I tried to push across the image of taking myself seriously, and I felt it was a responsibility to do so, because people were spending an awful lot of money on a horse. You ride for people like David Nicholson, Pipey, they were pushing the level of professionalism. Perhaps I took myself too seriously sometimes. But then you think: I have a responsibility to my family and myself and the position I have as champion jockey, not to end up with nothing.

Thanks in large part to his association with the trainer Martin Pipe, Peter enjoyed a record-breaking career. He rode 221 winners in a single season, and ended with an unprecedented tally of 1,678 over his career. He retired in April 1993, days after the void Grand National, with a winning ride on Sweet Duke at Ascot. He was 34 and entirely healthy. It was the same age at which his father had been forced into retirement.

PETER

I just felt, because Dad had that level of respect which comes through in the way people talk about him, that I had to command that. And I think that's one of the reasons I gave up: that I didn't want to drop off that level, which is probably slightly unprofessional. Dad had that bad fall, seeing other people drop off, other jockeys keep riding when they'd gone, and I just wanted to keep that air of respect. It's quite hard, when you're riding: there is that ticking clock. My father got smashed up. Did I ride till I got smashed up, or did I pull stumps myself?

I could have gone on to 40, but what do you do? I say to Luce, 'I would love to have ridden longer.' I didn't want to get smashed up any more, but I think my own seriousness, my own feeling of responsibility, was getting in the way in the end.

Since I've packed up, there's been many days I've wished I'd ridden till I was 45. You're young, everyone says you're fantastic, and you're earning a few quid: there's three things everybody wants out of life. But I did think there was a responsibility. I wanted to consolidate what I'd done. Was that slightly parental pressure from my mum? Was it the example John Francome had set, retiring at the same age? Was it slightly my own pomposity? I don't know.

We were making a good living, but we weren't rich people, and I'm not asking for anything to change. So I felt I had a responsibility to get out and do something. That's why I bought the farm with Nigel Twiston-Davies, and then suddenly I had the opportunity of a job at the BBC and a job at the *Daily Mail.*

Friends and supporters told Peter that his records would stand for ages. As it turned out, they were being rewritten within a matter of years by AP McCoy, who rode his first winner in Britain the year after Peter retired. McCoy soon inherited the job as first jockey to Pipe.

PETER

I suppose a little bit of me thought, 'Martin'll never be quite as good without me.' But he clearly was. All these things do you good. It depends how you take it on. You don't get too above yourself. There's some times when I say, 'Well, I wouldn't have won on that anyway.' The biggest jealousy I had was when AP won the Grand National, because I think that was a defining moment for him. But look, I've had so much luck – we've just won a National with Arthur. You can't worry about these things. You have your moment, milk your moment, and that's the way it goes.

Defer a couple of decisions in Peter's career and a couple of significant trophies fall into his hands. Had he stayed with David Nicholson for two more years, he'd have ridden Charter Party in the 1988 Cheltenham Gold Cup. Had he postponed his retirement for one more year, he'd have been on Miinnehoma in the 1994 Grand National. Does he ever dwell on such thoughts?

PETER

I don't really feel that. Of course I have regrets. But I think I felt at the time I gave up for the right reasons. And I didn't have a fall like Dad did. God forbid that Thomas ever has a fall like Dad did.

I remember when I rode my first winner, I thought: 'Great, I've done what Dad's done now. Another Scudamore's ridden a winner.' Then that figure of 500 winners he had when I passed that number of winners, then I did feel an equal to him. But I don't think there has ever been any competition among us. I've never felt competition with myself and Tom, or myself and Dad, over who was the better jockey. I think we've always respected each other.

Dad had a hand of cards. It might not have had the ace of clubs in it – he was never champion – but it had the king of diamonds and the queen of hearts in it. And he played those cards, I believe, the best he possibly could. I had the ace of spades: I had Martin Pipe in my hand of cards. I didn't have the king of diamonds: I didn't win the Grand National. But I played that hand of cards as well and as honourably as I possibly could, and I think my son has done it as well. I don't want to talk about who's the greatest. To me, that's a load of rubbish. As a sportsman, if you're the most professional you can be and at the end of the day you've got a house when you pack up, the rest is there for pub talk.

Peter invested the money from his riding career in Nigel Twiston-Davies' stable in Gloucestershire. The two had been friends from their first meeting at Pony Club, as, in Peter's words, 'two scruffy little kids' surrounded by well-spoken girls. Happy and productive years followed, during which time the yard had two Grand National winners. But Peter and his friend went their separate ways soon after the second of them in 2002.

PETER

I remember John Inverdale said to me, 'You shouldn't train, because there's so many people who've achieved things, tried to do something else and they lose the respect,' and I suppose I was quite conscious of that.

Nigel and I, things got unhappy. I can't even remember. There was just pressure. Nigel says it was the marriages going wrong. I don't think it was quite like that. I just think it was financial pressures. Nigel wasn't happy. I don't really know what it was. There wasn't a defining thing in the end. He offered me the money to buy me out and I thought, yeah, that's great. I'd always wanted to go back to Hereford. I could then see that that was my security, the thing that always worked for me all my life.

We had some other investments – we had a share in a pub called the Hollow Bottom, I had some land around the place, and I just sold it all up and bought this farm in Herefordshire that's there for the boys one day.

TOM

They'd been together a very long time, Dad and Nigel. I think they were both unhappy and something had to give. At one point, it looked like it was going to be Nigel, and then Bindaree won the National. I think he said afterwards, 'I'm not going to retire,' and it was a bit of a Tony Blair–Gordon Brown moment. That took a long time . . .

They're best mates again now, and they have been for six, seven years. But they went through a divorce, Nigel and Dad, and that particular break-up was harder on Dad than his own marital break-up, however awful that sounds. They were inseparable. Without wishing to get too flowery, they adore each other, and both of them were, in their own way, extremely hurt by it, and it took those wounds a long, long time to heal.

Happily, Peter is once more on excellent terms with Nigel Twiston-Davies, the pair of them having been induced by a mutual friend to make it up.

PETER

One day at Aintree, an old girlfriend of Nigel's came up to us and said, 'Look, you stupid fuckers, shake hands.' We were cuddling each other and saying how stupid we were for falling out. We've been friends ever since.

Their split in 2002 caused Peter to buy Eccleswall Court, a 19th-century Georgian farmhouse in 100 acres of land, three miles east of Ross-on-Wye. To Michael Jnr, who was on a school rugby trip to South Africa and Australia when the deal was done, the family move felt particularly sudden.

MICHAEL JNR

When I left home, we lived in the Cotswolds. When I got back, we'd moved in here. I'd never seen this place. I literally got picked up from school and driven back here. 'This is home now.'

Eccleswall wasn't immediately ready to be a racing stable, so to tide things over Peter got into business with Denis Caro at a more established yard in the area.

PETER

I was told Denis was looking for somebody to help him. I hadn't got the gallops in at Eccleswall and I thought, it gives me a couple of years to do that and keeps my owners happy. So that's what I did. And, in the meantime, I put the gallops in and got the place going.

But I just didn't get on with Denis at all. It's very difficult, when you're brought up in a totally professional unit and then people are doing it to enjoy training. I don't think Denis had my drive and anger, and I don't blame him, he was happy doing his thing. So that didn't last.

MICHAEL JNR

When it went wrong with Denis, 20 horses were literally coming back overnight to Eccleswall. So the licence just had to be done, carried on straight away from here. So rather than waiting six months for Dad to do it, it was just easier to put it in Grandad's name.

Michael Snr resumed the licence he had given up seven years earlier and, at least nominally, became a licensed trainer for another five seasons. But it was Peter's show.

PETER

I did the entering and dealt with 90 per cent of the owners. I was training in all but name. We probably had 25 to 30 horses. The best of them was a filly called Heltornic, who won some decent races. I always thought she would have won the three-mile handicap chase at the Cheltenham Festival in 2007: she was upsides in front when she fell two out.

We had Cheltenham winners, doubles and trebles. We had a lot of winners. Winners are always great fun. There were times when things were going well. We were making a living and that's the honest bottom line. I see people who've got licences just so they can get a 'J' or a 'T' label on the car, and that never interested me.

But it was hard work as well. You're back to basics and working hard, which is good. It was good for me. I'd had a very fortunate time. It cuts any arrogance out. It meant that, when Lucinda and I got together, I knew more about training. What doesn't break you makes you stronger. It wasn't that bad, I was earning good money. It was just that the BBC thing came to an end and the *Mail* cut down, which gave me a natural transition to training all the time.

I was very pleased for Dad. There had been times at Grange Hill when I saw Dad and he was struggling. I think he was worried that people would lose respect for him. I remember he said something to me one day: 'Oh, I'm just a burden,' or something. So I was always pleased that, when we got back to Eccleswall, he got his dignity back, I felt, with his training. His mates saw him doing well again and training again. And then, my marriage to Maz came to an end and Lucinda and I got going, and then it was an easy transition for Michael to take over the licence.

So that's how I ended up here in Scotland. Luce and I sat one day and discussed, 'Do we go south or north or go for the Midlands?' She said, 'Look, we've already got 30 or 40 horses here. There's an opportunity for Michael to take over your place.' So we got together and trained from here. Nobody ever seems to get the funny side of this, but I always say, I looked at her gallop and thought, 'Yeah, it looks like Martin Pipe's. This girl will do for me – we can train horses up here.' It's a very good gallop. She's been to university, she's far more intelligent than I am, so by the time I got there, she'd already designed the gallop correctly. You can't train winners without the correct gallops.

Obviously, you miss things. There's a lot of benefits up here as well. Sometimes I see people in the south and think, 'I'm very pleased I live where I do.' There is a clique in racing, a snobbery in it, and I think sometimes I'm happy out of that.

Maz and I get on better now than ever. She's brought up two terrific boys during a time when, I accept, I took her for granted. Really, your wife should be the most important thing in your life. But when you're a jockey, everything else comes second to your career. The children are easier to placate, as long as you're doing well, because you're their hero.

Peter followed a tortuous road, through several training establishments, to reach Lucinda Russell's stables near Kinross, just on the north side of the Forth Bridge. He has been there ten years, and One For Arthur has shown the heights that can be achieved by the Peter/Lucinda partnership. But part of him evidently struggles to move on from his days as a jockey a quarter of a century ago.

PETER

I have this dream that I'm in a race and things are going out of control. I'm in the weighing room, I can't find my colours, and the jockeys have gone out to the paddock. I'm late and I'm thinking, 'What am I doing here? Where's my boot?' In another one, I'm riding with Graham Bradley at Haydock and I go the wrong way. 'Christ!' And if somebody speaks to me right after that, I absolutely explode.

Sometimes you recognise what's happening and try to control it. 'Ah, I've had this dream before where I'm late, and I'm not going to let this happen again.' I get everything ready, and then I get down to the start and go the wrong way. The brain's playing tricks on you all the time.

It's funny, I don't have a dream where things go wrong for me as a trainer. Even though I'm not a jockey, obviously my brain still thinks I am. When Dad was dying he had that dream. He was on drugs for his treatment and woke up and couldn't find his car after winning the National. It was especially poignant for me, because I'm thinking, 'Christ, I'm having these dreams about being a jockey.' He'd never told me that he had that.

What will be the vivid moment that comes back to you in a dream, 40 years from now?

PETER

Maybe, I'll think, 'Bloody hell, I'm not champion jockey.' I'll look at the list and Dunwoody's in front of me . . .

John Francome was always so cool, said he didn't care about being champion jockey. One time, he was knocked out at Towcester. I thought, 'I'll be kind, I'll go to the ambulance room, see how he is.' He didn't know who he was talking to, he was on Planet Nine. And he said, 'How many winners has Scu ridden?' It eats you. Even him, who played it so cool. I thought, 'Yeah, you do care.'

4

BEING A SCUDAMORE: TOM AND MICHAEL JNR

'It's always worse for the people watching' –*Tom*

TOM

Mum and Dad, one of the reasons they moved to Hereford was, they were having trouble in their marriage. They kept trying, and gradually it had broken down. Dad moved up to Scotland in 2008. He'd met Lucinda, they got on, and it went on from there. It gradually happened, and then Dad was gone. I never felt it was bitter or acrimonious, because at the time it suited everyone.

The only time I got annoyed was just before Dad went, when Michael was just getting out of the rugby. I remember saying it would do Michael a lot of good to go and work for Martin Pipe for six months, or André Fabre, Criquette Head – go and get that bit of experience. Dad's response was, 'No. Why does he want to go there? He can learn just as much here with me.' I felt at the time that Dad was doing that for himself – that if Michael had gone, he was isolated in Hereford. I felt that he wanted Michael to stay because he's his mate, rather than for Michael's benefit.

And then, six to eight months later, Dad was gone, and suddenly Michael was in charge of it all, having had, I felt at the time, not enough experience to suddenly be left training racehorses. But he's done very well and turned it around.

PETER

I think, whether you learn from Fabre or Aidan O'Brien, it's not the training, it's the decision-making. And until you make decisions yourself, you can't get better at that. It's so easy to hide behind a trainer. Getting them fit is only a small percentage of it. It's where you run them, it's buying them, and of course when you go to the sales and the trainer buys one, well, you would never have bought it, would you? And he runs it there instead of here, and you would never have done that. But suddenly you're making these decisions . . . That's why I felt Michael should get in. Jump in the deep end, sink or swim, and you'll learn quicker. And he'd been in racing all his life.

MICHAEL JNR

When Dad first left to go up to Scotland, and I took over the licence, I was 24, 25. Very sudden. It's funny, looking back I cannot remember ever knowing that Dad was gonna go. I don't think we ever had that conversation, with him saying, 'Well, look, I'm going. You take over.' It was literally just, 'Where's Dad? Oh, he's up in Scotland. Oh, right, OK. He's not coming back?'

We were getting busy here, Dad must have been spending less time here, and Grandfather's health and memory and things were just beginning to get the better of him a little bit. We thought it would be time to move the licence over, but I didn't think it would be moved over and Dad gone. I thought it would be quite a nice way of gently getting into it with Dad, assistant in name, but probably actually running it for a good few years, until it worked out better.

If I could have chosen, yes, I would have loved to go to France or Henderson's for a year or something like that. But for us, it was either, take over at 24, or we sell the place and I have to go and do it a different way. Yeah, I made a lot of mistakes in the first couple of years, and looking back now I wish we could change a hell of a lot, but that's learning as you go along. You have to learn the hard way, but you learn quickly.

Grandad wasn't so much involved in the training side of things. Towards the end he was much more just doing the maintenance. He used to love doing the gallops. Even when he was 73, 74, he would still be up at five, half five every morning: he was always the first person up. He would get everything done: the gallops, go and feed the horses out in the field. And then you'd be wandering round at lunchtime or so and find him fast asleep in the corner of one of the barns. Because he knew if he came back in the house, Granny would be on to him to go and tidy this or clean that or take her somewhere. So the only peace he got, poor chap, was cuddled up in the corner of a barn somewhere. That always used to make me laugh, trying to find him.

PETER

Michael's a young man. I think his ambitions were towards rugby. He played for Ebbw Vale, and he had a Wales under-19 cap, and then realised he wasn't big enough. He started to ride a bit, but he was dieting so hard to try and ride, it was destroying him. I gave him a ride and he couldn't move on it: he was just too weak. But because he'd trained his body as a rugby player, I think he probably understood more about the training than I did. And he's proved it. He's a good judge of a horse as well. As you get older, you can't keep working at that level: you can't be riding horses and trying to train horses as well.

I think he's done fantastically well. And with Next Sensation he's had a Cheltenham Festival winner. He won the Eider Chase last year: he's got the ability to produce a decent horse.

MICHAEL JNR

Tom was always clear from day one: everything he ever did from a young age was about wanting to be a jockey. He never answered that question any other way.

If you're the son of a champion jockey whose father rode a Grand National winner, you might feel more or less compelled to follow them into the weighing room. Or you might hasten in the opposite direction: Michael's early diffidence about horse racing shows there is nothing inevitable about the outcome for those born into a dynasty like the Scudamores. But Tom's commitment to the sport has never wavered.

TOM

Growing up, I remember the acute disappointment of my dad not winning the Grand National or not winning the Gold Cup. You'd build yourself up. I remember the excitement before Desert Orchid's Gold Cup. That morning, it was snow, it was bottomless ground . . . 'Bonanza Boy's got a great chance!' Or going into the Champion Hurdle with Sondrio or Nomadic Way or Granville Again, thinking, 'God, he'll win the Champion Hurdle this year,' and the acute disappointment when he didn't. Growing up, coming back from Aintree, I remember thinking, 'God, he's got to win it one year . . .' I felt more disappointed when Dad didn't win Gold Cups or Champion Hurdles or Grand Nationals than when I haven't.

It was probably worse for us – we probably felt it more than he did, because I now know, riding, you pick yourself up and you move on. Horses win, horses get beat, and it's a great feeling when they win and it's a disappointment when they lose, but you don't go through the clouds. But when you're riding it, you're beat in the Grand National, you think, 'Well, it didn't quite get round.' You're worried about Market Rasen on Sunday.

It's probably different for me than for Dad. He won't remember Grandad riding the same way I can remember Dad riding, because he was born in

1958 and Grandad had retired in '66. And you couldn't watch it then like I could. We had SIS at home, so in the evenings I'd watch Dad. I'd watch him every Saturday and, more often than not, every Sunday as well, because in those days, with no Sunday racing, he'd ride in Ireland a lot more. There'd be a lot of English horses running in those big handicaps over there.

It is a mark of Tom's success that he has graduated from childhood excitement to the phlegmatic disposition of the mature jockey. Having once been desperate for his own turn to ride over fences, he is now a veteran of 20 seasons. The family name ensured he would get chances, but he has made fine use of them, forging a long and successful career. The teenage Tom could hardly take that outcome for granted, in view of the sheer number of excellent jockeys competing with him when he started out.

TOM

When I was 16 and first walked into the weighing room, you had Dunwoody, McCoy, Dickie Johnson, Charlie Swan, Paul Carberry, Jamie Osborne, Norman Williamson, Mick Fitzgerald, Tony Dobbin, Adrian Maguire . . . There'll be more that I'm forgetting, but that's ten straight away that, if you said, who's riding your horse tomorrow, you wouldn't care which one was. There are always great jockeys, there are always ones who would be unbelievable in any era. But I think at that particular moment in the late Nineties, the strength in depth was stronger than at any point.

PETER

I would watch the majority of Tom's races, 99 per cent of them. So in some ways I'm living it again. There's times I pick up the paper and think, 'What the fuck are you riding that for?' And I know Dad would think the same. 'Cos you're living it with them.

I don't care where he finishes. My first thought is, 'Has he finished?' He had a horrible fall at Uttoxeter and you couldn't see him moving. You know instinctively if he's got hurt. Is he hurt badly? And then you think, bollocks, he's got Thistlecrack coming up, I don't want him losing the ride on that. So the emotion is there to start with, and then the jockey in you takes over – Christ, you'll miss a winner! You've twisted your knee, so what? Go ride the next one!

It's a Scudamore trait: my father bore no pain. I didn't ask for any sympathy or expect praise for riding through pain, it was just what you did. Tom fell at Fakenham one day and he'd hurt his shoulder and missed the next winner. I'm thinking to myself, 'Well, he's not a Scudamore, he's just not!' And then he has another bad fall some time later, pushes his shoulder out and says, 'Well, I did dislocate my shoulder at Fakenham but I didn't tell anybody.' And there's me giving him no sympathy . . . That's the emotional roller coaster of it. I have to draw myself back about that and be sensible. He's not my child: he's a man making his own decisions.

MICHAEL

We watch Tom every day. And it's hell sometimes, especially if he hits the floor and doesn't get up, especially if they don't mention anything. It's worse than doing it yourself.

TOM

I think it's always worse for the people watching. When I'm doing it, you're not afraid. You're fully aware of the risks and accept the risks. But when I'm watching my kids showjumping, I'm in pieces, because you're aware of the pain and the dangers – you know what it's like to get hurt: it's a protective thing. I remember saying to Mum, 'How the hell did you cope with me doing it?'

She said, 'Not very well.'

Although Tom's mum, Marilyn, says she has eventually come to terms with watching her son ride in jump races.

MARILYN

I quite enjoy watching him. Obviously I hate it if he has a fall or anything that gets him injured. If I thought I could change the result by not watching it, I wouldn't watch it, but I'm not going to change the result, so I might as well watch it.

Peter has not just been a parent to Tom; he has also sometimes been an employer. It was a challenging new aspect to their relationship.

TOM

I remember riding a horse one day for Grandad when Dad was training them, at Towcester – I'd have been 20 or 21. It was the horse's first run over from Ireland, and I did something wrong. He'd said, 'Be as handy as you can be,' but it took off with me on the way down to the start and I thought, 'No, this would be the wrong way to ride it,' and I dropped it in. Of course, as soon as it jumped off, it didn't pick up the bridle. So then I'm pushing it after two hurdles, having jumped off in mid-div to back, having been told to be handy. I'm pushing it the whole way and it's a never-nearer fourth. If you're watching it, it didn't look so bad because I was flat out everywhere. But I got the start wrong.

He was furious. I remember coming back and he didn't say anything to me. I could just see he was angry. And we got in the car and he quietly just tore a strip off me. Didn't dress it up. There were no bad words used, just, 'It's not a game.' He always says to me that's what Fred Winter told him: 'It's not a game, it's a fucking war out there.' After he'd calmed down a few days later, we were able to laugh and joke about it.

Now, Peter is in Scotland and Michael Jnr is the trainer in Herefordshire. There is still conflict from time to time, but the brothers do their best to resolve it creatively.

TOM

We might disagree on one or two things, Michael and me, silly little things. We used to have a row of fences, baby fences and big fences. And we'd argue because I wanted to school this horse over the baby fences before I'd school him over the big fences. 'He's been running in Ireland – why are you wasting your time putting him over that?'

'Because we always do it that way.'

There would be arguments like that, because we'd all speak our own minds. But I can't remember there being any problems doing it. I just remember it being a lot of fun and really enjoying it.

MICHAEL JNR

We wouldn't hold back if we thought someone had made a mess-up or wasn't doing it right. Many a time has Tom had a go at me, if we haven't done something right here, or one's not fit enough or not schooled right or whatever. If Tom really thought something, he doesn't hold back, and in the same way, if I think he's given one a bad ride, then I'll say my piece. But we'll say our piece, give each other ten minutes and then . . . We're doing it to try and help each other. Yes, you'll get cross, and yes, you won't want to hear it, but you come back and think, maybe you are right. We will fall out but we don't let that stick; we will come back and talk to each other afterwards and say, actually, OK, let's work to make it better.

MARILYN

I think they've both been jolly lucky boys, to have never had a proper job, really.

Tom's much more mellow than Scu was, riding, definitely. I think it helps him a lot. I think he has a much better work/life balance than Scu ever had. Scu was totally consumed by it. And I don't say Tom has been any less ambitious or concentrated. It's just that Scu was far more consumed by the riding than Tom is. I think the only time he ever really switched off from it was when he was doing anything with the boys.

PETER

Tom has a different hand of cards. I think in some ways he's more talented than I am. He's a better athlete. The Pipes haven't hit the heights that they did in my day but he's ridden some very, very good horses. He's ridden nearly as many Cheltenham Festival winners as me. He's ridden over 1,000 winners, he's won a King George.

TOM

I've had ten Festival winners, so I'm three behind Dad. I might struggle to pass him for quantity of winners – I think I've got another 500 to ride – but if I can do him on quality, that'd be all right.

But honestly, I never feel like I'm competing against him. I think we're all very proud of what each other's done, but then we respect the difference in the generations. I know that if Grandad was around with my generation, he'd compete because he'd improve himself to, in the same way as Dad would. But at no point do I think, 'God, I've got that to live up to, or that to do.' I'm in competition with Richard Johnson, Sam Twiston-Davies and Aidan Coleman: I'm not in competition with what Peter Scudamore did. From the minute I started riding, I had that in mind. I'm in a constant battle with myself, really.

5

BEING A JOCKEY

'I may get hurt but I've analysed the situation and it's in my favour.'

'Winning the Derby makes you rich; winning the Grand National makes you famous,' racing folk used to say. While it is certainly possible to earn a lot of money as a jump jockey, surely no one is drawn to that line of work by the lure of the readies on offer. It is very obviously a dangerous job, and the risks do not seem to be reflected in the pay. At the time of writing, professional jump jockeys get £169.85 for each ride, plus up to 9 per cent of prize money won. An agent takes 10 per cent, you must cover all your own expenses, and insurance is required to tide you over when you're injured, because no one will offer you sick pay. There are surer ways to make your millions.

MICHAEL

When I first rode, we were getting seven guineas a ride. I think, about the time I finished, it was not far off 20. It might have been a bit more.

A rough calculation suggests Michael and his colleagues were faring pretty well in 1966 on 20 guineas (or £21) per mount, which would be worth about twice as much as the modern riding fee. On the other hand, getting a share of the prize money was no sure thing.

MICHAEL

You hoped you would get ten per cent off the owner. But it wasn't mandatory. It was up to the owner. One jockey rode a winner for a fellow at Chepstow one day and he gave him ten bob. He said, 'You'd better have it back – you want it more than I do.'

A lot of people used to send a cheque through the post and a nice letter. Others just gave you a dab in the hand there and then on the spot. I didn't miss out many times. Maybe a couple didn't pay up.

Michael recalls one success at Wye at the end of a season, when the owner was keen for him to commit to riding the horse in future but entirely reluctant to cut into his prize money. Michael's way of insisting on his share was to refuse to weigh out, the next time he was due to ride the horse, until payment was made.

MICHAEL

The trainer came in to get the saddle and I said, 'I haven't passed yet.'

He said, 'Why not?'

I said, 'I haven't been paid for the last one.' So he went down and got £20.

You've got to realise, the silly part about it is, we'd have done all this bloody lot for nothing, you know, 'cos we loved it. Half the jockeys would ride for nothing.

TOM

It wasn't a business: it was something you did before you got a proper job. That was why everyone retired at 30, 31. A lot of them were sons of farmers who got going pointing, and then it sort of overtook them.

In Michael's early days as an amateur, riding for nothing was more or less what he was doing. There could still be reward at times, beyond the pleasure of soaring over fences at speed.

MICHAEL

It was rather fun. I used to ride a very good horse called Tantivy for Tom Hanbury, a big, plain, old horse, a lovely horse. I won on him at Wincanton. Tom had been an amateur himself. He gave me two silk handkerchiefs the next time I saw him. Then he rang up and said, would I like to ride Tantivy at Wincanton again? I said I'd love to. When he won again, he gave me two polo-neck sweaters. Then he ran again and, bugger me, he won again, three in a row. Father said: 'I wonder what you'll get this time? Look, you want a decent pair of racing boots. You ask him for them.'

And, to be fair, Tom said, 'Go to Newmarket and get yourself measured up,' and those were my first boots. I think they were about 17 quid or something.

TOM

Grandad didn't want to become a professional. When I grew up, all I wanted to be was a jockey, but that wasn't seen to be a thing when Grandad was riding. It was something you became, it wasn't something 'I'd like to be'. You'd get going and have a few rides as an amateur, and all of a sudden they'd say, 'Well, you've got to come to the Jockey Club and have a meeting.'

In those days, a jockey did not choose for himself whether to continue as an amateur or try to make it as a professional. If he began to get so many rides that he could be said to be taking much-needed work from professionals, he would be called up to the Jockey Club's offices in London for a quiet chat and a ruling about his future status. Michael was summoned along with a small party of other riders including Peter Brookshaw, who rode Hillmere to win the Fox Hunters at Aintree in 1950, and Ted Greenway, who would eventually become Red Rum's vet.

MICHAEL

My second season, I had 150 rides, and the stewards said I should have to go to London and decide whether I'm going to be an amateur or a professional. I had to prove I was getting £1,000 a year, other than racing. I said I was farming and this, that and the other. I didn't want to turn, because I thought I'd be too heavy, but it was the best thing that ever happened, because I kept my weight down, and I was getting paid for what I liked doing best.

All three Scudamores discovered, on entering the weighing room, a series of unwritten rules, the most important of which insisted on respect being shown to more established riders.

PETER

We were taught by our elders, you don't go on the inner of a big boy, and you cut your hair, you turn up smart. This macho thing, you don't go up someone's inside . . . When you go back to it, it was a ruffian sport of very, very tough men, and it's hard to get rid of that completely. It's always going to be there.

Far from helping to get rid of that attitude, at Newbury in 1988 Peter rather entrenched it, when engaging in a furious war of elbows with a rival jockey, Bruce Dowling. Peter felt Dowling was trying to sneak up his inner when he had no right to do so. Dowling later insisted there had been room to run into, and that his rival had not been close to the inside line. They collided on the approach to the cross flight, where Dowling's mount fell.

PETER

I would say I was defending myself. He was coming up my inside, taking my run, putting me in danger. Somebody said, 'He could have sued you for that.' I, in my small mind, being a jockey, thinking you're bigger than the law, never considered that something like that would happen. I thought you didn't let anybody up your inside: that was just the code of honour. It was the pirate's code. You were meant to be tough, and you were meant to have respect. Arthur Thompson was a respected man because people didn't go up his inside. Famously, if you went up his inner, he'd push the bridle off the horse, he would push your foot out of the iron. You just didn't do it. So how do you get that respect if you don't put somebody through a wing? And if you let him up your inside, then you get beat. That's what we were taught.

Among those who instilled this lesson in Peter was Michael, who used to tell a story of the time he rode against Lester Piggott at Hurst Park, in the days when the great Lester was still prepared to test his luck in occasional races over hurdles.

PETER

He says Lester tried to get up his inside, and they pushed Lester against the rails, and all he could hear was the iron scraping against the rail. Lester said to Dad, 'If you'd let me out, I'd have won there.' You go back to the pre-camera days, the inner was sacrosanct.

Peter was given a three-week ban, the longest of his career, for what he did to Dowling – though the happily uninjured Dowling also got three weeks for his part in the collision. Twenty-seven years later, Tom was involved in a similar incident when holding to his line on the approach to the 'elbow' on Aintree's run-in. A rival who was trying to nip up his inner ran out of time and collided with the rail. Tom was found at fault by the raceday stewards, but an appeal panel ruled he was justified in standing his ground.

TOM

Where do you think you're going? Right, if you go there, the emphasis is on you. Good luck with that. If you carry on the course that you're going, you're going for that wing. But I'm not moving out of the way. If you're on a good enough horse, good luck to you. Otherwise, you're eating plastic.

If someone tries to go up your inside, you'll hold your position. You'll stop them from going there, but you can't do what Dad used to do. In my mind, if someone wants to go up my inside, I'll keep straight, and if you've got enough horse to go there, then that's up to you. If I've come off my line, I'm half asleep. If you're jumping the second paddle of hurdles from the rail and something goes up your inside, that's your own fault.

I remember getting run away with one day at Newton Abbot, and there was nothing I could do. I ended up going up AP's inside because I was on a very keen one. I was cheeky, but I had nowhere else to go, I was clipping heels with him. And there was just a gap appeared on the inside and I went through it, and he wasn't very happy about it. But then we came back and watched the replay of it and there wasn't a lot of choice.

That reference to the legendary McCoy underlines a basic truth of race-riding: that the most successful jockeys can impose on their peers and influence the way the game is played.

PETER

Certain people will, by personality and achievement, command respect down at the start. And they tend to dominate the race. If you become the dominant character, then you're going to control the race more often. So if John Francome says, 'I'm going to make the running; don't take me on,' most people won't take him on. But if Joe Bloggs says, 'I'm going to make it; don't take me on,' Francome might say, 'No, you don't: I'm making it.' And that's the way it is. If Joe Bloggs doesn't behave himself, he gets ostracised in the weighing room. Most people want to fit in, so they find a way to do as they're told. But if someone new comes along who won't fall into line, he eventually commands his own respect because people think, I can't bully him. If there's a kid in front of you, you say, 'Bit of light on the inner!' And if they don't move over, you go into the weighing room and say: 'Well, he's a shit.' But the strong man: you respect that man. The weak man, who lets you up the inner, fails.

Not so long ago, we had a jockey called Graham Watters. He came in after one day at Ayr and said a senior jockey was going to hit him because he kept going down the inner, because we keep telling our jockeys to go down the inner. And I said, 'Well, to be perfectly honest, Graham, I'd pay that jockey the same amount of money as I'd pay you. Either you dominate the inner or I'll pay him to do it. It's quite simple.' So it was still happening a few years ago, and you have to be tough enough.

TOM

You can see the ones that are going to be good jockeys because they've got a good understanding of it and they're making the right decisions. And they're willing to learn, and they have an innate understanding. I remember riding with Ryan Moore on the Flat when we were both amateurs, and even at that stage you knew there was something. He'd appear from nowhere. He had an uncanny ability to read a race and make the right decisions. And that was when he was 16, 17. He didn't look great in a finish, none of us did, but he just had this amazing ability to make all the right choices at all the right times.

PETER

I saw lots of people who could ride well but just didn't have the attitude when they got to the track – were probably too intelligent, or just weren't so thick, or weren't as brave. I saw people who mentally couldn't take it: they'd beaten themselves, they'd talked themselves out of it, they doubted. I used to get down to the start and listen to the boy who was hesitating and seeing what happens – I'm sorry, he's not going to make a good jockey. McCoy was a great jockey because of his mental strength.

You've got to be positive in a race, you've got to be positive in your attitude, you've got to be positive in the way you speak to people. If you have that, you have a chance. I get some people whose persona gives them no chance. They may be great doctors or solicitors, but they're not going to be jockeys. It's just a fact of life. They're waiting to see what happens. Once you start having negative thoughts come through, then you're beat. It's no use going out, thinking, 'This is going to fall.' You've got to go out and say, 'It's not going to fall.'

MICHAEL

It's always in the back of your mind you can get a bad fall. If you can get by and not let it worry you too much . . . But there are some jockeys you know are going round just for a living and they're not enjoying it.

PETER

I think there are other people who didn't care. Francome had a great attitude, he wasn't frightened of getting beaten. And some people accused him sometimes of stopping one because he looked so cool, a bit like Gower with cricket. I had a different approach. I was so thick-skinned and stupid, if it got beat I didn't think it was me. So I wasn't frightened of getting beat, therefore I wasn't tense.

Dad was a very nice man, which probably cost him as a trainer. Undoubtedly, he didn't make it as a trainer because he wasn't hard enough. He would have said that himself.

I didn't ride against him, so I don't know if that affability affected him as a jockey. But watch people like Francome and others, who are the nicest people in the weighing room, but once you got onto the racetrack, no quarter was given and it wasn't expected. And if you did give it, you didn't command respect. You wouldn't have commanded the respect of Fred Winter, Josh Gifford, Stan Mellor, if you were in any way soft, because they had no softness in them. So Dad must have been a tough man once the tape went up.

He would refer to it as an unwritten law: early on in a race, you helped your fellow jockey, you gave a bit of light going into a fence, you didn't take him on. But then there comes a point in a race when that is not asked for, or given. When you get to the big races, that point is very much earlier. Your adversaries, you're travelling to the races with them, you're sitting in the weighing room with them, and on an ordinary day at Worcester or Leicester, you'll help them. But at Cheltenham, nobody gets any help at any stage. Dad said you didn't fall out with somebody, because you'd be struggling in a novice chase one day, wanting some help, some light going to a fence, and if Fred Winter doesn't give it to you, you turn over. Occasionally, once a season, maybe three times in your lifetime, you do need help, and I've helped people and people have helped me.

One of the games that goes on between jockeys is trying to find out in advance how a rival horse will be ridden.

TOM

It can be a game of poker. You might discuss it, but you're not going to give away everything. You want to ride the race to suit you. You're trying to get little nuggets of information. There's one or two lads who will always take the mick. There's a senior jockey just now who has a reputation for telling complete lies down at the start, but then it catches you out. You just don't believe them; you ignore everything he says.

At the end of the day, if you're fiddling around, asking everyone what they're doing, you really haven't done your homework. You're relying on other people, but you should know how a horse is ridden or what its strengths are. If you're riding one around Exeter and one of the others has been doing its winning at Newton Abbot, it's probably going to be quicker than you, and its emphasis will be on speed rather than stamina. Watch their races, see what they're like: you'll know their strengths and their weaknesses and what they're likely to do. Unless there's a sudden tactical change. You have to have in mind, if X has been very disappointing being held up for its last seven runs, they might try something different. If that suddenly goes ten lengths clear and it's a stone lower than it won off three years ago, you've got to be aware of that: you don't want to let it go 20 clear.

PETER

We talk to each other in the weighing room: 'Who's gonna make it?'

'I'm gonna make it.'

'No, I am.'

So you get in the paddock and say, 'They're gonna go quick here.' So the trainer tells you to drop in a bit. Everyone else is saying the same thing, so you end up going no gallop.

MICHAEL

I rode with Frenchie Nicholson a bit. He was getting to the end of his career, and I'd sit next to him in the weighing room and always looked up to him. One day at Chepstow, I said to him, 'You'll win here.' I was fishing a bit, trying to find out . . .

He said, 'Boy, never kid one who's kidded millions.'

For all the complexities of working with and against his fellow professionals, Peter was more comfortable doing that than dealing with less experienced, less accomplished riders, whose effect on a race could be unpredictable and disruptive. In 1982, he found himself lining up at Aintree against the amateur jockey Norman Babbage.

PETER

It was the two-mile handicap chase before the Grand National, which is always a terrible race to ride in because you don't want to be injured and miss the National. Aintree was a very fast track and you get fallers there. So you're down at the start with the fastest two-mile chasers in the country, and Norman Babbage says, 'I'm going to make it.' And all the boys are saying, 'For fuck's sake, Norman!'

Anyway, we jumped out, and he says, 'I can't hold my horse!' He comes flying by us, taking us along too fast. But instead of turning left around the grandstand bend as he should, he goes straight on over the Melling Road towards the first fence on the National course, taking himself out of the race.

So that's an extreme example of an amateur buggering up a very important race for us, because at the end of the day we're professional jockeys trying to earn a living. I used to tell the story in after-dinner speeches, saying Norman Babbage was the only man to refuse at the first before the Grand National had even started.

MICHAEL

There was great camaraderie in the weighing room, unbelievable. But the one thing you should not do if you didn't want to get into trouble was ring up a trainer and try and get a ride off another jockey. That was murder. And there were one or two that did it and got away with it. In our day, Tim Molony, who was champion jockey for three or four years, he was a bit naughty, ringing up. I thought the world of Tim. It always left a black mark when people did that.

PETER

Somebody who rang for somebody else's ride was really unpopular. At the time, there was an advert for making phone calls, with a little bird called Buzby. The jockey who was ringing up for rides was known as Buzby. I remember when Ronnie Beggan – he was the first jump jockey to have an agent – sent his card to Martin Pipe. I was really miffed. You don't do that sort of thing. It was the pirate's code again.

I never saw a serious fight, a blood thing. Ringing up for the ride, that was worse than punching somebody. You just didn't do it. But you can't blame people. There are others who got their rides in the bar afterwards – they went and saw the owners. There are ways of getting your rides. But the weighing room was, surprisingly, a non-violent space, for the level of competition and the violence and the stuff that was going on outside – violence in the sense of getting kicked around by a horse.

TOM

If you're approached to ride a horse, it's different. But if you approach somebody, owner or trainer, and try and pinch that ride, it's considered bad etiquette, and some people have a very bad reputation for it. It has led to disagreements, confrontations. Sometimes it can be a case of wires crossed, and you think somebody is sniffing for a ride but actually it's the owner or trainer talking to them, or somebody getting the wrong idea. However, there are jockeys renowned for it, and they certainly wouldn't be respected in the weighing room.

Despite those and other tensions, jockeys prepare for competition alongside each other day after day, literally rubbing shoulders with those who have just carved them up on the track, or been carved up.

PETER

Is there any other sport where a man changes next to his opponent and does it every day of the week? In a tennis tournament, you can hate your opponent, because you see him at Wimbledon, and you won't see him again until some match in America in three weeks' time. In racing, I had to sit next to John Francome for ten years of my life, and if I didn't get on with him at some level, it was to my detriment. So although Richard Dunwoody and I were in determined competition, there was a respect. You have to get on with certain people, or you don't survive.

A kind of seniority system exists, whereby the most senior jockey at a track on a certain day gets to change under the 'top peg', the next most senior is beside him, and so on around the room to the 17-year-old no one has seen before, who keeps his eyes on the floor at all times.

PETER

I think it meant more to certain people. It was almost a thing that the valet was bullshitting to you about: 'I've got you the top peg!' Where's the top peg in a square room? Francome and I very often changed opposite each other, so we both had top pegs. It was there and it wasn't. Steve Smith Eccles always thought he had a top peg, and he'll swear that he did, but I never went in and thought, 'Oh, I've got the top peg today!' It's a lovely legend, myth, part of the stupidity of horse racing. It was a badge of honour if you weren't champion jockey or you weren't commanding respect.

MICHAEL

You wore a neck scarf, which they always said helped you, stopped you breaking your neck. You always had a scarf and a polo-neck sweater, and then you'd put your colours on top of that. And when they called the jockeys out, you used to get up and go to the valet and get him to tie your hat. I got that I could do my own, 'cos I saw Gordon Richards do it one day, so if he can do it, I can. But I'd often see a queue of two or three jockeys waiting to have their hats tied up.

Different people have different ways of controlling their nerves. There were three or four – we used to play rummy for a penny a spot. At the races or on the train, we always used to play this rummy, kept your nerves in peace. Then this one official, he was ever such a nice chap: his job was to call, 'Jockeys out!' I remember him one day, he walked round the table, saw I'd got a good hand, so he hung on for a bit.

PETER

Fear makes you humble. I had an element of fear, because you're riding in a 17-runner novice chase and you can get hurt. You realise that. You don't get cocky, because if you win that, you're in a 17-runner handicap hurdle next.

You always get a young man coming through that is braver and stronger and better than the rest. And you can see him changing. Dunwoody was one, Adrian Maguire was another. Comes into the weighing room just at the end of my time, fearless, absolutely fearless. I talked to Adrian about it recently and he said, 'Yes, when I was like that, I was like the little kid in the back of the class, playing with the compasses, not taking any notice. But you get a few slaps. . .' And he had some horrible falls. He said, 'Suddenly, I'm the little boy at the front of the class, putting my hand up, answering all the questions.'

You get people come in, they're not brave, they're stupid, and they'll ride stupidly until they get hurt. And then you get the people that are brave. Francome was very, very brave. I saw him one day at Fontwell, he jumped the first, went round the bend and pulled up at the second. That's bravery, because he said, 'This horse is going to fall and hurt me.' A great many jockeys would have carried on regardless and very possibly got hurt. A show of machismo never mattered to John. But at other times, when he analysed the risks and said, 'I have a better than 50-50 chance of standing up on this horse,' he was the bravest man that rode. The stupid one says, 'I won't get hurt.' The brave one says, 'I may get hurt, but I've analysed the situation and it's in my favour.'

When I was 23, 24, 25, I was as brave as a lion. And then you think, 'Hang on – I'm not going to last.' It's a gradual realisation: 'I'm going to have to change my approach a little bit: I'm smashing myself up all the time. I'm going to have to use my brain a little bit more, rather than trying to be the bravest man that's ever done the job.' I wasn't getting to the end of a season, and it was costing me the chance to be champion. After I came to that thought, I won on horses that I wouldn't have won on before. And I probably won on a few before that I wouldn't have won on after.

TOM

When you're first riding, you're afraid of losing. The more success you get, you're not afraid of bollockings, you're not afraid of getting beat: all you're interested in is winning, or how do we win next time? You're getting off them saying, 'Right, sorry about that, that's a complete balls-up, I did this wrong, this wrong,' or: 'You told me to be fourth or fifth, but I couldn't lay up there. If I rode the race again, I'd jump out to make the running . . .' Or nobody wants to make the running, and you'll think, 'I'm on a 10-1 shot here . . . Hmmm . . . Sod it!' You go against instructions. You're not afraid: all you're interested in is winning, and getting yourself the best opportunity of winning, or finding out how this horse can win. And that's where experience and confidence come in. That comes in at different stages, depending on how successful you've been or who you're riding for that will back you to the hilt.

PETER

For a jockey, the moment of winning is the highest point. You get the biggest adrenaline, even if you're odds-on favourite. People will say anyone could have won on it, but anybody didn't win on it: you won on it. It was your partnership, that you and the horse worked out together. Then as you come into the paddock the adrenaline quietly drops down. The trainer says, 'Well done,' the adrenaline goes up a bit more, and then you come into the weighing room, it drops – it gradually drops down from there. I think that's what was the obsession to me: that moment of winning, whether it was a short head, a walkover or whatever. That's what became the drug.

It's easy to stand back and say, isn't it all fantastic? It's not. When you're in it, Dad gets jocked off Linwell, I didn't win a Grand National or a Gold Cup, I rode Chatam instead of Rushing Wild in a Gold Cup and, Christ, if Rushing Wild had won instead of being second, what an idiot I'd have looked. Within it, it feels mostly down. But obviously it's mostly up; you just don't see it like that. And I think Thomas feels it.

TOM

I'd entirely agree with that. It's not mostly down, but you're not getting carried away with the emotions because it's such a thin line between being right and being wrong. You don't want to make the wrong decisions: which horse to ride in a novice hurdle, which meeting to go to. You're grateful to be in those positions, to ride the good horses, but the mental side of that is quite difficult.

When I won the King George on Thistlecrack, the high of that lasted until I got beat on the next one. I got beat in a handicap hurdle on Dell' Arca and probably should have won on him. I remember coming back that night, saying to Joe Tizzard, 'We'll meet up for a drink at some point, have a bit of a celebration . . .' We've never got round to it.

Because there's racing the next day, the enjoyment is winning it, and then it's done. It might be different if you win a National or a Gold Cup, perhaps. I see jockeys win the Gold Cup, arrive the next day very hung-over for the Midlands National and never kick on from there: that's the highlight of their career – it's a downward spiral from there.

One minute you're in fashion, then you're not. It's very easy to get into a thing where you start moaning, 'Oh, I should be riding that.' You just have to keep positive and keep moving on, but it's very easy to get down. There'll be times when it really pisses you off that you're not riding certain horses, or you made the wrong decision, but luckily, if you've got enough horses to ride, there's always tomorrow.

With their physical wellbeing as well as their employability at risk each time they go to work, it's no wonder that some jockeys get a bit superstitious, in the hope of influencing events over which they have little control.

PETER

I remember Richard Linley gave me a pair of gloves once because he said they were unlucky for him. He kept falling in them. I was going well – I think the others were saying, 'That'll stop him . . .' And I'm taking them, thinking: 'Fucking gloves aren't gonna stop me . . .'

People would say, 'You're on a good run.' I'm not on a good run: this is what happens all the time! You have to think positive. New colours, new boots, new saddle – anything out of the ordinary has to be pushed out of your mind. So the hardest thing was when you got down to the start and there was an amateur – that's what disturbs you, because it's breaking the ordinary. You control the ordinary; it's the extraordinary you can't control. 'It's a dangerous job, but I've evaluated it and I'm prepared to take the risk' – but when you throw another risk in, my little monkey in my head says, 'That's not right!'

TOM

A lot of the Irish lads have crosses of St Christopher. Some will touch wood just before they go out. But I can't think of anyone who's particularly superstitious. In Dad's day, Hywel Davies was said to be superstitious. He'd leave a rolled cigarette in the hope that he'd come back and finish it off.

Some jockeys found that it was bad luck to be superstitious.

TOM

Jim Best the trainer, when he was riding as an amateur, he told the valet, 'I was on the way here and I thought I saw a magpie, and I said, "Hello, Mr Magpie," and it wasn't: it was a speed camera, and it flashed me.'

Where I might be superstitious is, you try and do the same routine as when you had a nice winner the year before. You try and walk the course at the same time, do the same things in the same order. But that's more putting your mind in the right place than actually being superstitious. It's trying to harness that positive energy, trying to get the same concentration, the same feeling as you had when it was successful, when it worked.

If things went wrong, there would sometimes be a way for Peter to escape serious criticism, a way that is no longer open to his son.

PETER

When I first rode, there were no camera patrols. You went off to Fakenham; obviously no trainer went to Fakenham. If you fell off it three out, you went and gave the travelling head lad a tenner: 'Say to the guv'nor that fell.' You go into the clerk of the scales and you say, 'Fell, sir.' And you hope the *Sporting Life* results man was taking it off the clerk of the scales. You could do extraordinary things when there was no camera, which we just accepted.

There's stories of Frenchie Nicholson jumping in on a foggy day at Wincanton, having cut across the middle. You could put people through the wing, you could push people's bridle off, and you could be a big, tough man that dominated things and not follow the rules, because they couldn't prove it.

The arrival of cameras at every racecourse was also a huge step forward for those whose job it is to police the sport, and catch those running a horse with deliberate defeat as the aim.

PETER

Dad said you didn't stop horses for bookmakers. If a trainer had told you to give a horse a quiet run, you gave a horse a quiet run, because that's what we accepted, never thinking we were defrauding the public. There were no bumpers in Dad's day: the horse had to be educated, and lots of horses got their education on the track. The difference between educating a horse and stopping it is a very, very thin line.

I grew up with Grandad's stories – he told them over Sunday lunch – about this kind of thing. Perhaps they knew they had a good horse, but it wasn't for the public to know yet. Their justification was, the horse was being educated. But Dad said, once it had been placed, once it was public property, you then had to do your best.

In defence of that attitude, I'd say that definitely, if you give a horse a hard race first time, you can destroy its career. I've done that: I've given horses a hard race first time as a jockey, even without hitting them, and they never ran good races again.

I stopped a horse one day when I was very young and green. I won't name the trainer because he's still alive, a right bastard. I stopped one for him because I was told to, and I was had in. The stewards let me off. One of them came afterwards and said to me, 'I saw what you were doing. Don't be stupid: don't do that again.' And I never did. That put me on the right side.

In my time, I was only ever once rung up to stop a horse. And I wasn't even riding the bloody thing. It was before the overnight declaration of jockeys. I'd decided to go to Ludlow instead of Ascot. Somebody rang me up and said, 'If you win on that horse tomorrow, you'll get shot.' And I thought, 'Well, that's bad luck for Jimmy Duggan, 'cos he's the one who's on it.'

If racing was crooked in those days, I was riding lots of odds-on favourites for Pipe and nobody ever came up and asked me to stop them. And I'd been in the company of Brian Wright, the drug smuggler who's in jail for the rest of his life – he's supposed to have corrupted jockeys. He never asked me to stop a horse.

We had punters. We constantly had people ringing for tips – it was part of our way of life. They were London people; some were owners. You say, 'This'll win today,' and they give you a few quid if you're right. It was accepted by everyone that this went on. One of the jockeys in my day asked his trainer for a bigger retainer; he needed a bit more money and felt he deserved it. The trainer says, 'Just get some more punters.' But now Thomas couldn't possibly behave like that.

The regulation of betting now is far, far superior than in our day. The worst thing, in hindsight, is that I didn't care if I was in the first four, if I was beat. It wasn't till later that I understood the value of each-way punting. I wasn't riding for the punter, I was riding for myself, and now I think that's wrong. I remember dropping my hands for third or fourth place one day, and I got away with it, but you're getting booed. But we were never taught, and how were we meant to know? I wouldn't know anything unless my father told me. There was no lesson, no, 'You must ride out for third, because some of these people may have backed you to get it. You owe it to them and you owe it to racing, because we need them to keep coming back.'

TOM

That has changed so much from when Dad finished and when I started, because the nature of betting changed. I was never approached by anyone. Dad had his punters, and I remember being in the car when he talked to them. You wouldn't have them now. When Dad retired, spread betting came along, and then Betfair. Before, OK, it was against the rules, but it was slightly accepted that you had your punters. Members of the Jockey Club would be punters for the top Flat jockeys. That's the way it was. But then, with the advent of Betfair, people can make more money out of knowing what's going to lose. And that becomes a different thing altogether. You don't want punters. Once you're in their grasp, you're just gone. You don't want anything to do with them.

The problem, I suppose, arises when you're 18, 19, and someone offers you a lot of money. Say they offer you ten grand for information, or to do something. If you're in a position where you're desperate, you do desperate things.

Martin Pipe always taught me, never accept any money off anybody. If you're in trouble, you come to me. If someone offers you ten grand, what an enormous sum of money. But that's not your yearly wage. In the big picture, what's ten grand worth? You could end up making £100,000 a year. Why would you go and throw it all away for £10,000? Because the next time they come for you, it won't be with £10,000. It'll be nothing. It'll be a gun or a threat to expose you. They've got you by the balls. And he made that clear to me when I was 17, 18, when I was just getting going. He said, 'There are going to be people who'll want to speak to you. Just be very, very careful.' I remember that being a very good piece of advice, and because of that I'm always wary of people when I meet them for the first time, if I'm honest. I can be a bit standoffish, because I don't know what their motives are. Maybe it's me being over-precious, but I just have that mentality, I'm afraid.

While jockeys might always be trying, they tend to find their efforts meet with more success at some places than others.

TOM

It used to annoy Dad if it was said he was no good around one track. There'd be tracks, he would tell me now, he rode better than others. He said it took him a long time to work out Sandown, and there are tracks now that I ride that I don't feel as comfortable on as others.

A lot of it's down to where your trainers run their horses. For some reason, myself and David Pipe have a very good record around Cheltenham and Newbury, so I love going there. We have a shit record around Kempton. I think in the last ten years, I've had five winners round Kempton, and three of those have been Grade Ones. I don't mind riding round Kempton but it's just that David won't send his really good horses there: they'll wait a week and go elsewhere. Whereas Nicky Henderson, his stats at Kempton, Newbury, Cheltenham are fantastic, whereas there'll be other places, Aintree, for a long time: rubbish. And yet you'd think, 'If you're so successful at Kempton, you'd be very good at Aintree,' but I don't think he had a winner at the Grand National meeting for about seven years at one point, until Irish Hussar won the novice chase.

You can look too deeply into some things. Dad was never a massive fan of Sandown, always thought it was overrated. But he still rode lots of winners round there. He won the Mildmay Cazalet Memorial, which used to be a really big race. Grandad loved Sandown, absolutely best place on earth.

PETER

I knew you didn't go down the inside at the three Railway Fences at Sandown, because in my father's day, the inside had a little bit of a drop. If you meet the first fence right, you're then supposed to meet the other two right. But things like that used to play on my mind. I used to be so conscious of meeting the first one right that I'd meet the second one wrong, and think, 'This is a load of bollocks anyway.' Sandown was Dad's favourite track. I never got it like he did.

TOM

There's always somewhere you feel more comfortable. Dad always used to say Plumpton was an idiot's track; didn't particularly like riding round there. I've had loads of winners there; I really like riding round Plumpton. I don't mind Sandown, but it wouldn't be one of my favourites.

When Dad was riding, Haydock was fabulous. Now I think it's a dog track. It's a very different course to the one Dad rode round. They've turned it into a sharp, front-runner's track, whereas before it was as good as Newbury: a great, big, fair track. Now, if you don't get the right position, you're beaten after three hurdles. It's like Southwell now. They've turned it into Southwell. The chase course used to be right on the outside, and the hurdles course just inside that, and then they moved it right inside. At least it's still a racetrack, because the other option was that jump racing wouldn't continue there, and it does exist and they have good prize money there.

PETER

'Dog track' is going too far. I have huge admiration for the administration at Haydock. They sat me down and said, 'Look, Flat racing's making money, jumping isn't. In some ways, Flat racing is subsidising the jumps.' So it was a commercial decision to move the jumps course inside the Flat track. Of course it's changed, but so has the Grand National course. So has Leicester. There's a picture from the 60s of Oxo and Nicolaus Silver jumping the water at Leicester. You see how high they're getting, because the fences of the time were so stiff and you didn't touch them. They're Grand National horses: that's why they're not touching it.

I loved Haydock because you didn't have to give them a ride. If you gave them a ride or you rode like a hero, you turned them over. The horsemen, like John Francome and Neale Doughty, were good round Haydock. You had to go down the middle, because they were big fences that had a drop on the inside. You'd turn over if you didn't. You had to look at the whole fence for many, many strides out. It suited those lovely old staying chasers of Gordon

Richards that Doughts used to ride. You didn't sit up the neck. They needed wagoning round there.

TOM

Dad could be dismissive about Lingfield. I think Lingfield's a brilliant track, but apparently before they put the all-weather in, it was absolutely brilliant. I remember Dad saying they completely ruined Lingfield: they changed the layout of the track. And yet I wish there was more racing there. It's very fair, lovely fences, all in good positions, you can ride any sort of race. Those are the courses you like best, the ones that are fair. Exeter's a fair track, and so are Ffos Las and Newbury. Taunton is generally suited to front-runners, Sandown is very hard to make the running round. Carlisle, very hard to make the running round there, because it's so stiff. You turn into the straight and you don't kick, you wait. I remember Neale Doughty saying to me, 'Jump the fences up the run-in. Don't go for him – wait, wait, wait, wait, wait. If you're going well, just stay going well.' At Carlisle, when you think about kicking, you wait ten seconds.

At Stratford, when they get over the mound in the back straight, they shoot down, and because of that you've got to be in a position three furlongs before that, so you're not caught out. Your first ride round there, you think, 'I'm going really well here . . . Fuck me, where have they gone?' And you can never get it back.

You jump the last down the back at Newton Abbot, fences or hurdles, in general you can't be any more than three lengths off the leader. Fakenham, going out on the final circuit, you've got to be in front or second; otherwise, you're getting pushed round them all the time.

PETER

Leicester, we always used to go and speak to the groundsman to find out where the better ground might be. When it was heavy there, you were usually better on the outer. Fontwell, I used to go under the hedge, because the hedge has drawn up the moisture, so the ground isn't so soft. I remember getting beat on one of Neville Callaghan's there; I turned into the straight and, as I remember it, I was gonna get beat and I switched to the inner. He gave me one of the biggest rollickings I ever had. He didn't put me up for a long time, because he said I should have come down the outer.

I learnt a huge amount off Martin Pipe's father, David, who was a bookmaker. He used to say to me, 'The top jockeys come down to Newton Abbot and ride it the same as they do Newbury: they sit in behind and think the second-last there is like the second-last at Newbury.' I knew you had to be in a good position jumping the last down the back at Newton Abbot, so you were in the right position to turn into the straight.

I remember at Lingfield trying to make ground up the hill. Fred Winter told me, 'You've got to be in position at the bottom of the hill. Sit up the hill, travel down the hill.' Cheltenham's very much the same. You can drop them in but, once you turn down the back, by the water, you've got to be making ground up, so you're in a decent enough position.

Towcester is idiosyncratic. Horses win there that don't win anywhere else. Stan Mellor said, 'At Towcester everyone thinks you hold up,' but it's hard to make ground when you're going down hills, up hills or round bends. And what are you doing most of the time at Towcester? You're going up a hill, down a hill or round a bend. Stan said Towcester is a make-all track: it's hard to come from behind.

I try to tell my jockeys to get into position for the final bends. It's no use getting to the bend and then panicking, or trying then to get a position if there's a lot of runners.

When jockeys chat about how courses have changed, it is never long before talk turns to the quality of the obstacles. It is an article of faith among the older generation that the fences were bigger, or at least stiffer, when they had to get over them. Michael claimed he was able to walk along the top of some steeplechase fences half a century ago.

PETER

I've got a picture of myself, as an amateur, jumping at Fontwell – it's hanging on my bedroom wall. Tom got it for me. It's taken at such an angle, the fence looks very small . . . Of course, when you're lying on the ground and 20 horses are galloping over you, it doesn't make a difference what the size of the fence is.

Although we say it is much easier now because the fences are softer, the jockeys are having more rides, therefore they're having more falls. I think it was one in 13 when I was riding, probably one in ten when Dad was riding, and now it's about one in 16. But you multiply the number of rides, and the number of falls remains the same.

Are the fences really softer now than 30 years ago?

PETER

Yes, it is definitely the case, and if you went to a clerk of the course, he would say, 'Don't say anything, buddy, but we have softened the fences.' Look, I've got a son going round, I don't think it's a bad thing.

TOM

When you watch the old races at Cheltenham, you realise the fences now are not as stiff as they were then. You're not getting the ditch falls, when they dropped their hind legs in the ditch and turned over, which they did when Dad was riding. I think the design has changed a bit as well. They had the gorse in front of them when Dad and Grandad were riding: that's completely gone.

It does change from course to course. Some places have a reputation. It's basically down to whoever's building the fences. Somewhere like Ludlow used to be very soft and didn't take much jumping. The last couple of years, they've made a concerted effort to turn that around. I think they've done a good job there because before it wasn't a fair test. Something could get half-way up the fence there and it didn't stop them. You'd ride something that was a really good jumper round there and it would get beat.

You don't want them being unfair. When Grandad was riding, people didn't like Plumpton. And then when Dad was riding, Taunton had a reputation, because of the camber of the bends. I think Grandad said Ascot wasn't much fun to begin with, when it took over jump racing from Hurst Park in 1965, because the fences were stiff.

Even if the fences have softened, a jockey's life remains a bit of a grind. But the grind can be addictive, and it can shield you from some of the tedious chores faced by those with less exotic jobs.

PETER

The thing I found most difficult when I gave up, which I still do, is: I'm not riding today – where is racing, where's the racing results? I felt it was a badge of dishonour if there was racing on and you didn't have a ride. And in some ways it's hiding your head in the sand, because if you go to Plumpton for one, you don't have to face the bank manager, go shopping, do all the things in ordinary life. That's the bubble that you live in. It's the most important thing in the world, being a jockey, being part of the circus.

TOM

One thing I find very difficult is when you get hurt. You become so institutionalised to knowing what you're doing at entries and declaration time. If my girlfriend says to me, 'What are you doing next weekend? We've been invited somewhere.' Well, I don't know. I'm not thinking that far ahead. This week, I'm thinking, 'I've got tomorrow off, probably Towcester on Wednesday, don't know where I'll be on Thursday, and I'll have to decide Ascot or Haydock for Saturday.' That's as far as it goes. I'm not thinking about Easter coming up, or the girls are on half-term this week. So as soon as you get a gap, you feel completely lost. If I'm injured for a bit or suspended for a week, it's a really weird feeling. You want to look at entries and declarations, and if they don't concern you, it's a really hollow feeling. It's horrible.

It's a very sheltered life. You have everything planned for you. You're in bed at 9 p.m. because you know you've got to be up at 5 a.m. to get to the yard at 7.30. I'm in the first at Plumpton, that's 2.15, so I've got to be there at 1.15, which means I've got to leave at 9. That's all you're thinking about. And then at the end of the day, can I be back home by 9, in which case I can have a meal? Or do I stop at Marks & Spencer for a sushi thing?

PETER

Sometimes you've got to grow up. Undoubtedly, to be a sportsman, you're a spoilt child. It's a game, isn't it, really? You're going out to play and getting paid for it. As Francome used to say, 'A bomb's gone off in Lebanon but you don't care.' You say: 'OK, I'm very sorry about that, but what's going to win the novice chase?' There's a war on, or a bomb goes off in London – as long as it doesn't affect racing, plough on! It's wrong: insulated, very immature, almost childlike. People do change. I was perfectly aware that I had to grow up.

I remember when my grandfather died, I wasn't going to go to his funeral. And my grandmother said, 'You're going to his funeral.' I think racing must have been off in the end, so I did go. I would have gone to Plumpton for one ride. 'I'm sorry, but you dying gets in the way of my . . .' Of course it's wrong. I didn't go to my sister's wedding: I went and rode at Perth. Nicky had no issue with that whatsoever. But now I look back, it's wrong. Clearly wrong. It's only now that you look back and think, life is bigger than that. Being sport, of course it's tough. But it's not the real world. You're extending your youth to your mid-30s or whenever. Don't come out and be sad about leaving. Come out and say, 'I was bloody lucky to have done it.'

6

THE POINT OF IT ALL: WINNING AT CHELTENHAM

'No, no, I'm quite happy not to have ridden a winner here . . .'

Year after year, jump racing folk try to convince themselves that there's a whole season full of races to aim at, and that success in November can be just as gratifying as success in the middle of March. But, for as long as most folk can remember, the Cheltenham Festival has been the place where everyone wants to win.

PETER

There's no other meeting like it, even Grand National week. At Cheltenham, every single race is a life-defining moment. It was three days in my time, the be-all and end-all of everything. You started on the Tuesday, and suddenly you're walking out of the weighing room on the Thursday night. It's all rushed into one, and the emotional turmoil of that is draining.

TOM

At Cheltenham, you find out who the champions are. You're riding expensive horses – Moon Racer and so on: they haven't been bought to win a race, they've been bought to win at Cheltenham, and here it is. This is it, this is why people are spending six figures. Western Warhorse, 33-1 no-hoper for the Arkle – he'd cost £125,000. He was bought to win at Cheltenham. And that's not even top-of-the-range: that's the average. That's what you're dealing with.

If you get beaten elsewhere, you're very disappointed; you might be grumpy about it, but you might learn something from it. You come to Cheltenham, that's not the time to learn: you have to win. You can't come back and say, 'I tell you what, we were unlucky there. If I'd ridden him a bit more positively . . .' If you get beat in the Christmas Hurdle, you're given another chance. If you get beat in the Champion Hurdle, you get the sack.

Nor is there any escaping the atmosphere, no hope of doing something else to distract you in the hours before the tape goes up. Most jockeys get to Cheltenham early, to avoid being stuck in traffic. It means they are in the weighing room for hours with nothing to do but pore over the form and fret.

PETER

I always remember a jockey I rode with called Mick Williams. Before he went out, he used to smack his stick on the table. If he did it at Wolverhampton or Worcester you'd be annoyed, but you could just shake it off. When he whacked his stick on the table at Cheltenham, that monkey came flying out of you – you'd just –

Scu is rising from his chair as if for a fight, roaring with pent-up aggression.

PETER

You go to Cheltenham on an ordinary day and there's two with a chance. At the Festival, there's seven with a chance, and 12 or 15 that think they've got a chance. The intensity is different. The circus has changed. You've got Irish people coming in who are not members of the circus, northern people who are not members of the circus, you've got people coming for their one big break in life, riding a horse that's going to make them or break them.

We didn't know what was happening in Ireland. The *Sporting Life* in those days would be dominated by Uttoxeter or whatever was going on in England. When Tied Cottage and these great Irish horses turned up, you hadn't seen them on telly. The BBC might have shown a glimpse of the Irish Gold Cup. I'd think I had two aces in my hand and then these Irish would come across, horses looking like hat racks, and they'd gallop into the distance.

Now, of course, we have pre-Cheltenham talks, and everybody's got an opinion whether the Leopardstown novice hurdle was a good race or a bad race. But you had no opinion in those days.

TOM

I remember going to the Festival with one chance and hoping to God. And then I've had years where I'm going with seven or eight chances, and that makes life a lot easier. 'If Dell' Arca gets beaten, I've got Kings Palace to look forward to' – you're still walking on air. 'Cor, I wasn't expecting Western Warhorse to win! Today's my crap day and I've had a winner, so imagine what tomorrow's going to bring . . .' Because of that, you're really level: you're not pinning everything on one hope, you're not going out for the one race thinking, 'It's going to be a long week if this doesn't go in . . .'

I remember I'd be the one watching AP and those guys having winners, and you could see how relaxed they were. They'd come in, changing their colours, have a bit of craic with the valets. I'd be getting down, Noel Fehily sitting next to me would be getting more and more pissed off as every single one got beat, and you'd see AP having winners and Dickie having winners – you'd just see the relief lifting off their shoulders – and then they'd go and have another one, and suddenly they're a barrel of laughs. They're not getting on your nerves or anything, but you're just watching them . . .

And all of a sudden it flips. I'd be the one coming back in, laughing and joking. Looking around, I remember AP getting more and more pissed off, kicking things. Dickie was pretty level, Noel getting fucked off with it all. It goes like that. But you leave them to it: you don't say, 'Oh, it'll all change tomorrow,' because you don't want that. You're not giving them a pick-up, but at the same time you're trying not to say, 'Cor, wasn't today great? I was amazing! Did you see that?' They've got no interest in that, and you've got other people to speak to about it.

Peter spent the first half of his career wondering when the wheel was going to turn his way at the Festival. It was a place that repeatedly frustrated both him and his main employer, 'the Duke', David Nicholson, whose Condicote stable was close to the track. By contrast, Cheltenham glory came easily for the Yorkshire-based Michael Dickinson, who famously trained the first five home in the 1983 Gold Cup.

PETER

I couldn't ride a winner at Cheltenham for years. Dickinson was making us look pretty stupid. Unbelievably stupid. What are the chances of getting the best five steeplechasers in your yard? Millions and billions to one. He's dominating in sheer class, and when your nickname's the Duke, you don't want to be dominated.

You were almost going out there feeling like fodder. It was a social thing. 'Oh, it's Cheltenham, we've got to have runners.' It was on the Duke's doorstep: half of them wouldn't have run if he wasn't based there. So the thing was becoming self-perpetuating. He's living in the Cotswolds, he's got Lord Vestey as his main owner, and his dad, Frenchie, had ridden Golden Miller. It was difficult.

Badsworth Boy [trained by Dickinson] may or may not have been the best two-miler of all time, but his dominance at the time was so supreme. I rode Artifice against him: Artifice would carry 11st 10lb and win the two-mile handicap chase round Aintree. He was a very, very fine horse. But by the time

I'd jumped two fences at Cheltenham, it's over: Badsworth Boy only has to stand up. Dickinson horses were that much better.

I half had a thought: 'Well, if I don't ride a Festival winner, I don't ride a Festival winner. I've been champion jockey.' It wasn't eating me, it wasn't affecting my confidence or anything like that.

It's sad, when I try to pull away from myself – I wasn't aware until Dad's death, really, of the number of winners he rode round Cheltenham. I was quite arrogant, I suppose, or thick or stupid. I thought, 'Well, maybe the Gold Cup wasn't quite such a big race in those days.' But that's thoroughly unfair. I'm just saying how I coped with it. I thought in my own mind I was a better jockey. Dad rode with his stirrup leathers long. Jockeys weren't as good in those days. But that's just the stupidity of youth coming through.

My burning ambition was always to be champion jockey. I really do think that. I might not get a winner at Cheltenham, but if I rode three at Wolverhampton on the Friday, that was great.

In the end, Peter got the Festival wins that allowed him to set aside such rationalisations. Tom has also achieved success at Cheltenham in March. A packed and entertaining Festival could be made out of all the races there that have fallen to a Scudamore at one time or another.

THE SUPREME NOVICES' HURDLE:

- 1950 Sir Charles (Michael)
- 1961 Greektown (Michael)

The first Scudamore victory at the Cheltenham Festival came in the last race on day one in March 1950. A few months shy of his 18th birthday, and still riding as an amateur, Michael rode Sir Charles to win the second division of the Gloucestershire Hurdle, now known as the Supreme. The horse was trained by Michael's father, Geoffrey, and allowed to start at 25-1 by a sceptical public which at that point had no reason to respect the surname. 'Sir Charles was never out of the first three,' reported the next day's Sporting Life. *'He won by a length, his rider Mr Scudamore keeping his mount going well.'*

Eleven years later, Michael won the race again, this time aboard the Willie Stephenson-trained Greektown, who finished strongly after being held up to win by three lengths, despite giving weight to all his rivals. These were the only two wins over hurdles at the Festival for a jockey who gained much more admiration for his riding in steeplechases.

The Festival has grown enormously in fame and importance since the war. Cheltenham did not dominate the thoughts of jockeys or define their careers in the 1950s as it does now; that, at least, was the impression left by Michael on both Peter and Tom. While he enjoyed his share of success there, those memories did not come up in conversation as often as Oxo's National.

TOM

He never said much about his Cheltenham winners to me. I'm sure the first one, on Sir Charles, trained by Great-grandad, must have given him enormous pleasure. But I can't really remember him talking much about the others.

Greektown was basically his favourite horse, I think. He used to love riding him. He'd have been just about the best hurdler Grandad rode. They won the Gloucestershire Hurdle and they had a go at the Champion Hurdle in 1963.

THE ARKLE TROPHY:

- 1964 Greektown (Michael)
- 2014 Western Warhorse (Tom)

Dunkirk was sent off favourite for the 1964 Arkle, or the Cotswold Chase, as it was then known. He fell at the second-last, but was behind the winner at the time, and the Sporting Life*'s Tom Nickalls had seen enough. 'There is little doubt that the best horse won,' he wrote. 'This was the big, handsome Greektown. His jockey, M Scudamore, confirmed to me afterwards that he jumped like an old hand.'*

PETER

The two races Dad talked about were the Gold Cup on Linwell and Greektown's Arkle. It was Greektown's first time over fences, an extraordinary achievement in itself. He said Greektown was a tearaway, and he used to joke that, when he went to school him, he'd have his breakfast beforehand because he didn't know whether he was going to survive to have his breakfast after. I don't think Willie Stephenson schooled his horses all that much. Dad said Greektown was frightened of his fences, and that's why he stood off so far.

TOM

Grandad was convinced Greektown had been got at when Dunkirk beat him 20 lengths in the Champion Chase in 1965. Dunkirk was supposedly a great horse, but Grandad said Dunkirk beat him a lot easier than he should have done. Greektown gave him absolutely no feel that day. Whether he was really got at, or whether it was just an excuse, you couldn't be sure. Now you can blood-test them and find out the horse is actually sick. But I do remember Grandad being pretty convinced. That was one of his biggest disappointments.

Half a century after Michael's success in this race for the fastest novice chasers, his grandson followed up on Western Warhorse, whose main achievement beforehand had been to antagonise everyone around him.

TOM

He was an absolute bastard. He really was a bastard of a horse. The lads that rode him out at home, you wouldn't know what he was going to do next. He was a complete runaway and would just bolt. It took three people to get me on him, because he'd bolt otherwise. David Pipe was there, legging me up, Gerry Supple was there holding one rein, and some brave bugger was leading him up, literally in front of him, holding on to his bit. And they're all hanging off him. And as soon as you got on him, he would just go. You just had to be pointing in the right direction. He wasn't much fun.

At Kempton on Boxing Day, he'd buried me. I'd got on him fine, got down to the start and I got my girth checked. And as I did that, he bolted through some rails and I fell off him. After that, I thought, 'I'll never get my girth checked on him again.'

The next time I rode him was at Doncaster, two miles three: he made all and won, but was hanging on at the end. Jumped brilliantly, and it wasn't a bad little race, but it was a fast-diminishing neck at the end. He didn't show an awful lot of speed. And he's by Westerner, who won an Ascot Gold Cup. We all thought when he turned up in the yard that he was going to be a three-miler – that's what he was bought for.

But after I rode him there, I spoke to his owner, Roger Brookhouse, and he goes, 'I know what that horse needs.'

'What's that, Roger?'

'That'll win the Arkle. I'll run him in the Arkle.'

He clearly wasn't quick enough to run in an Arkle, and this was going to be an above-average Arkle, with Dodging Bullets, Champagne Fever, Trifolium. Western Warhorse was rated 129. I was thinking, 'He'll win a nice little handicap somewhere on a Saturday round Sandown or something. Flipping Arkles are something else.'

I said, 'I'm not sure about that, Roger, but, look, you pay the bills. Whatever you want to do, but I'm not sure the Arkle's the race for him, if I'm honest. I don't think he'll be quick enough.'

'His jumping'll stand him in good stead.'

Roger's one of those people that, once he's made his mind up, that's it. You've got to respect him for it. Some people, you can try and turn them, but Roger's had horses a long time, so fair enough.

I remember schooling him in the hood just before. They put the hood on him for the first time, and I remember an ear flicked out of the hood and got stuck underneath it, and he bolted down the track. Luckily, he stopped just before hitting something. I couldn't get off him soon enough after that.

But the speed of the race suited him. He jumped the first few nicely, and Ruby went on and I was able to sit fourth or fifth. When they all came past me, I was expecting to drop back, but his jumping kept him in there. At the top of the hill, Daryl Jacob came past me and I just let him in, because I thought, 'We're going back a bit here, they'll quicken away from me.' And I pulled him out and he started running down the hill. I thought, 'I'll be placed here.'

And then we winged the fence down the bottom of the hill, and suddenly I'm in with a chance. In the end, when we winged the last, I thought we'd go away, but Champagne Fever kept on battling and we were only in front two strides before the line. But I knew going across the line. Ruby knew he'd been beaten and I knew I'd won, however tight it was.

He was an absolute headcase, and even coming back in after he'd won, he was trying to disappear off in every single direction. Martin Pipe normally likes leading in the winners, and he went to lead him in. He forgot that this horse was a lunatic. He's gone to grab him and the horse has gone to bolt again. I've said, 'Mr Pipe, just leave it!'

Everyone was just so shocked and excited that he won. And it wasn't a fluke. He was the best horse on the day.

It was bedlam after that. And it was such a great way to start the week, because I knew I had loads of good rides later on. If you'd said to me, which is my ride with the least chance at the Festival, it would have been him. He's had one run over fences, he's 33-1, he's rated 129. He should have been 100-1. But he won and Roger was right: he was an out-and-out two-miler. At the beginning of the season, I'd have given him to you as a Pertemps horse, or maybe one for the Kim Muir. Not the Arkle. He was 20lb better than we thought he was.

PETER

I sometimes wish my children did something else. Because I never rest. Tom rides at Uttoxeter this afternoon and, because of modern communications,

I'll be watching. I know Dad used to go to a betting shop in Hereford to watch me in races, or find out the result. He must have wasted his life, partly. Now, I can look at the phone. Dad was distracted the whole afternoon; I'm distracted for a few minutes, because no matter what's happening, I'm checking to see if he's got round. And if he's fallen, I call or I text, and then he doesn't answer . . . You're telling yourself, 'He's all right, he's all right, he's all right.' And then as soon as you get a text, you don't need to answer: you just know that he's still alive. It's soft but it's true.

So, Western Warhorse, it's done him at Kempton, and you think, 'God, has he landed on his ankle?' I'm worried for him, and you're thinking, 'Bloody horse!' And then the bloody horse that's threatened him has ended up giving him one of his biggest moments. So my emotion in the stand that day was almost a forgiveness of Western Warhorse.

THE FESTIVAL TROPHY HANDICAP CHASE:

- 1986 Charter Party (Peter)
- 2008 An Accordion (Tom)
- 2016 Un Temps Pour Tout (Tom)
- 2017 Un Temps Pour Tout (Tom)

Peter's win in 1986 came just two hours after his first ever Festival success, Solar Cloud in the Triumph Hurdle, which ended years of agonising frustration for him. Having watched Dawn Run's Gold Cup from the weighing room, Peter went out to ride Charter Party, a 12-1 shot. All Festival-related tension had drained away. Gone was the urgent need to break his Cheltenham duck, to prove that he deserved his status as champion. He approached his remaining rides in a relaxed frame of mind.

PETER

I didn't give a shit. And he won because I didn't. I rode him with such confidence. I probably rode him closer to the pace than normal and, even though we were racing, going to the last, I don't move on him. And then we land and he quickens up.

You can't ride a winner for years, and then you get two on the same day. And then you could admit it was a monkey off your back. Not riding a winner at the Festival meant you weren't good enough to perform at the highest level.

You tootle off to Wolverhampton on the Friday and life goes on. But you haven't got Cornelius Lysaght from BBC Radio Gloucester coming to you before Cheltenham next year, saying, 'Oh, you haven't ridden a winner at the Festival! Does it get to you?'

'No, no, I'm quite happy not to have ridden a winner here . . .'

Next year, we can talk about something else.

Twenty-two years later, and after a change of sponsor, the same three-mile contest won by Charter Party would provide Tom with his first Festival winner. Like his father, he had been made to wait for a taste of Cheltenham glory, which finally came in his tenth season with a licence. Tom had just endured vexing defeat on a fancied runner, Osana, beaten a length in the Champion Hurdle. Osana's owner, Thomas Barr, wasn't happy, and insisted on using other jockeys the following year.

TOM

He got stuffed in the next year's Champion Hurdle. I don't think he ever won another race over hurdles. It was a bit galling, but time's a good healer, and they were wrong.

Just before I went out to ride Osana, I was having a couple of minutes to myself in the weighing room. I like to cut myself off and go through the job in hand, but I might have looked nervous. And I remember Fitzy [Mick Fitzgerald] coming over. I wouldn't say we were mates or anything, but he said to me, 'If the horse is good enough, you're certainly good enough.' He didn't need to do that, and I don't know what made him do it. He was riding in the race himself. For such a hard man, it showed another side of him: it showed the admiration and respect that most of us have for each other. It's not all about tearing each other apart. I always felt grateful to him for that. It's the mark of a lot of the men I ride with that, even in the most pressured environment, little things like that can happen.

Less than an hour after Osana, Tom got the leg-up on An Accordion, a 7-1 shot. Prominent from the off, An Accordion made mistakes and threatened to stop once in front, but got home under a strong drive.

TOM

It was wonderful. It was obviously for David Pipe, so that was great, but the owner was Brian Kilpatrick, who also owned Sabin Du Loir and gave him to us when Dad retired. Dad and Sabin basically retired at the same time. So the first horse I ever rode was Sabin Du Loir, and I schooled him over hurdles at home when I was ten. He was the first horse I rode over fences. He was the first horse I rode up the gallop, all those sorts of things. So to then get my first Festival winner for Sabin's owner, who was a very old man by this point, was lovely.

The other thing I distinctly remember was seeing Grandad standing in front of the weighing room as we came back in, and he gave me two thumbs up. That was a big monkey off my back, a massive relief.

PETER

It had all been coming back to me, the struggle of it. Was he ever going to ride a winner at Cheltenham? He was never going to be seen as a good jockey until he did. When he won on An Accordion, it was a monkey off my back as well.

Among Tom's tasks at the 2016 Festival was turning around the form of Un Temps Pour Tout, a David Pipe horse who had not won since the French Champion Hurdle the previous summer.

TOM

Un Temps Pour Tout had been disappointing over fences. We'd thought he was an RSA horse and he probably was an RSA horse as it turns out, but he kept getting beaten. He'd been favourite for his first three runs, and I got a bollocking for his second run. 'Made too much use of him. Went too fast.' No, I didn't. We didn't have words, myself and David, but as close to it as we ever got. He wasn't happy. He said, 'What would you do again differently?' I watched that race over and over . . . When I jumped the ditch, I couldn't get beaten. And this chestnut thing came past me. And there's miles back to the rest. We have pulled so far clear and they are some good horses.

Some bits of form look a lot better a couple of seasons later. The horse that so frustrated Tom by beating Un Temps Pour Tout in mid-season was Native River, no star at the time but subsequently the winner of a Hennessy, a Welsh National and a Cheltenham Gold Cup. Un Temps Pour Tout really was as good as trainer and jockey had hoped, and he won his Festival handicap by seven lengths at 11-1, the first time he hadn't been favourite that season.

PETER

Tom's still my kid on the football pitch. Part of me doesn't want him to make a fool of himself, part of me is saying he's better than anyone else. Part of me says he's still making mistakes and he's a little kid, you know? But watching Un Temps Pour Tout, I can see his sympathetic handling of the horse. I thought it was very, very good.

While he was an easy winner at the 2016 Festival, Un Temps Pour Tout was so disappointing in the Hennessy eight months later that David Pipe opted to send him back over hurdles.

TOM

Thistlecrack was going out of that division, and Un Temps Pour Tout had won a French Champion Hurdle. We thought, maybe he's slightly better over hurdles than he is over fences. He doesn't have to be that much better over hurdles to suddenly be a Stayers' horse. But it didn't work out. He was third in the race at Ascot, sixth in the Cleeve, and we just said, nah, let's go back over fences. He wasn't going to win the Stayers', so put him in the handicap chase. And he went and won it again.

I was a little bit more on edge because I knew he was one of my only two chances at the 2017 Festival, him and Starchitect. They were chances: that was all. I was more wound up, purely because, if I had a chance, I had to grab it. So when he won, I really enjoyed that. He only got home about an inch in front of Singlefarmpayment. Makes all the difference.

THE CHAMPION HURDLE:

- 1988 Celtic Shot (Peter)
- 1993 Granville Again (Peter)

PETER

I didn't want to ride Celtic Shot, I wanted to ride Celtic Chief, who was trained by Mercy Rimell and started favourite. Thank God the owner insisted I rode him. That was a really special moment, because it was about Fred Winter, really. He was a God. I felt very privileged to be part of Uplands. I've been to Anfield, and you go into the trophy room there; it was a bit like walking into the yard at Fred Winter's. There weren't trophies, but there were stables where Pendil, Killiney and Lanzarote had been – 'Millionaire's Row' it was called – these horses I'd grown up with. Everything was done properly. You knew you were playing for Liverpool.

There's a picture of Fred in his office, when he's ridden the winners of the Triumph, the Champion Hurdle and the Gold Cup in the same year. Everybody's saying you're a good jockey, but every morning you're looking at a picture of him that reminds you he was arguably the best of all time. Some people, if they tried telling you how to race-ride, you'd think, 'You don't know what you're talking about, and you can't do it.' When Fred told you what to do, you knew he could do it, and if you wanted to be compared to him, you had to do it.

But things had gone wrong: Fred was falling apart and Charlie Brooks was holding it together. Fred had fallen down the stairs, he was ill, he had all the symptoms of having had a stroke – he couldn't talk properly. You went and sat with Fred and you made small talk. When he'd been healthy, you never made small talk with Fred Winter. Celtic Shot was a good way for him to end his time as a trainer.

I'd been second in Champion Hurdles on Cima and Broadsword, and I suppose it felt good for me to bury those. Cima was beaten by Dawn Run, probably as good a race as he ever ran in his life. I got murdered on Broadsword going to the last, and I thought I should have won. I couldn't believe he got beat. But the couple of times I watched it afterwards, on reflection, For Auction was probably a better horse.

Seconds are terrible things, but when you eventually ride the winner, those seconds promote themselves a little bit. Suddenly, it's not That Awful Race That Will Be The Death Of Me One Day: it's the race I always do well in.

TOM

Celtic Shot winning the Champion Hurdle was one of my earliest memories, because of the nun running down the street who was my schoolteacher.

I was five, and at a Catholic school in Chipping Campden. I got picked up by Wendy Rollason, who is now godmother to my eldest, and she was outside the school in her little Mini, listening to the radio. I remember Wendy going bananas when Dad was coming up the hill and Classical Charm chasing him. On the radio, they were saying, 'Classical Charm is coming . . .' I just remember shouting, 'Go on Dad!' – me and my brother and Wendy, shouting in the car! Anyway, he held on and won, and then there's Sister Helen flying out of the school gates and doing a dance up the road. It wouldn't surprise me if she'd had a bet – she used to love her racing. She was magic, Scouse lady, absolutely brilliant. I think she went off to work in Africa. She's the reason I support Everton. I think she had us all supporting Everton.

I'd been aware that Dad was a very good jockey, but Celtic Shot was the first time I have a memory of realising, 'Oh, that's mega . . .' I wasn't aware, but Dad had been second in three Champion Hurdles, on Broadsword, Cima and Gaye Brief. And he jumped the last upsides or in front basically every time he'd ridden in the Champion Hurdle, and something had come by him. I hadn't realised what a monkey off his back that was. He probably would say it wasn't a problem.

Peter's second success in the Champion Hurdle, aboard Granville Again, might never have happened, following disaster the previous year when he fell at the second-last flight on the same horse.

PETER

I felt Granville Again would have won the Champion Hurdle but for falling, and he wasn't a good loser, the owner. You think, 'I don't want to lose the ride on this because I'll win the Champion Hurdle next year.' So we won the Scottish Champion Hurdle the next month and I'm good again, and I keep the ride on him. That's why I had too much to drink the night before I won the Scottish National on Captain Dibble – because I was celebrating the relief.

I knew I had to go and ride him in the Kempton race, the Christmas Hurdle, which in those days was the same day as the Welsh National. If he won and I wasn't riding, there'd have been pressure to put somebody else on him. But he was only third behind Mighty Mogul, and I missed three winners at Chepstow.

That was his third defeat in a row. He was breaking blood vessels, but then Michael Dickinson comes in and helps Pipey stop him doing that, tells him what to do. I wanted to ride this other horse, Valfinet, that was pissing up in these semi-Champion Hurdle trials – he beat Kribensis five lengths in the Kingwell. But Pipey kept saying to me, 'Come down and ride Granville.' Without actually telling me to ride him in the race, he was doing everything possible to steer me that way, so I rode him.

It was just a surreal feeling. He felt magnificent in the paddock, and then the whole race went really well. He settled straight away, and I'd learned to go on the outside of these fields, as Steve Smith Eccles had told me. I got to the front too soon. My biggest problem was making sure I jumped that second-last. If you look, I sit up at that.

It probably wasn't a very good Champion Hurdle. I probably won two Champion Hurdles on ordinary horses. He was a good horse, not a great horse, and neither was Celtic Shot. Granville beat Royal Derbi, who came out of a seller. They weren't Pearlymans.

THE BALLYMORE NOVICES' HURDLE:

- 1990 Regal Ambition (Peter)

This influential race has been the first Festival win in the careers of Istabraq, Hardy Eustace and Faugheen, who all went on to land the Champion Hurdle. Perhaps Regal Ambition's name might now trip off the tongue as theirs do, had things worked out differently.

PETER

He really was a steering job, probably one of the best horses I rode. Run For Free makes the running but, if you watch me, I'm only just waiting for my chance to get to the front and, going to the last hurdle, first time around, that's it, the race is over: he goes to the front and I don't have to move on him until the last, and he just strides away. He was a very, very good horse on that day. They sold him to America and he broke down there the next month and had to be retired.

TOM

This was the first time I went all three days to the Festival, when Regal Ambition won. He was brilliant, as good a horse as Dad ever rode. There's some good horses in this race. The Illywhacker, he was second in a King George. Run For Free won a Scottish National and a Welsh National. Tinryland, he was a good horse. We'd have been standing down there somewhere, me aged seven and my brother aged six, on the lawn in front of the stands. That's where we watched all the races at that Festival. I remember just jumping up and down.

He was no good on the Flat, Regal Ambition. Useless on the Flat. But he'd won at every single point in this race. He just killed them. And you don't see horses going up the hill like that: he was just relentless. You talk about Faugheen and all those, he's up there with them.

THE RSA NOVICES' CHASE:

- 1957 Mandarin (Michael)
- 1991 Rolling Ball (Peter)
- 1992 Miinnehoma (Peter)
- 1993 Young Hustler (Peter)

While he became a legend of jump racing, in the spring of 1957 great things were evidently not expected of Mandarin, as he was allowed to start at 8-1. The prize seemed to fall in his lap as there were more fallers than finishers and the hot favourite, Stroller, a Champion Hurdle runner-up, went out of the race at the very first fence. Michael was credited in the press with achieving 'a miraculous recovery after Mandarin had crashed through the last fence in most perilous fashion'.

Eventually, under a succession of other jockeys, Mandarin would win two King Georges, two Hennessys and, at the age of 11, the Gold Cup and the Grand Steeplechase de Paris. But Michael was hired, as Peter recalls the tale, because he could be relied on to get the horse jumping at a time when his novice season was threatening to go wrong.

PETER

Another jockey was riding him and he was falling, and they put Father on him because of his skill over a fence. He was a small horse, didn't stand off a lot: you had to let him fiddle – Dad worked that out. I think he was from a day when that kind of horseman's skill was more revered, like Ted Dexter playing a wonderful off-drive. Everyone says, 'Oh, dear old Ted' – but then Viv Richards comes along and hooks it out of the ground.

TOM

He said Mandarin was an unassuming little horse and fences were the making of him, that he was a good, neat jumper. But I don't know if he thought he was going to go on and be as good as he was.

When Peter got his big chance in this novice chase some 34 years later, the trainer in question seemed to think his jockey only needed to stay aboard.

PETER

Rolling Ball's a certainty and, in Martin Pipe's language, a certainty really is a certainty. It's going to win. And then, first time down the hill, he makes a right mistake, and you just think, 'Ah . . . Is it such a certainty now?' He was a bit mad, Rolling Ball. I didn't ride him at home, but he wasn't easy on the racecourse. He went from very extravagant to pissing awful at times.

I couldn't ride a finish because he was stopping, and I was just throwing everything at him, screaming at him to keep in front up the run-in. It wasn't pretty. I remember a Frenchman I rode for saw a video of it: he said, 'You are champion jockey, and you ride like that?'

The following year, Martin Pipe once more ratcheted up the pressure on his stable jockey, making no secret of how much he expected from his latest star novice chaser.

PETER

The first time I rode Miinnehoma over fences at Newton Abbot, Pipey told me, 'If you get beat on this, don't come back.' When we got to Cheltenham, he told me again, 'This cannot get beat.'

There was a serious rivalry between Nicky Henderson and Martin at this stage, and Henderson had Mutare. And obviously Josh Gifford's staff fancied Bradbury Star, but I couldn't see that. No way was Miinnehoma going to get beat, I thought he was such a certainty.

Mutare had fallen at the fence down the hill and, horrible jockeys, you thought, 'Good, that's gone.' And then going to the last, this can't be right, Bradbury Star can't be good enough to be upsides me? And he put down on me at the last, Miinnehoma, which allows Bradbury Star back in, but he runs on and wins.

It took a year or two for him to come back to his form. He wasn't right the next year and then, the year after, he won the National.

Judgement and diplomacy were necessary for Peter to win this race, then known as the Sun Alliance, for the third time in a row. He had to talk Martin Pipe into letting him off to ride a more fancied runner for Nigel Twiston-Davies.

PETER

Young Hustler – I just loved him: a square little horse. I couldn't even make him make a mistake.

I was very brave: I got off Martin's Capability Brown, despite having been on for his last four wins, including the Reynoldstown. I didn't think Capability Brown would get round. Adrian Maguire rode him and gave him a right ride. But it's war, as Fred puts it. I go out on the second circuit and he's with me again, Capability Brown. I thought to myself, 'If he comes with me, he'll turn over. I'm sorry, Adrian, but I'm going to have to . . .'

So we turned down the back and just raced. Capability Brown stretches at the first in the back and lands on his head, survives, but then he crashes through the ditch. He just didn't have the ability to jump like Young Hustler. I was able to ease off then, school round, and have enough to get home. It was a great thrill to ride a winner for Nigel. Two little pony club kids to combine for a Cheltenham winner: that was a special moment.

Nigel would be like Pipey: his horse couldn't possibly get beat. That's the attitude great football managers have, isn't it, and it instils confidence in you. You know if you get beat, it's your fault.

THE QUEEN MOTHER CHAMPION CHASE:

- 1987 Pearlyman (Peter)

Having broken his Festival duck the year before, Peter was now embracing cutting-edge technology in pursuit of quality rides.

PETER

I'd bought a mobile phone. It had a huge battery you put in the back of your car, and this phone went by your handbrake, between the front seats. You've been conned into buying this phone by some salesman and you're conscious of money. It's gotta pay for itself, this phone. I need somebody to ring to justify having paid for it. But I couldn't get a signal anywhere: it was red all the time!

Anyway, two days go by and nobody's called me on this bloody thing. So I'm driving into Burford and there's this sudden noise. 'Christ, what the fuck's that? Oh . . .' Pick it up, it's John Edwards. Would I ride Pearlyman? Great! Phone paid for.

And then I was on the same road, a bit closer to home, the phone goes again. It's someone from the press, saying the Queen Mother is going to be the race of the meeting. I thought, 'Is it?' Because you didn't have computers or the pre-Cheltenham talks. Cheltenham just came along. It was only the Friday before when you'd start building your rides up. Make sure you get a ride every day: that was the thing.

So here's this man saying it was going to be the race of the meeting, because of Desert Orchid, Pearlyman and Very Promising. He'd won the Grand Annual, Pearlyman, and John Edwards was a very good trainer of Cheltenham horses. But it was hard to see him winning, purely on his form. He'd won his trial, and he must have been second or third favourite, but I wasn't thinking this was a steering job.

I drop him in and, over the ditch in the back straight, Little Bay falls. Now if I'd been tracking Little Bay . . . all over! I don't know what decision made me not do that, but I didn't. So we got to the top of the hill and he came back on the bridle. These horses are so good, but you don't really appreciate how fast you're going because it's in their rhythm. 'OK, I'd better have a feel of this . . .' – and he took off with me. 'Christ! Woah, woah, woah!'

So I come down the hill and I'm going to the last, I'm upsides and I've got it won. But I meet it long and he puts down on me, because he wouldn't go long, he was a bad jumper. It allows Very Promising back at me, but Pearlyman gets going again and wins a neck.

It was a victory with particular meaning for Peter, who had endured an acrimonious split with David Nicholson, trainer of Very Promising, at the end of the previous season. Very Promising had given Peter 'a bit of a kick in the bollocks' in November, beating him in the Mackeson, in which he was second on Half Free.

THE CORAL CUP HANDICAP HURDLE:

– 1993 Olympian (Peter)

PETER

We've got this horse from somebody else. Pipey says, 'This'll win the Imperial Cup and the Coral Cup.' This is just after Christmas. You think, 'For Christ's sake, Martin, I can't think that far ahead.'

The only danger with Olympian was his starting, and the more he raced, the more hesitant he got at the start. The Sandown race is just two miles, and he was good enough coming out of the gate. It's only a few days later at Cheltenham, you're lined up at the two-and-a-half-mile gate with orders to make all. And of course Pipey wouldn't consider he would be slow coming out of the gate. 'You're an idiot: you only have one thing to do, so don't tell me you can't get this thing out of the gate. I'll put somebody else on it who will . . .'

So you're lining up at Cheltenham with 20 others who all want to make all. He's slow, they're gone, and you should give him time to get his breath, don't rush him there. But I rushed him, and by the second I'm in front. I came to the top of the hill, still running away, still hard on the bridle, I'm just not going to get beat. You don't often think, 'Let's get a good picture,' going to the last. But I was in such control, I thought, 'I'll sit up the neck at the last.' And he pissed up the hill.

Neale Doughty fell three out and says he would have beaten me. And he actually did beat me at Aintree on the same horse. But by then the weights were different and Olympian wasn't as good. He'd done his thing, so it's not a fair comparison.

It was my last Festival, and I rode three winners. To ride a treble at Cheltenham in those days was a good thing, because there was less racing. Not many people were riding more than three at one Festival. I was very proud of it. From not being able to ride a winner there to go out with three was quite nice.

THE CHAMPION BUMPER:

- 2015 Moon Racer (Tom)

TOM

Moon Racer was great at home: he would work over everything. You'd sit on him and straight away be thinking, 'Crikey.' He'd just lob along – he was a push-button horse, a real classy animal.

But talk about things going wrong! This was the last race on the Wednesday, and the first two days had been frustrating. Kings Palace was well beaten,

Dell' Arca fell early. In the race before this, the Fred Winter, I'd ended up missing the start and being miles behind and finishing eighth. David was fine, but he said to me afterwards, 'I was gonna ring you up that night and just say, "It's all right, you've still got two days left."' He could see me beginning to get wound up.

So of course there's a false start for the Bumper. Now it's a standing start: we line up down the inside and the fucking bastard hesitates. I've been told to be handy, and now I'm near the back and a wall of horses in front of me. For the first three furlongs, all that's going through my head, I remember it very distinctly, is, 'Fuck, fuck, fuckity-fuck,' all the way.

The thing is, the Bumper's a really rough race. I remember going to the first bend and I'm right down the inside, mid-div, the worst position. If you picked the one position you don't want to be in, I'm in it. There's 20 runners, they're all good horses, they can just wipe you out of it. It's law-of-the-jungle stuff.

And, bless him, he held his position. I thought then, 'Here we go, that's all right.' And after that, it was pretty straightforward. Everywhere I wanted to go, he just took me. That's the beauty of Cheltenham, where it finds out the best and the worst of them. There is no hiding place.

AP had a horrendous time on Yanworth, finishing fast, and everyone's like, 'Oh, that's the one to take out of the race – he was unlucky.' He wasn't unlucky. At the vital times, he wasn't good enough to hold his position. AP was in the right position, but the horse can't hold it. I was in the wrong position and I could go and take his. The real good ones get you out of jail, and Moon Racer was one that got me out of jail that day.

PETER

He got into trouble, but I'm watching it, knowing Cheltenham. You know they all want to be up there but, because the pace is so solid, he still has a chance, and you're thinking, 'Don't panic.' And he didn't panic. Gaps kept coming, and then when he got to the bottom of the hill, he quickened up, and it looked like a Ruby Walsh ride, completely perfect. But it was like the swan: it looked beautiful on top, but you knew underneath the legs were paddling like hell.

THE RYANAIR CHASE:

- 2014 Dynaste (Tom)

A popular grey, Dynaste was sent off the 3-1 favourite, and won tidily enough to justify that status. But punters might have been more wary had they known quite how tricky the horse had been to prepare.

TOM

He was a funny horse: we couldn't school him at home. He was a brilliant jumper at the races, but over fences at home he wasn't very good, so in the end we just stopped schooling him. It didn't make any difference. Dad'll tell you the same about a really good horse he used to ride, Run And Skip, who was fourth in a Gold Cup and won a Welsh National. Same: couldn't school him at home. Run And Skip would refuse, Dynaste would hurdle the fences and cut himself or do something stupid. In the end, I just said to David, 'What's the point?'

And the other thing, we took him for a racecourse gallop about three weeks before the Festival and he worked horrendously. Absolutely embarrassing. He wouldn't have beaten a seller that day. But then you hear the story of Mr Mulligan, who supposedly did the same thing before he won the Gold Cup. There were long faces that afternoon, because we were worried. Was he wrong?

That was the beauty of David's place, because we did all the tests and he was fine. But he was a terrible work horse, terrible in most of the things he did at home. When you'd school him over hurdles, then you'd realise he's got something about him, he's a bit different. Other than that, you wouldn't have any idea he was a 169-rated chaser.

The race didn't go swimmingly. I was struggling for a long, long way, but the thing is with Dynaste, you could keep throwing him at his fences and he'd keep getting you out of jail. He'd do that all the way down the back straight. I remember pulling him out, thinking, 'I've got to get a run here: I'm not going very well,' and he just jumped his way into contention.

Coming down the hill, I'm further back than I'm meant to be, and if you're watching from the stands, I'm getting a bollocking. But I'm not afraid. It's just the way it's worked out. The only thing in the back of my mind is, 'If I finish with a rattle and finish second, I'm in trouble.' But what I did know was that I was going a gallop that he could maintain, and that was the important thing. And because he was the best horse in the race, he's ended up winning quite easily.

I was delighted for the horse, because at that time he was looking a bit of a bridesmaid at the top level. When he was taking on the Cue Cards and the Silviniaco Contis, he might have finished second, he'd probably finish third: he was probably 7lb short of them. But he was just such a tough horse. He always had issues behind, pelvis and things. I was pleased for him that he had his day.

THE STAYERS' HURDLE:

- 2016 Thistlecrack (Tom)

In racing as in life, opportunity is enormously important. Getting on the right horse at the right time can be no more than a matter of luck.

TOM

Ruby rode Thistlecrack one day at Ascot and won on him. Then Ruby couldn't ride him in the Imperial Cup, so Aidan Coleman rode and finished fifth. I keep winding him up about it – he managed to get Thistlecrack beat off 135! How'd he manage that? It was soft ground, over two miles, he should have been an absolute certainty!

I Broadway.
Tynemouth.
Northumberland

Dear

I am sending this extract (below) to the relatives of all the crew.

My Son writes me that they are being well treated. and are feeding fairly well, but this is thanks to the Red Cross parcels of which he speaks very highly.

I trust you are hearing regularly, and the news is as good as can be expected.

Yours Sincerly.

J Bridger

Extract from letter dated 10/9/43 from

F/Lt John Cameron Bridger. D.F.C. P of W.

.... I have been in Germany nine weeks. We've ust had a bit of real news. The fall of Italy. I an make no comments, I can only hope to be home oon. I feel I had better mention how I happen tobe ere. My aircraft went down in a routine manner. with ull crew aboard, finishing up on a hill-top. My afety harness saved me from any serious injury, but ost of the crew were hurt, those who were conscious howed courage and fortitude of the first order. particularly in the case of Sgt Scudamore who received acial injuries and lost a lot of blood, dispite this e acted in a way that made me proud to be a fellow nglishman. In the air when we were in difficulties gt Groom, dispite his youth, acted like a hardened eteran. I had a great crew. It is very saddening to inish up as we did. But it could have been worse. e live........

Clockwise from top left: A letter from Flight Lieutenant Bridger letting the families of those involved know what happened in the plane crash over Mont Rigi in Belgium; Geoffrey Scudamore, 1944, painted by a Russian prisoner of war in Stalag IV-B, one of the larger POW camps in Germany; From left to right, Fred Winter, Michael and Arthur Freeman jump a hurdle together at Sandown in 1957; Point-to-point rider, Geoffrey Scudamore, jumps a fence in 1938.

Left: Michael (right) and Legal Joy jump the last alongside eventual winner Teal in the 1952 Grand National.

Below: Michael rides Greektown at Windsor in 1965.

Left: Linwell is led in after winning the 1957 Gold Cup at Cheltenham.

Below: Gerry Scott and Surprise Packet fall alongside Oxo and Michael in the 1959 Grand National.

Above: Michael looks over his shoulder as he wins the 1959 Grand National. Tim Brookshaw in second on Wyndburgh has his feet out of the irons as his right stirrup had shattered at Bechers.

Right: The Lambourn Horse Show and Gymkhana during the 1950s. Leading jockeys of the age took part including Michael, Tim Molony, Fred Winter, Bob Turnell, Reg Hobbs, Dave Dick and Jack Dowdeswell.

Below: A hero's welcome home for 1959 Grand National winner, Oxo.

Above: The Cheltenham Gold Cup 50th Anniversary Dinner 1974. Former winning riders were invited, Michael is third from the left.

Left: Peter's dress sense could cause a flare up with his father Michael (centre).

"I remember the end of the race. I jumped the last upsides Josh Gifford. On the run-in he was pushing me over. It was a photo-finish and if I hadn't have won I'd have objected." Peter Jones

Three Grand Annuals: left Peter and Pukka Major, 1989, preceded by Josh Gifford, trainer of the second, beaten again in the race by a Scudamore, above Peter Jones and Fortina's Palace, 1970, trained by Michael who also rode a Grand Annual winner in 1961, and below Tom and Next Sensation, 2015.

Golden Freeze and Michael Bowlby (left) take on an ultimately disappointing Carvill's Hill ridden by Peter in the 1992 Cheltenham Gold Cup.

Peter and Michael in the paddock at Cheltenham.

Anyhow, so it came to Aintree and I didn't have a ride in the race, simple as that. And Aidan was asked to ride him; he had a choice between Thistlecrack and I think it was called Parish Business of Emma Lavelle's. And he chose that over Thistlecrack and the rest, as they say, is history. I won a Grade One hurdle on him round Aintree and he was 25-1.

Joe Tizzard did say beforehand, 'This is a good horse.'

And I was like, 'Yeah, yeah, yeah, whatever.'

Joe said, 'Ride him like you want to. Ride him like a good horse. Just make sure, whatever happens, we'd rather see you finishing than looking good and stopping, so just drop him in.'

So I just dropped him out the back and hunted him round, thinking, 'I'll run on and finish fifth or sixth, 25-1, they'll be delighted with that.'

But Thistlecrack won, cementing his partnership with his new jockey. The following season they were unbeaten in five races, the highlight coming in the Festival's World Hurdle.

TOM

The one I was concerned about was Cole Harden, because of what he'd done the year before. I didn't want to get in a battle with him. I thought, 'If I was on Cole Harden, I'd want me to appear at the top of the hill and try and take him on there, turn it into a battle.' But Thistlecrack travelled so well into it, he went past Cole Harden going to the second-last and he was just doing a half-speed. That was the extraordinary thing: there was never a moment's doubt. All the way through, you were just completely in control. He is able to maintain a gallop near to flat out for as long as you want. Over hurdles, I used to think what stops him being a Champion Hurdler is the first mile of the race – you didn't really feel much. He would take a bit of time to warm up and get going. Over two miles, by the time he's up and going, they're away.

PETER

Whenever Thistlecrack runs, I get terribly nervous, because I believe he's the best horse the Scudamores have touched. You always want to get on the favourite, but then the risk is that you get the favourite beat. To me, it was one of the great Cheltenham performances I've seen. What he's beat, I don't know, but the command with which he's won it was awe-inspiring.

THE MILDMAY OF FLETE HANDICAP CHASE:

- 2012 Salut Flo (Tom)
- 2014 Ballynagour (Tom)

Having finally broken his Festival duck on An Accordion, Tom was made to wait another four years for the follow-up. He could hardly imagine that much better years were coming. In the case of Salut Flo, just getting him to the races was cause for celebration.

TOM

He was a good horse but he had a lot of injuries. He didn't run for a long time: he was very, very brittle. He came over from France, broke down, they got him back, won at the Festival, broke down again.

It was a nice win, because Grands Crus got beat the day before, and he was many people's idea of the banker of the meeting. Salut Flo I just remember being a massive relief. He was fancied. He'd run really well in the December Gold Cup, then made a bad mistake at the third-last. So they thought, 'We'll just leave it till Cheltenham after that.' Fair play to the owner, Allan Stennett. When your horse hasn't run for two years and the trainer says, 'Well, he's run well today, we'll put him away until March now . . .' There's a nice race at Ascot, a nice race at Haydock – there's all those nice races. But he wanted a winner at Cheltenham, and it happened. Not everyone's willing to do that, especially when you know they can go wrong like Salut Flo did.

He made all the running. He jumped better that way: that was the key. He wasn't the best of jumpers. It was just a case of getting him out and into his own rhythm, and it just so happened it was in front. If he was amongst horses, he could end up rushing a little bit. There weren't that many front-runners in the race: we got a good start and jumped the first two fences well, and the rest of the time he didn't miss a beat, which, for him, was rare, because most of the time you knew there was a Horlicks coming. He wasn't very big. And it wasn't as fiercely run as those handicaps sometimes can be. For a Cheltenham race, we got a relatively easy lead.

He was delighted, Allan. He took me out for lunch about a month later. You could see the pride he would get. He wasn't an extrovert. You ride for some people who are amazing in victory and horrendous in defeat, whereas you get some that just don't show an awful lot. You can see how much it means to them, but at the same time, when horses get beaten, they don't drop off a cliff. The higher your excitement takes you, the further you've got to drop.

Two years later, the same owner, trainer and jockey combined to win the same race with Ballynagour, a 12-1 shot who performed like a hot favourite.

TOM

He'd won from the minute he jumped the first fence. Very rarely in a big race is it as straightforward. That was about the easiest winner I'll ever, ever ride. It was mad.

At that point, he was very inconsistent. He'd blown them away a year before on his first race at Warwick, and then bombed out at the Festival. You were going out there thinking, 'Well, if he turns up he wins, but . . .' On his day, he was a flipping brilliant horse. It gave me a massive thrill, winning that. As it turned out, he was 15lb to 20lb well in. He was a Grade One horse running in a handicap, and it felt like it.

The following year, things did not go so well when the same team tried to win the Plate with Monetaire.

TOM

We had the false start, which led to a standing start, and Monetaire was a bad starter. He was slowly away and ran on to be second. Allan took that well, where a lot of people wouldn't. No, he was as good in defeat as he was in victory, and that makes it a lot easier.

After years of Festival frustration, Western Warhorse, Dynaste and Ballynagour gave Tom three winners there in 2014. It was a significant and satisfying moment, even if there was barely any time to pause and look it in the eye.

TOM

It just felt that I'd gone into that elite level of success. It was myself, Davy Russell, Barry Geraghty and Ruby Walsh, all finished the Festival on three winners, and Ruby's ridden more seconds, so he was top jockey. On the Thursday night, after I'd had the double, I remember coming back and Charlotte had some friends round and they were celebrating. I think I had a glass of champagne and went to bed. I remember coming back after Dad won the Champion Hurdle and thinking, 'The house'll be absolutely rocking,' and Dad had gone to bed.

That's the thing: there's no time. It's that sort of quiet satisfaction, when you're on your own. You might watch it a couple of days later. That's where you get the sinking-in feeling of what you've just achieved. It might take a week or two, but there'll be a moment when you suddenly think, 'Yeah, that was great.'

THE TRIUMPH HURDLE:

- 1956 Square Dance (Michael)
- 1986 Solar Cloud (Peter)

Square Dance's success does not count as one of Michael's ten Festival successes, as the race was run at Hurst Park in those days, transferring to Cheltenham in 1965 and becoming part of Festival week in 1968.

Peter's win 30 years later was rather more significant, as it provided the first Festival winner he wanted, needed and feared he might never get. The day before, Peter had ridden Bolands Cross in the Sun Alliance Chase, a horse so strongly fancied he was sent off at 5-2 in a 30-runner field. The outcome provided a serious test of Peter's stoicism.

PETER

There were so many fallers at the ditch, I landed on a jockey. They were all turning over there. So I'm sitting in the ambulance with my mate, Hywel Davies. He says, 'We were right, then: you'll never ride a winner at Cheltenham if you can't win on that, isn't it?' Fucking hell! Your head's absolutely gone.

After that experience, Peter approached the next day's first race with no enthusiasm. The Duke's runner, Solar Cloud, was due to start at 40-1. Rod Simpson offered Peter the ride on the fancied Tangognat, but the Duke flatly refused to allow his stable jockey to jump ship.

PETER

I know Solar Cloud's just a social runner. Typical Duke: 'I've got 20 runners at Cheltenham,' and he's never had a winner there. So he tells me to hold it up. And I think to myself, 'It's got no chance. If I hold it up, I'll be tailed off by the time I come to the third. So I'll whizz him out of the gate, they'll come past me, but I'll have given it some sort of ride.'

So I whizzed it out of the gate, and I was still in front at the top of the hill. And it's in my mind that he pulls up in front, this horse. So I just kicked. It was a moment of madness or genius, and I kicked and went clear. And I've hung on to win a short head.

I clearly had an intuition or a positiveness about me that allowed me to win races like that, against all orders. Maybe in the back of my mind I knew the horse better than the Duke did. It's hard to know what makes you think in a point of pressure like that. It's part of being a good jockey. You've got to read a situation as it comes to you at the time. If you visualise that situation beforehand, I think you're affecting your decisions, because you're beginning to dream. You have to have a clear mind, going out. On the day, I got the tactics absolutely spot-on.

Dermot Browne, he should have won, he comes flashing by me on the line on Brunico and says, 'I've won! I've won!'

I thought, 'Oh fuck, I've just got beaten on the line.' And the Duke definitely thought I'd got beat, he said so.

Afterwards, it was quite ironic to me, having fallen on the good horse the day before and then won on a horse I didn't want to ride. And I thought, 'Why do I get so wound up about it? Why do I try so hard when the hand of cards is there?' Something's coming round the corner and there's nothing you can do about it.

THE CATHCART CHALLENGE CUP:

- 1956 Amber Wave (Michael)
- 1964 Panisse (Michael)
- 1987 Half Free (Peter)
- 1991 Chatam (Peter)

The Cathcart lasted for almost 70 years, but was killed off in 2004 to make way for what is now known as the Ryanair. If you are prepared to stretch a point and say the Ryanair is basically the same race, this would then be one of two Festival races which all three Scudamores have won, the other being the Grand Annual.

Panisse was only second past the post, but was awarded the race by the stewards after Michael objected to the winner, Wayward Muse. She had hung across Panisse on the run-in and was only a head in front at the line. Michael's other Cathcart winner had also been by a narrow margin, when the game mare Amber Wave held on by a neck after making all.

PETER

Half Free was always one of my favourites. It was difficult, because he was Richard Linley's horse, really. But he must have been hurt – he used to dislocate his shoulder. Anyway, I won on him at Wincanton in October. He got a penalty for that in the Mackeson: he carried 12st 4lb and got beat. I thought I'd ridden a good race, but Fred half gave me a bollocking. He thought I'd given him too much to do. But we got beat very little distance, giving weight to Very Promising. I thought the penalty got him beat.

The Cathcart was the last race at the Festival, and I'd just had a bollocking for riding I Haventalight in the three-mile handicap chase. That's when Fred said to me, 'It's war out there – it's not a fucking game.'

So, I'm riding Half Free and chasing Hywel, on Western Sunset, and he was a most remarkable horse. It puts you in awe of these horses. You think you're flat out all the way. OK, you're close enough, but you're thinking, 'This isn't running well.' And then when you come down the hill and straighten up, he picks up from two out. He wasn't a big horse, but he just runs up that run-in. And it makes you look so good, because it looks as if you've timed your run perfectly. But you haven't: you've been panicking all the way through, because it's not a game, it's a fucking war. That's ringing in your ears, and you're gonna get beat, and Richard Linley would have ridden him better . . .

He was a Cheltenham horse: better there than anywhere else. And the Cathcart showed why, because he could pick up off that bend. You're in such awe of the bravery and the talent and ability to jump. He didn't go long: he was just so quick over his fences.

It's a pity there wasn't a Ryanair when I was riding, because it would have been perfect for Beau Ranger, Half Free and Sabin Du Loir. Half Free was one of the best I ever rode, and he didn't have a classic distance to race over. I remember arguing about it with Philip Arkwright, clerk of the course at Cheltenham. He was worried that a two-and-a-half-mile championship chase would take runners away from the Gold Cup and the Queen Mother. And he was right, but there's one there now anyway.

Chatam's Cathcart made Peter top jockey at the Festival for the third and final time, but the horse's heroics were undermined by Celtic Shot, who'd just been a disappointing seventh in the Gold Cup. Their jockey was feeling deflated.

PETER

Chatam had been to the three previous Festivals without winning. It seemed that you couldn't win the top races, so you slotted into one like the Cathcart. I'm not knocking it in any way, and I loved Chatam. But I had more fun winning it on Half Free, and my greatest thrill on Chatam was winning the Hennessy eight months later.

NATIONAL HUNT JUVENILE CHASE:

- 1952 Signal Prince (Michael)
- 1956 Segnor IV (Michael)

Michael's skill with inexperienced jumpers is proved beyond question by the fact that he twice won this mad race, restricted to four-year-old chasers. To the relief of all jockeys, it was killed off in 1958. Racing's authoritative historian John Randall once wrote that, in a typical running, 'hardly any of the field had run over fences before, and many had not reached their actual fourth birthday or been schooled properly. There was often wholesale carnage with few finishers.' But Michael evidently picked his way through the mayhem to score on Signal Prince for Fred Rimell in 1952, and Segnor IV for Fulke Walwyn four years later.

Reporting on Signal Prince, the Sporting Life*'s man wrote: 'M Scudamore, who rode such a good race on the winner, was told not to go to the front until clearing the last fence, instructions he carried out to the letter.'*

Michael's second win elicited further praise from the same source: 'Scudamore is very strong and, thanks chiefly to this, Segnor IV battled off Square Shooter from the last.'

TOM

That race scared the shit out of him, he didn't mind admitting that. It obviously wasn't much fun to ride in, because he never spoke about it with much enthusiasm, and he'd won it twice, so he should have liked it more than anyone. But he did have a great reputation. I don't think it was any coincidence that he was asked to ride the likes of Linwell and Mandarin in their novice seasons.

PETER

I think he was very pleased that they got rid of the race. It's a bloody stupid idea, having a four-year-old chase anywhere, let alone the Cheltenham Festival. And I've never heard of Segnor IV. Even within our own family, these horses weren't massively talked about. We talk about Cheltenham now as the Olympics of jump racing. It clearly wasn't in those days. It was a social gathering that had begun as a lot of bad people getting together to get pissed for a couple of days.

Peter is invoking the spirit of the Reverend Francis Close, rector of Cheltenham in the early 19th century, who railed against horse racing and published a pamphlet detailing its 'evil consequences'. His followers so disrupted the races on Cleeve Hill that a new site had to be found, in the grounds of Prestbury Park, now so familiar to followers of jump racing.

PETER

It was almost a pagan festival, marking the end of winter. The Gold Cup didn't have the status it has now: until the war it was a trial for the Grand National. This is what Father's living through: the Gold Cup and the Festival leaving those times behind.

Having struggled for so long at the Festival, Peter ended his career with 13 wins there. At the time, only Pat Taaffe and Fred Winter had ridden more. Tom now has ten Festival successes, becoming the third Scudamore to break into double figures. He hopes to match his father's record, or perhaps even pass it . . .

PETER

You ride a winner at Cheltenham and, as soon as you pass the post, everything is gradually downhill. You go past the post, it's an immediate high. Everyone's cheering as you walk back in front of the stands and that's quite a high. You have a little burst again as you come into the paddock and the owner and trainer say you're marvellous. Then you come into the weighing room and everyone says well done. And then gradually it's the realisation that you're just back to normal and off you go again. Three weeks later, they put someone else on the horse . . .

7

SENSATION

'He worked so badly. You can't send a horse to Cheltenham working like that.'

The last day of the Cheltenham Festival in 2015 was supposed to be about two things: the Gold Cup, of course, and AP McCoy, who was taking his final rides at the race meeting before retiring the next month. For Tom and Michael Jnr, it also meant the thrill of being able to team up with a Festival runner. The brothers had Next Sensation in the Grand Annual, the final race of the week at Cheltenham.

Expectations had been high for Next Sensation in the previous year's Grand Annual, for which he had started third-favourite. Tom was unable to ride, being committed to a useful horse of David Pipe's, so Richard Johnson got the leg-up.

MICHAEL JNR

Everything had gone really well that year. He'd won three out of his last four. We were torn between the Arkle and the Grand Annual, and decided on the Grand

Annual, with Dickie on board, which was great, him being a Herefordshire man, and the owners knew him well. It was all working out perfectly.

TOM

Dickie went too quick on him, but it wasn't Dickie's fault. Next Sensation's a big, keen, awkward bugger, and there was a delay at the start because Oscar Hill bolted and had to be withdrawn.

MICHAEL JNR

Oscar Hill tore off with the chap before the race, and he did two circuits round the inside of Cheltenham, out of control. The camera was switching between him getting run away with and all the runners down at the start, and you could see Next Sensation, he was losing it, the longer he was walking round. As a young horse he was a real hothead, really difficult to cope with. And here he was getting himself wound up and you could see the sweat coming out on his neck. Once the tape went up, that was it: he was just gone like a bat out of hell.

TOM

I've never been as fast before or since. Lads in the weighing room still talk about that Grand Annual when Dickie made it on Next Sensation – he was just a passenger. For him to still be in front after the last and look like he was going to win halfway up the run-in, he had to be good.

Michael always thought that could have been his chance of a Festival winner. It was a huge blow, but it didn't get him down, and off he went. He's pretty level. Even if it didn't outwardly affect him, there wouldn't have been a day gone by that he wouldn't have thought about it until Next Sensation could have another go the next year.

MICHAEL JNR

How fast he'd gone, you thought, 'He's going to walk at any stage . . .' And so to hang on and be fourth . . . Typical Cheltenham: it was only the last 200 yards that got him. He ran a great race. You came away delighted but deflated at the same time. 'What if that other horse hadn't bolted . . .?' And in the back of your mind, you knew he had his wind issues, and therefore you're thinking, 'Was that it?' Was that your one shot at it?

Then the next year he was never right, he hardly ran a good race all year. He started out at Ascot, ran terrible. Went to Cheltenham after that, ran terrible. He was much better back at Newbury just before Christmas. We thought, 'OK, we're going back in the right direction.' So we got his wind done, and then it was all about getting him right for Cheltenham.

We took him for a racecourse gallop to work him with some of Dave's, and it was embarrassing. We set off in front. Everything passed us by the time we entered the back straight, and he was trotting as he came up the run-in. He worked so badly. This was two, two and a half weeks before Cheltenham! You can't send a horse to Cheltenham working like that. The only good thing about that day, his wind was perfect. Maybe he didn't go fast enough to push it. I was shaking my head, thinking, 'This is embarrassing – I've come here with all of Dave Pipe's Cheltenham runners . . .'

And Dave said, 'Don't worry: Dynaste worked like that last year, just before he won the Ryanair.' They scoped him, they did everything, he phoned the owner and said, 'Look, we can't run, he's worked so badly . . .' Got him home and there was nothing wrong with him, and they decided, 'Let's just run him and see what happens.'

It was a bit the same with Next Sensation: we got him back, there was nothing wrong, and we thought, 'It's been the plan all year – we've got to go for it.'

The good news was that Tom was free to ride, having decided the Pipe runner this time was an insufficiently tempting alternative. With Next Sensation perking up a bit in his home work, the brothers were just hoping for some drying weather.

MICHAEL JNR

Of course, it rained like hell on the Thursday night, Friday morning. I rang the owner, Mark Blandford, before we left, and asked, 'Is it worth going?'

He said, 'Because it's Cheltenham and it's close, we'll go and see what it's like.'

Had it been Aintree, we probably wouldn't have even left the yard.

I went and spoke to Tom after he rode in the Gold Cup, and he said, 'It's probably not worth running him: it's too soft out there.'

So we said, 'Right, shall we pull him out?' And I don't know why, one of us just said, 'Oh, come on – it's Cheltenham, we're here, there's nothing else for us apart from Aintree in three weeks' time. If he's not enjoying it, pull him up at the top of the hill, and it's been a nice blowout for him, and it'll set him up for Aintree.'

Their hesitation was entirely understandable. The Grand Annual is not the sort of race to be tackling just for the hell of it. Run over jump racing's minimum distance of two miles, it's a race for fast horses who aren't quite good enough for the Champion Chase, and tends to attract a packed field. Bravery in the saddle is required, even more than usual.

PETER

If yours missed the cut for the Grand Annual, you don't think, 'Oh dear.' I rode in it once on Fu's Lady. Lot of runners, and I remember turning at the top of the hill and you just have to throw her down it. Because of the type of horse she was, you know you're loading things against you. She was very tall and leggy, so if you met one wrong, she wasn't going to shorten. She was flat at her fences. You're going so fast that, if you meet it wrong, you know you're going to turn over. And you're not even frightened. Concerned, I suppose. It's almost a pride. There's a moment in your life, whatever you're doing, when you think: 'This isn't for everybody.' And you think, 'Yeah, OK: I accept it.'

Fu's Lady and I did turn over coming down the hill. And you get up and shake yourself off. I was younger: falls were part of the fun of it. It's a stupid thing to say, but you think you're unbreakable. There's still a slight madness to you when you have a fall like that. You're half taking the mickey out of yourself. Yes, you're still young, and you can laugh about having a fall.

The Fu's Lady tumble came a year after Peter won the Grand Annual on Pukka Major. It was a victory that did much to cheer him during the 1989 Festival, when he might have won both the Supreme and the Sun Alliance Novice Hurdle if he had chosen the right horses.

PETER

Pukka Major was a reluctant starter, and he was slowly away that time. I was always behind where I wanted to be. He was absolutely flat out at the second-last, a fair way behind Clay Hill. I've got a great picture of it, not a pretty picture but an absolute 'racing' picture. I was panicking because he's slow out of the gate and you're forcing him, forcing him. And it's funny, then you have this feeling it's all coming together, coming down the hill, although you've got plenty to do.

I always think, with horses, it's the mental as well as the physical part of getting them to run. You need every single sinew, every emotion, pleading, cajoling, everything. Physicality on its own will not do it. He's going: 'I can't, I won't, I can't, I can't, I can't, all right, I might, I might . . .'

Come on, please!

'All right, I'll do it for you.'

And that picture is almost the point when he says, 'OK, I'm going now.' I love the picture from my point of view, because I can see the beginning of it. Although it looks a hopeless cause from the stands, to me it's not. It's that moment that it's beginning to change.

It's one of the later races, after the carnival, so you know you're not going to get headlines. But at least you've walked away from the meeting with a '1': you've ridden a winner, which is vital. I remember Monty Court writing in the *Sporting Life* in his summary of Cheltenham, that perhaps the riding performance of the meeting was Pukka Major. That, to me, was very important.

It also mattered that Peter was repeating his father's success in the Grand Annual, which Michael Snr won as a jockey on Barberyn in 1961, and then again as a trainer with Fortina's Palace nine years later.

PETER

Fortina's Palace was a big, powerful, hard-pulling horse. Dad rode him at home. Nobody else in the yard could ride him. I saw Dad's superb horsemanship then.

I'd have been 11 when he won the Grand Annual. Cheltenham was more of a racing people's environment then: it wasn't the wild publicity that it is now. Because I lived with the horse, and the horse is a great big strong thing, like a rugby centre, and he's gone and scored the try, there was real private pride that your hero's gone and done it. It wasn't, let's go down the pub and the whole village is gonna come and see him. It was much more private. I didn't think, 'Oh, that's great, Dad can train at the highest level as well.' I knew he could.

Having emulated his father by winning the race himself some 19 years later on Pukka Major, Peter took pleasure in learning the significance of the Grand Annual, which was first run in 1834 and is therefore the oldest jumps race still being staged in Britain. At one time, it outranked the Grand National in importance, and its barrel-like trophy is a reminder of that status.

The 1847 Grand Annual, in which Fred Archer's father was the jockey on the narrowly beaten runner-up, is said to have been the inspiration for the poem 'How We Beat The Favourite', by Adam Lindsay Gordon. A favourite of Peter's, it tells of a tough, stamina-laden mare who outbattles a successful racehorse masquerading as a hunter, ridden by a professional jockey pretending to be an amateur, who has a steward in his pay. Here is a flavour:

A hum of hoarse cheering, a dense crowd careering,
All sights seen obscurely, all shouts vaguely heard;
'The green wins!' 'The crimson!' The multitude swims on,
And figures are blended and features are blurr'd.
'The horse is her master!' 'The green forges past her!'
'The Clown will outlast her!' 'The Clown wins!' 'The Clown!'
The white railing races with all the white faces,
The chestnut outpaces, outstretches the brown.

PETER

The man who wrote it is obviously a dreamer. He's ridden out for these people in Cheltenham: these jockeys are heroes to him. And they're gamblers, they're bad people. So there's this man, he's gone to public school, and his father is an army officer. He's obviously a very clever man, but a waster, and he's fallen into bad company. And this is his dream. Some children want to score the winning try for England or the century at Lord's. He doesn't want that: he wants to win the Grand Annual. And this poem is about riding against his heroes. He has pure admiration for the courage of this horse – how it picks up, how it goes across the ploughed field. I'm getting emotional, talking about it now, because what he describes is all that we do it for. And that spirit, to me, is still there in Cheltenham.

Perhaps some of Adam Lindsay Gordon's buccaneering approach to life was in the two younger Scudamores as they looked at rain-soaked Cheltenham and decided to run Next Sensation anyway. It was a decision that, about 30 seconds into the race, Tom nearly regretted.

PETER

I was standing in the hospitality tents opposite the second-last. They'd just gone past me on the first circuit when he made a terrible mistake and disappeared, and I thought they'd fallen. He's that type of horse: he lives on the edge. His jumping is fantastic, but there's very little room for error, so you've always got your heart in your mouth, watching your son and having ridden in that race. You don't want to turn over in that race, 'cos you've got 25 others to gallop over the top of you.

TOM

I don't know how he stood up. He was a big, bold jumper, but stupid as well. Especially early on, he'd take a chance with one. Once he'd done that, then he was a brilliant jumper. It would sort of put him right. I didn't school him at home very much because he was so big and bold and stupid. You'd school him once a year, maybe. When he got on the track, he was fine, but he'd make a mistake early on and you just had to hope you'd get away with it. On telly, it doesn't look like much, until you pause it and see how low he's got. He was such a big, strong horse, it just switched him on.

MICHAEL JNR

It was a horrific mistake. You thought that was your luck gone. I never thought he'd fall: I thought he'd unseat Tom. Nothing against Tom, it's just that from the moment he's taken off and how he's hit the fence, I thought he'd find a leg and keep himself up, because he can do that. All his career, just about every race, he's always taken a liberty with one, and it almost seems like he needs to do it to gain respect for the fences again. He's so big and powerful, I think he just thinks they're nothing to him. Jumping was probably his biggest asset, and actually, after that, he's hardly touched a twig.

PETER

I saw him disappear and thought, 'Oh, fuck it. I hope they're both all right.' Then he came up again on the other side of the fence. And after that you see Thomas is controlling the race from the front. He comes down the hill and jumps that second-last in front of me.

Because he's a weak finisher, you think McCoy's going to come by him. And it's doubly important, because it's McCoy's last ride at the Cheltenham Festival. But Tom hasn't moved on him. And it's a skill, not to panic. He's not going to go much faster when you let him go, but Tom's held him, held him, made sure he jumped the last.

MICHAEL JNR

All the way, you think, 'Yep, they're gonna come and get him. They're gonna come and get him.' And there was just that moment when they jumped the one at the top of the hill, something fell in behind, and the camera changes from upsides so you can see them all coming towards you down the hill, and everybody else was just niggling and pushing. I thought, 'OK, if we've done enough with him and he keeps going, he'll win now.' When he jumped the last, it was just screaming from there.

The commentator was getting all excited, thinking AP was gonna come and do it. Tom always gets very cross whenever we watch the replay. There's some line, the commentator says, 'Next Sensation's paddling and the others are closing,' and then as he says it, he realises the others are not closing and he has to change it.

TOM

Because of his wind issues, I didn't want to get after him too soon. It was just holding on, holding on. Jumped the last and, as Grandad would say, kick like hell.

That was the best of the lot. It tops everything. I started crying like a baby, all the way back in. It was just fabulous. And I remember taking it all in, coming back in, all very vividly. The only bad bit about it was, normally my girls go to the Gold Cup on the Friday, and this was the only time they didn't go. I can't remember why – they didn't go that week at all. They've been every other year. It would have been lovely if the girls had been there.

PETER

It's my greatest moment in racing, watching Michael and Tom winning the Grand Annual. Even above the Grand National, or being champion jockey: to stand there and watch them winning . . . Chris Coley, who used to organise hospitality at the Festival, watched it with me, and said he'd never seen anybody so delighted. He wrote me a lovely letter, saying, 'It was the most joyous and fitting end to my 34 years of working there, and I shall cherish the memory.'

You think back to Dad then – he'd only recently died. He was probably closer to Tom and Michael in some ways, and prouder of them than he was of me. To him they're babies, aren't they? He's watched me grow up and become a man, but with your grandchildren it's slightly different.

It's only Aintree and Cheltenham and certain occasions that you think of this Scudamore thing in racing, and you think, 'Christ, that's fantastic.' Aren't we lucky? Without the history of the sport, we're nothing anyway. We are part of that history, and most of the time it's earning a living, but occasionally the romance and the history comes out and it is emotional.

MICHAEL JNR

It meant everything. It was the first Cheltenham without Grandad. Mark Blandford, the owner, was Grandad's godson. Mark's parents introduced Granny and Grandad. Mark's father, Roy, would always go off racing with Grandad, and they would stop in every pub on the way home. You couldn't have picked anybody better to have won for.

Dad was there. Everybody was there. The year before, you were thinking, 'That's your chance of a Festival winner gone,' but if he had won then, he'd have gone up the weights and he probably wouldn't have won the year Tom rode him. It's funny how sometimes these things just work themselves out, from not wanting to run him 40 minutes before, to suddenly there he was, somehow getting his head in front.

TOM

I was due at Kempton the next day, but I did go out that night with Dad and had a couple of glasses of champagne and something to eat. We went back to the Hollow Bottom near Nigel Twiston-Davies' yard where I grew up. It was nice going back somewhere I'd spent so many teenage nights after Cheltenham. Michael was going to come and join us, but he got carted off to the Plough instead because his new girlfriend was there, which is fair enough.

It was me, Dad and Nigel. We had a few glasses of champagne, and they had a big screen where we kept watching and watching it, much, probably, to Nigel's annoyance, because I'm not sure the poor old bugger had had a winner that week. From his point of view, it must have been fucking annoying to be surrounded by Scudamores watching this race over and over and over again.

It was just a lovely time.

PETER

I think Brough Scott or somebody said the Scudamores are a golden thread through racing, and of course Lucinda's mother loves that and quotes it to anybody who'll listen. But if there is a golden bit of binder twine through our time in racing, the Grand Annual is it. It'd be lovely if it was the Gold Cup or the Grand National. It's not a flash race, but at the same time it's the type of race that jump racing is all about, and we've all won it. I like that.

8

FOOD, DRINK AND HOW TO AVOID THEM

'My God, I do like to see my jockeys have a drop of port in the morning!'

PETER

You have to live the life of a jockey to know the importance of weight. It governs everything. It governs the comfort in your life, and your ability to make a living. So the first conversation is: 'How's your Harry Tate?' How's your weight? If your weight's good, life's good. It's just the oddity of being a jockey.

Wasting's a pretty fucking miserable, awful thing. You can't have a social life and waste. People would say, 'Come out to supper tonight!' Well, I've got 10 stone to do tomorrow . . . You feel such a miserable fucker, not going out, or going out when you're dieting. If you're a footballer, you go out and drink water, but you can still eat and have a social life. But a jockey . . .

TOM

The heaviest I remember being was when my eldest daughter was born, and it was during the September break. My weight went up to about 10st 10lb, and I had ten stone on my first day back, which meant I had to be 9st 11lb [to allow for the saddle and other kit]. I got it down to 10st 6lb by the Thursday, so that was 9lb to shift in two days. It was just running and sweating and very little intake. But you don't stop the intake: you still have to have a nibble on chocolate here or half a cup of tea there. You'll feel very, very tired afterwards. It's amazing what your body can get you through. But in the old days, people were doing that a lot, the Biddlecombes and all those, day in, day out.

MICHAEL

Some were better at it than others, but I was born with bad feet, so I'm not much good at running weight off. Some of these Flat racing jockeys would go and run three or four miles before they go to the races. I mean, it's amazing.

On a normal day, if I was going light, I might have a poached egg before I went, and half a cup of coffee. If you're going light, you wouldn't have anything till after you passed the scale. Once you've passed the scales, you go and have a cup of tea. They used to laugh at me, because I'd take the ham out of the sandwich and chuck the bread away.

PETER

I notice now that four or five jockeys a meeting will be running round the track. In my day, nobody ran round the track. I mean, nobody. I'm not proud of that. But you'd lose more in the sauna than running round the track, and you were always rushed. You'd ridden two lots and you had to get to the races. You got there an hour before your ride – you wouldn't have had time to run round the track.

TOM

A lot of the time, when the new doctors come in, they say everything is wrong and they try to change it all, but they don't understand racing and the demands upon us. So yeah, in an ideal world it would be marvellous not to have any saunas whatsoever. Jerry Hill, the BHA's medical adviser, wants to put in Wattbikes at the racecourses, so that you put your sweatsuit on and lose weight on a bike. That sounds brilliant – I'd love to do all that – but when you've been riding out all morning and you get to the racecourse, you've got half an hour to lose 1lb . . .

You speak to dieticians and they say, 'We can get your weight level at 10st 4lbs.'

Well, I don't want to be 10-4. I want to be 10 stone. The diets, again, are so much better, but there's sometimes that lack of understanding.

'Well, we can get you 10-2.'

OK, 10-2 is fine, but every now and again I've got to be 10 stone. 'Well, we can't do that, because your weight will balloon up . . .' Well, that's too bad.

MICHAEL

I always made sure I had a meal, one meal a day. One or two people said, 'You've gotta look after your health: you can't just go riding and not eat at all.' OK, I know one or two jockeys, when people asked them to go light, they just gave up eating for 24 hours. But I always used to say, 'I'm gonna have something' – it was usually a steak. And of course there was no Sunday racing, so Saturday night you had a blowout.

PETER

My father constantly repeated a story. A trainer approached him and asked him to do light. He said, 'I can't do that weight.'

The trainer asked him what he was going to do when he got home. Father said, 'Well, I'm thinking about having my steak with an egg on it.' And the trainer said, 'Well, think about it and, when you get home, don't eat it.'

My father thought a steak with an egg on it was a good diet. But didn't the footballers have a good steak and chips in those days? We didn't understand diet.

When I was a young man, as an amateur, because I'd heard Biddlecombe had sat in the sauna with a champagne cocktail, I did it. But after a while, it's obvious that it's bad for you. I think if I sat there solidly, I could lose 2lbs an hour. It got harder as you sat there. Some days, if you were dehydrated and tired, it was harder to sweat.

My father used to sit with a rubber suit on in what he called a sweat box. It was a chair, and then round it would be a box with a slope to it like this, and his head would come out of the top. You'd see them in *Carry On* films. That's his way of losing weight, with electric fires and so on inside.

TOM

I remember the first time I went into the sauna when I started riding, and two Flat-racing jockeys came in with a pint. They shared a lager. I remember thinking, 'That can't be right.' I think with the Flat boys, the likes of them having half a lager would knock the edge off the pain of wasting, and they could sit in the sauna for an hour. Every now and again you get to the races a little bit heavier than you thought you were gonna be. There is no alternative. But the days of people taking piss pills have basically gone, because you're getting drug-tested.

The mental turmoil some of those Flat boys must be in . . . I've seen Adam Kirby when we had the mixed race meeting at Sandown. He rode in the first race, went for a run, came back and he needed to lose half a pound, and he had ten minutes to do it. He put his sweat gear back on, went in the sauna and jumped up and down on the spot. And that's every single day. And George Baker told me he'd have a meal every other day, a pint of water . . . That's why they're miserable. A lot of them are.

Even when their riding days are behind them, ex-jockeys find it hard to leave behind the habit of treating food as a kind of enemy.

MICHAEL

You could have a sweet, a decent breakfast. I didn't wanna get fat. My father got really big, 'cause when he was a prisoner he was down to 9st 7lbs. He was about 16 stone when he finished up. And some jockeys, when they give up, they go to fat. But I'm going that way 'cause of this treatment I'm on. It's a thing for prostate cancer: they give me an injection once every three months. The other day, my great-granddaughter was sliding down the stairs. I was down the bottom, catching her and, about the third time, she said, 'You're fat!' Spoiled my day.

PETER

I've taken pee pills. But people said they were bad for you, and it didn't take a lot of working out. A pee pill was not going to be good for you. People used to say they'd get cramp if they used them, but I only ever took a quarter of one and I pissed like hell, got very light. David Nicholson told me not to take them, and I never did after that.

I would never have a steak with an egg on it, like Dad. If I was doing light, I'd have nothing. Nothing until after I'd weighed out or after I'd ridden. I rode better with an empty stomach, felt better. It never affected me. I never felt weak or physically affected by it. But that was my constitution. I'm not saying it fitted everybody.

The hardest thing is, if you're at Plumpton or somewhere and you've gotta drive home, you haven't eaten all day and they've got a Scotch egg and a steak and kidney pie for you on the counter, which you can't eat. That's why I used to take fruit with me and stuff like that, try and have this controlled thing. I had this Hay Diet: a cup of tea and some fruit in the morning as a normal thing, and then a sandwich at lunchtime, and then try and have meat at night. But if you were dieting, you cut things out.

I remember I had to do 10 stone in the Scottish National. Everyone else was going off to party. I had a Scotch to sleep and went to bed. If you're in bed, you're not hungry. You have a Scotch because, if you're hungry, you don't sleep well. And then Little Polveir won the Scottish National.

It's funny, that Piggott effect. Your hero – you knew the wasting didn't get him down, did it? It was discipline. It never got me down. I wasn't the type. I didn't get depressed because of it: it was just something you had to do. People would come in the weighing room: 'I haven't eaten anything and I've put 2lbs on . . .' That's a lie. If you don't eat something, you lose weight.

I don't think I ever felt weak for dieting. The lightest I can remember being was 9st 2lb, to ride Gaye Brief in the French Champion Hurdle. Everybody's eating and drinking marvellous food, this social thing, and I thought, 'I haven't got the mental strength for this,' so I had de-appetisers. They were like speed. Didn't stop you sleeping, but I knew it was making my heart race. And I dehydrated myself. It was very, very hot that day in Paris. So hot, I remember the Orangina, when I came back to the car, was almost too hot to drink. And I could not keep anything in my stomach. We had to drive up to ride in Belgium the next day, and I drove from Paris. I was peeing out me arse. That was the illest I made myself, and it frightened me, but I must have had some salt and some drinks and I was all right the next day.

And what happened to Gaye Brief?

PETER

He fell at the practice jump and fell again in the race!

It'd make you laugh now. Steve Smith Eccles, Francome and Hywel Davies are probably lighter than when they were riding. At least I'm bloody heavier than when I rode. I'm probably not eating that much more than I was then. Of course I didn't have gravy . . .

For those jockeys who fail to boil themselves down to the required figure, there are two options. You can admit it to the trainer and the owner, jeopardising what may be important sources of work. Or you can cheat.

PETER

Dad had cheating boots with no soles, so that saved you half a pound. And then you'd come back in the changing room and put your proper boots on. But clerks of the scales weren't stupid: they'd been at it longer than you had. If you came out to weigh with clearly a pair of cheating boots that didn't fit you, that looked like a pair of wellingtons without any soles, they would say to you, 'You are going to ride in those?'

You'd say, 'Yes, sir.' You'd got caught, so you had to ride in the cheating boots. Very dangerous: you could kill yourself doing it. They had no heel on them, these boots, and a very thin sole, so your foot could go through the iron and then you'd get hung up by your ankle if you came off – one of a jockey's worst nightmares.

Peter recalls how a jockey being weighed would sometimes engage the clerk of the scales in conversation to distract him from another jockey wedging the toe of his boot under the base of the scales to buy his friend a pound or two.

PETER

Francome had the balls to try something like that. I couldn't possibly do it. The other thing, it was another jockey who designed it, but Francome loved it, something like this: you put your cap on your knee and the long piece of silk used to tie the cap hangs down. So they used to cut the end of the silk bit and put a coat hanger up the silk, and then you could look round and look at what weight you are, and push the coat hanger against the ground. You could push a couple of pounds off . . .

Digital scales and vigilant officials have made such antics a thing of the past. Meanwhile, a team of experts at the Liverpool John Moores University has been advising jockeys, including Tom, on what food they should and should not be eating.

PETER

They're so much further ahead. Dad just wouldn't think like that. In Dad's time they stopped and had a port and brandy on the way to the races. He knew every pub on the way. He told me the stories: 'We got there early and we had a sherry and we walked out. Do you know what happened? The bookmakers bought us another sherry as we went out!' Whether it happened or not, legend believes it happened.

MICHAEL

Biddlecombe, once he got his licence, we used to share [the driving]. Our trouble was getting him home. I always remember one day coming back from Southwell, and I don't think he was driving yet, he wasn't even drinking. We called at this pub, the Chesford Grange, outside of Warwick.

'What's that?' he said.

Sherry. Because, if you're wasting, you mustn't get too much liquid in you.

'Oh,' he said, 'I'll try one of them.'

When he'd finished that, he'd look at someone else. 'What's he got?'

Gin and orange. 'Oh, I'll try one of them.'

Well, he was so pissed. His mother blamed me. And he never looked back. About 11 o'clock, he said: 'What time is it? Oh, bloody hell, I was supposed to meet our Tone in Ledbury at nine o'clock!'

Peter remembers his father telling him how jockeys in the 1930s would sometimes have a port and brandy under their seat in the weighing room, as a reliable source of courage before they went out to ride. Dick Rees, a five-times champion jockey, is among those said to have shored up their nerves in this way. Courage would have been all the more necessary in those days of stiffer fences, poorly schooled novice chasers and medical assistance of variable quality.

MICHAEL

Captain Bobby Norris was a lovely man. He used to train in a big park just outside Banbury. He was a great character, and he used to ring me up to go schooling. And one morning he said, 'Scudamore, come in, come in, have a glass of port!'

I said, 'Well, I'm not riding today, I will have a glass of port.'

So he pours himself one and drinks it, then pours me one, looks at me: 'Have another one!'

I said, all right. 'My God,' he said, 'I do like to see my jockeys have a drop of port in the morning!'

And the other lovely story about him was, when Paddy Cowley rode for him at Newbury one day and he went out to ride with a coat on, on a cold day. And he said, 'Cowley! Jockeys are bloody soft today. Before the war, they were tough men – they didn't put coats on! Come out to ride half-pissed and my God wouldn't they give them a ride!'

And Cowley said, 'If I was half-pissed, I wouldn't half give this a ride . . .'

But by the time Peter was riding, attitudes to alcohol were changing.

PETER

Francome didn't drink, Jonjo O'Neill didn't drink. So I think I was beginning to see that, if I wanted to get on, I had to have a different perception.

I tell you what changed me. I remember once, standing in a bar at Aintree with John Burke, who was not that much older than me, and he was having maybe two half-pints. And the next day he turned over on Andy Pandy in the Grand National. I would say he was sober when he went to bed, and it can't have affected him the next day, but people said, 'He had a few beers – that's why he turned over . . .' And I was just at an age when you were so impressionable. I thought, 'I'm never going to get caught like that. I'm never gonna get accused of having a few drinks and being beaten.'

TOM

With the advent of the breath test, it's frowned upon to have a drink the night before. I'll have a glass of wine, a couple of beers, but certainly not to the level of Grandad's day, probably not even Dad's day. The likes of John, Jonjo, Dad and then McCoy, Dunwoody, they set the standard and you copy them. They didn't drink, so if you want to be a professional athlete and continue at the top, you've got to make sacrifices, and it's not really a big sacrifice to make.

Dad says he didn't drink the night before, but he got absolutely off-his-head drunk the night before Captain Dibble won the Scottish National. I think Nigel said to him, 'You ride better when you're drunk.' He'd won on Granville Again the day before, so maybe the pressure was off. And Nigel might have been right: he was as brave as a lion on Captain Dibble. It was a bloody good ride – I watched it the other day. Dad had obviously wasted ten years, staying sober . . .

PETER

From my point of view, it's a PR exercise. You've got to get on. Francome got on in his way, Piggott got on in his way: I had to create an image to get on. I thought, 'People are paying a lot of money for a horse in training and you to ride it: they don't want you coming in saying, "This is jolly good fun!"'

9

AINTREE: WHAT COULD POSSIBLY GO WRONG?

'I remember jumping the first, thinking, "Christ!"' – *Tom*

It might come as a surprise to those who remember it, but Strands Of Gold's exit from the 1988 Grand National is now the cause of mirth in the Scudamore family, or at least among its youngest members. There is, of course, nothing funny about horse and jockey taking a crashing fall at Becher's Brook but 12-year-old Margo and ten-year-old Myrtle, daughters of Tom, are royally and repeatedly entertained by watching their grandfather get off the Aintree turf and hurl his whip back at the fence in a vivid act of frustration. In the background, an advertising hoarding says: 'I bet he drinks Carling Black Label . . .'

TOM

The girls find it hilarious. Oh, yeah. Especially the youngest one, she's a proper Scudamore, she is: utterly, utterly ruthless. There's no holds barred.

She screams with laughter when she sees this, because of Dad's reaction. They get him on the phone and everything: 'We've just seen it, what were you doing?'

Up to the moment of take-off, what Peter was doing was winning the Grand National. He was aboard a highly capable, well-handicapped nine-year-old that had not long since joined Martin Pipe. Hard against the inside rail while his rivals congregated in mid-track, Strands Of Gold was lobbing along and had masses more to give. 'Would have been concerned in finish had he got round,' was the verdict in Timeform's Chasers & Hurdlers. *But at the second Becher's, he only got halfway up.*

PETER

He would have turned over at any fence. He was a fabulous jumper but Mark Dwyer, who had been riding him, told me he would just miss a fence out. He did it again with me at Ascot. He's clearly able to jump. But he didn't come up, did he?

TOM

He was cantering, absolutely cantering. You watch it back now, he would have won. It's just scary how well he was going. I mean, look at him – how often do you see a horse going that well? And he did win the Hennessy later that year. But the height he got at Becher's, it wasn't the drop that caught him out, he'd have turned over at the water jump, doing that. Everyone says he shouldn't have gone down the inside . . .

PETER

Pipey pulls my leg about it. But my thing was to go down the inner. You're either 100 per cent committed or not. I didn't really alter my riding attitude when I got to Aintree. I wanted to win, not finish second. On reflection, we'd only just had Strands Of Gold. He would miss a fence out now and again, and you didn't want to be in front too long. But we rode everything up in front. He was going to stay, he was fitter than everything else, so I was up there, down the inner, because that's what we did. It's easy afterwards, but if I'd jumped it, landed the other side, got ten lengths on everything else and won a length, everybody would have said it was brilliant. There's a quote from Bryan Marshall: 'You either go down the inner or the outer, and not many races are won down the outer.' I don't keep awake at night worrying about it.

An under-explored aspect of Strands Of Gold's fall is that two strides before take-off, he passed an ambulance man standing on the track itself, a full stride in front of the hedge which famously signals the approach to Becher's. In the age of Twitter, punters would have been demanding an investigation before the winner got to the finish. Was Strands Of Gold distracted at just the wrong moment?

PETER

He was standing in a position he shouldn't have been and I fell. I didn't see him. Whether Strands Of Gold saw him . . . I'm not making excuses, but it is a possibility.

The five-year-old Tom was making his first visit to Aintree that year, and the excitement of that first journey north stays with him. As it turned out, he was the first person who dared to approach his dad and open a discussion about what had happened.

PETER

Thomas was a very serious little man. Things were very black and white to him.

'Is Dire Straits the best group in the world?'

Tom, that's a subjective thing.

'Are they world champions? Are you the best jockey in the world? Are you going to win the Grand National?'

I'd been teaching him to ride, and one of the things I told him – I still say it to people now – was: 'If you touch a horse's mouth going to a fence, you affect him.' Once you touch their head, you affect them, and they may make a mistake. Even when you're trying to shorten their stride going into a fence, you don't want to be pulling on their mouth. So if you hold a bit of mane, you can pull against them: you can give them all the signals to pull back without pulling on his mouth. So I used to say to Tom, 'Do that. And you won't fall off, either, because you've got a hold of his mane.'

So Strands turns a cartwheel at Becher's and I've thrown my stick across the track. I'm livid. I walk into the weighing room and this little figure comes in and says, 'Daddy, were you holding on to the mane?'

TOM

I remember him being in the shower and nobody had spoken to him. I went and gave him a bollocking for not holding on to the mane. Aged five. He's feeling that and I've gone marching over . . . I don't think he rode a winner that week. It was a long journey back.

After that, I remember going up full of excitement every April, and coming home bitterly disappointed. Oh, it wasn't that bad. We have very fond memories of it all. Strands Of Gold was the only disappointing one. There were ones when you'd go up thinking, 'Good old Bonanza Boy,' but never really feeling that he was going to do it.

Even after Dad retired, we went up every year. He was working on the telly and he was involved in the horses at Nigel's as well. I remember the night before Earth Summit won, it was pissing with rain, which was ideal for him. That was just a brilliant night all round. I was 14 or 15, and going out in Liverpool was just amazing. There was this tiny restaurant, and in it was Richard Johnson and Choc Thornton. I think Dickie had just turned professional; Choc's an amateur at this point. Obviously, Carl Llewellyn was there, Alice Plunkett, Arthur Moore, Graham Bradley and his wife Bob. I remember Bob dancing in the window and they all started piling in, thinking it was a strip joint.

Just three years after being starstruck by his fellow diners in Liverpool, Tom was taking part in the great race. The fence that had claimed his father and Strands Of Gold also proved too much for him and the 50-1 shot Northern Starlight.

TOM

I just remember being phenomenally excited. If I'm honest with myself, I probably got a bit carried away by it all. I was 18. Now, I go out there and I think, 'OK, keep him calm, get to Becher's, it's just another race, this is where I want to be at this point of the race,' and so on. Whereas on Northern Starlight, all I could think about was, 'I'm riding in the Grand National, I'm riding in the Grand National, I'm riding in the Grand National!'

I remember jumping the first, thinking: 'Christ!' And then, 'I've jumped another one!' I remember him putting down on me at the ditch and thinking, 'Cor, here we go . . .'

'I've jumped another one!'

'I've jumped another one!'

And then I fell off him. Well, his saddle slipped. I wouldn't have got any further, because two fences later there was a massive pile-up and I was upsides Jim Culloty and Warren Marston and they got stopped, so it saved me getting a kicking.

Things were rather different when Michael made his Grand National debut in 1951, exactly half a century before Tom. For one thing, it was the first year when the race no longer featured a short stretch of ploughed land. This had moved around the racecourse, and was at one time sited just after Becher's, but eventually found a settled position on the run to the first fence, where it took the edge off the field's flat-out charge. In 1951, as jump racing became more professional and moved away from its hunting roots, the ploughland was finally grassed over. Coincidence or not, there were a dozen casualties at the first that year.

MICHAEL

They went like lunatics. Alf Mullins, another jockey, a great friend of mine, took me to the races. He said, 'They'll have their whips up, going to the first.'

I said: 'Don't be bloody daft.'

Well, I didn't see anybody whip up, but they didn't half bloody go, I'll tell you that. And 12 of us went at the first, over-jumped or brought down, you see.

In his disappointment, the 18-year-old Michael could take some comfort from the company he was keeping on that landing side. Others who got no further were Jack Dowdeswell and Bryan Marshall, who had both been champion within the previous four years, as well as Dick Francis and Pat Taaffe.

MICHAEL

After that, Lord Sefton used to come in each year and stand in the weighing room door and tell everybody to go steady. Well, that was like a red rag to a bull. Put it this way, he was a lovely man and I rode some winners for him, but he was the wrong man to do it. Because what experience has he ever had round there? Nobody laughed at him, but they took no bloody notice. If your trainer says, 'Jump off and be up there with them,' you've gotta go. I mean, he pays the wages.

PETER

Lord Sefton giving them that lecture is like the man who plays fly-half for the local rugby club coming to tell Barry John how to play fly-half. He just shouldn't be doing it.

The next year, 1952, Michael had an altogether happier experience when he was booked by Fulke Walwyn for the eventual runner-up, Legal Joy, on the recommendation of his main employer, Fred Rimell. Walwyn arranged an unusual preparation for the horse, who had evidently been held up in his home work.

MICHAEL

Fulke rang me and asked would I ride him in the National for Dorothy Paget? Would I go up to Aintree and have a canter on him on the Thursday and the Friday and the Saturday – give him a canter in the morning because the weather had been bad: they couldn't do much work at Lambourn. I've never known a horse go one, two, three like that. When I got on him, he was nice. Second day, he was better. The third day, I couldn't hold him.

He gave me a hell of a ride. I know Fulke was very pleased – everybody was very pleased.

We went home the next day. I hadn't got a car: I was too young to drive. Alf Mullins took me home to Much Dewchurch. I remember going round the bend in the road, there were bloody colours all over the telegraph poles and a dozen, 15, 20 cars there – they were having a booze-up on us being second. It was a great party.

But finishing second on Legal Joy did not turn out to be as financially rewarding as Michael had been told to expect.

TOM

Dave Dick used to ride a lot for Dorothy Paget, and he told Grandad, 'She'll pay you up front, you'll get a bonus, and then on top of that you'll get another percentage of any prize money.' If he won, he gets an extra ten per cent; if he's placed he'll get five per cent or four per cent.

Grandad never got the money. He always swore that someone else had pocketed it.

Anyway, Martin Pipe, being the great racing nut and historian that he is, went and bought a lot of Dorothy Paget's things when they came up for auction, and they include loads of letters. He rang up Grandad to tell him, about six months before Grandad died, that he had found the letter Dorothy Paget had written to Fulke Walwyn, setting out what he was to be paid.

By the time of his career-ending injury in 1966, Michael had ridden in 16 consecutive Grand Nationals, a record that stood until Richard Johnson made it to 20 in a row some 50 years later. Michael reckoned he had learned a few things about tackling those famous fences, and passed them on to the Scudamores who followed.

MICHAEL

I had my own way of doing it. I used to jump out of the gate and go to the Melling Road, and then take a pull and get back, balance and look for daylight.

The first circuit, it was just a matter of survival, and a lot of the sensible jockeys looked to get round the first circuit and then think about riding after. In 1960, I think it was, they put more belly on the fences, on the take-off side. So, pre-1960, if you got in very close to a fence and your horse didn't know how to bend, you were in trouble. But they pulled 'em out in the bottom, basically made more slope to them, so when you got in close to one, you'd got a better chance of getting away with it.

Then, 50, 60 yards before you get to Becher's is a footpath, and I used to give them a kick then, because my father always said, 'When you jump a big drop fence, make sure you're going quick enough at it, so you jump out over. You want to be going that angle [more forwards than downwards] when you're landing, not doing that [coming down steeply].'

I rode in 16 Nationals, I got round in five, so I would have jumped Becher's ten times. And I rode in numerous other races there: the Becher Chase and the Topham. I went through it one day, and I reckon I attempted to jump Becher's approximately 28 or 30 times. And I fell off once and got knocked off once. And they say Becher's takes a lot of jumping!

You see some horses, in the past anyway, getting in too close and going straight down like that, they tipped up. If you're going at that angle [a longer jump with a less steep descent], you might stumble a little bit, but you don't go straight down, head first into the ground. I often wonder whether half these jockeys know that. I should think Peter's jumped it a good many times, and Tom has. Perhaps I told them, perhaps I didn't.

PETER

I had the same approach, only because he told me. You used to extend your horse to Becher's from the hedge, so you'd jump out over the drop. It's like going into a tackle in rugby: if you go in fully committed, you're less likely to hurt yourself.

But, on Strands Of Gold at least, Peter did not follow another bit of his father's advice, about the risk of approaching Becher's up the inside rail.

MICHAEL

We used to sit for hours, talking. 'Where are you going? Are you going down the inner or the outer or up the middle?' You always want to go the safest route. I used to try and go as wide as I could: up the outside, not too many about. Becher's, middle to the outer, was, in those days, not half the drop. It was about, I don't know, two foot less of a drop than the inside. I think it cost Peter a National.

Then again, paternal advice doesn't always lead directly to success, as Michael found the first time he rode over the Aintree fences, aboard East A'Calling in the Becher Chase of 1950.

MICHAEL

I jumped off in front and I was only 17 at the time, going to Becher's in front, and he hurdled it. And as I landed, I thought, 'What the bloody hell's all the fuss about?' And of course I went to the Canal Turn . . . A thing Father taught me was, always present a horse straight at a fence. But the Canal Turn, you have to cut across. I jumped him straight and probably lost three or four lengths, and finished up getting beat a neck or something. If I'd cut across, I think I would have won.

At the time of writing, Tom has yet to win a National, but he has won two other races over the famous green fences: the 2014 Grand Sefton aboard Poole Master, and the 2016 Becher Chase on Vieux Lion Rouge.

TOM

When I'm riding around Liverpool, I think about exactly what Grandad said to me. Both winners I've had over the National fences are down to Grandad.

He'd say to me, 'It doesn't matter whether it's the Grand National or another race there: you get to the water. It doesn't matter how. Your first six fences, middle-outer, survive: don't take any risks. Get to the Canal Turn first time,' he said: 'ideally you don't want to be on the inside, because they'll cut you up. You jump the Canal Turn, then you drop onto the inside, and it's a pretty free run then from Valentine's.'

Once you get to the water jump, then you've got to improve your position, because in most Nationals – you watch – from the Canal Turn the second time, the positions don't change enormously. Suddenly, there's a group in front and the winner comes from there.

One For Arthur was unusual: he came from a long way back – but the second, third, fourth, fifth and sixth didn't. You remember Amberleigh House and you remember One For Arthur because they came from further back. In any sport, something Dad always drums into me, you have to play the percentages.

So you jump the water, and then you improve your position all the way down to Becher's: you keep going forward. That doesn't mean you're suddenly getting them racing, but you have to go forward.

Dad'd say, 'Don't go right down the inner at Becher's.' Graham Thorner would disagree: he said he'd won the National because he jumped down the inside. But for every one of those, there's nine that turned over. It's all very well being that one, Grandad would rather be one of the other nine that win or might be second, because he's jumped it middle-outer.

'Second Canal Turn,' he said, 'there'd be more room, so then you're thinking of getting that angle right. From the Canal to the third-last is a long, long way, so just jump along there, don't do anything silly. If your horse is going forward, go forward. But if you're in third place and they're getting away from you, don't chase them. You can't make it go quicker than it's capable of. It's still a long, long way.'

He'd be absolutely fanatical about how you get from the last to the winning post: try and jump the last fence down towards the inside, and then you've got to get the angle to the elbow so right. He said, 'Don't pick up your stick: pull it through to your left hand, slap him down the shoulder. It's about momentum: just keep him going forward, don't try and win your race from the last to the elbow.' You can lose the race, like Crisp against Red Rum, like Liam Cooper on Clan Royal – there's so many you can name where the mistakes were made from the last to the elbow.

Keep him going, get to the elbow, get that rail, pull your stick through to the right hand and ask him for everything. After four and a half miles round there, or even two and a half, they're not going to be able to sprint. All you're doing is getting that last little bit out of them, keeping them concentrating and balance, balance, balance. Make sure you get that because, when I was on Poole Master, Sam Waley-Cohen was in behind me and he's looking for me to make a mistake, and I didn't.

The opposite happened when I won the Becher. Highland Lodge was in front, got to the elbow and drifted wide, off the rail. I had the momentum. If he'd stayed on the rail and I had to switch around him, I wouldn't have got there. And all I had going through my mind from the back of the last was Grandad talking me through.

It's funny, Poole Master was amazing over the National fences when you schooled him at home. On the track, only once did he do it, and I think he had four or five runs over there. And he'd shown no form at all. He'd gone into races before that in brilliant form and run terrible. When he won the Sefton, he was 25-1. I thought my good ride that day was something else, and all of a sudden I realised, going to the Canal Turn, that we were bowling along. I remember jumping the last and Grandad talking to me all the way up the run-in. You're aware of all the other things going on, but at that point you're distinctly aware of it.

Poole Master meant a lot. Dad was standing down by the winning line – he just happened to be down there – and that was a great thrill, because Dad never won a race over the National fences, and I was the first Scudamore to have won one there since Grandad had won the Topham in 1963 on Barberyn. Grandad had died that summer, in July, so it was only five months later.

While Peter didn't win a National, he showed significant skill around Aintree. Of his 13 rides in the big race, Strands Of Gold was the only one from whom he was parted mid-race. In other years, on other horses, he finished third, fourth, fifth, sixth and sixth again. All it would have taken was a bit more luck in running or in choosing the right mount from those on offer.

PETER

I was asked to ride Party Politics before he won in 1992, but Nick Gaselee always wanted commitment months and weeks before and I couldn't commit, in case Martin wanted me to ride something in the race. That was the only National winner I possibly could have ridden.

A horse I rode, Little Polveir, he won a National, two years after I won a Scottish National with him. But I never thought, 'Oh, this'll win a Grand National.' Because of the handicap system, I never thought it was worth setting your stall out to ride a particular horse in the Grand National, because the odds against you were ridiculous.

On one memorable evening in the spring of 1985, Peter was trying to shed a few pounds in the sauna at home when the phone rang and he was offered a ride in the National on Hallo Dandy, who had won the race the year before. Minutes later, the phone went again and he was offered the ride on Corbiere, the 1983 winner. He chose Corbiere, which was the right decision, inasmuch as Hallo Dandy then fell at the first.

PETER

There were certain people you rode for who gave you instructions or asked you to do things that you knew were beyond the capability of you or the horse. So then you just switch off. But Jenny Pitman knew her horse really well. She marched you round, she told you where she wanted you to go.

It's fascinating, the respect you have for National horses. Corbiere's athleticism was extraordinary. I'd ridden him round Chepstow, and won on him. I remember getting on him in the paddock, expecting to be getting on an armchair and I couldn't possibly fall off him because he's won a National, but in fact I was looking on his nose: he had no neck on him. I thought, 'Christ, I'm going to fall off here.'

When you first go to a fence on him, he'd be slow. So you'd go, 'Come on, you've got to lay up,' and he would put down on you, because he thought, 'I'm going too bloody fast.' Then he got into his rhythm, and then he could stand off.

Now that Peter was familiar with Corbiere, he had every hope of being involved at the finish of this Grand National. But he nearly missed out on the ride altogether after taking a shocking fall two days before on Burnt Oak in the Topham. A slightly reckless front runner, Burnt Oak put both front feet into the fence and turned over at speed, splatting his jockey straight onto the ground.

PETER

It was the one before Becher's. Thank God it was: I'd have been dead if it was Becher's. I'm knocked out. I break my nose and I smash my legs up. They're not broken, but I cannot walk. And Jenny won't let me ride Corbiere on Saturday unless I've proved that I could ride on the Friday.

I remember I was staying with a friend of mine, Michael Sampson, who always looked after me when I was in Liverpool. On Friday morning, he found me a physiotherapist in one of those smart, old houses. I promise you, I couldn't walk in: I had to be helped in. I was thinking, 'This is a waste of time.' Anyway, this lady strapped me up and I rode that afternoon, so I got to ride Corbiere the next day. If you look, I've got waterproof breeches on because my leg was so swollen: I couldn't get my normal breeches and boots on.

I think every time you set off in a National, you've always got hope. And also, you've got pride in yourself. You think, Ben de Haan's won on this horse; I'm better than Ben, I'll win on it as well. You have to think like that.

This is his third National, and Dad always used to say, and I think it's right, it wasn't the height of the fences, it was the width of the fences. It's the width of the ditches that gets them. The only mistake he makes is the first ditch. If you've been to war a few times and you know what it's like to have a bullet shot at you . . . I think with these horses, when they've been round a few times, they're starting to think, and it's the ditches that are worrying them. I think Corbiere had had enough by this stage. This was his last real go at it. I never thought he'd do it again.

He never left the inner. At second Becher's, all the others have landed in a heap. Look at the ground he made there and two fences later, at the Canal Turn. Then, I thought he'd win. And that's when it's in your mind: you feel your father riding with Tim Brookshaw, you can't help but think you're making history now. The late, great John Burke was standing by the rail on the run back from Valentine's – he'd been on a fancied horse of Toby Balding's. He's leaned over and called to me, 'Go on, Scu, you'll win now!'

I thought, 'Christ, I'm going to win the National . . .'

And with that, Phil Tuck comes by me. I could hear him, and thought there must be a loose horse. I thought I was well clear. I thought, 'I'll still get back up,' but at the second-last he put down on me.

Corbiere stayed on gamely to be a good third behind Last Suspect and Mr Snugfit, carrying over a stone more than either of them.

PETER

In those days, you were very pleased to jump round. It's sport at its very highest. That horse has never left the inner. If I'd gone any closer to the inside, I'd have been on the road. Unless you take lead out of the weight cloth, he couldn't finish closer. He and I put in every ounce of energy that we possibly could. So I never felt any disappointment. What more could you ask?

While Corbiere was undoubtedly the best of the rides available to Peter that year, it's easy for a jockey to make the wrong choice, or put themselves in a position where they can't make the right one. Tom's best chance of a National winner sailed past him when he was just 19 and got on Smarty, runner-up the previous year, rather than Bindaree, trained at the Nigel Twiston-Davies stable where Peter was working.

TOM

I committed to riding Smarty during the winter because he'd been second the year before. I was young, a conditional jockey, and I got offered a job riding all the horses for those owners. And I accepted. I remember Dad encouraging me, thinking it would be a good move, that I'd have some horses to ride. But it was just a complete disaster for all parties. Cost me a National winner. Mark Pitman trained them, and I never really saw eye to eye with him, at least partly because I was so young and headstrong.

On another day, I'd have ridden Bindaree, but then you quickly put that to the back of your mind, in the same way as I'm sure Dad, every now and again, thinks that on another day he could have ridden Party Politics.

PETER

We fancied Beau in the race. Beau was a great big horse who could stand off everywhere. I never fancied Bindaree at all, really. Thomas could have ridden him, but he had taken the ride on Smarty. Thomas and I were barely speaking after this, but I insisted he ride Smarty. Thomas lacked experience round Aintree, and Bindaree wasn't straightforward. I thought for just his second ride round there, Smarty was a better conveyance. Smarty had been second, he was going to be a good ride round: there was no reason why Smarty couldn't have won – and then wouldn't you have looked stupid if you'd got off? Tom wanted to get off Smarty but I said, don't. Father always said to me that, within reason, once you'd agreed to ride one, you stuck to it.

Carl Llewellyn chose Beau. Beau stumbled after the last, first time round, unseated him. And so Bindaree won.

Michael also had his near-misses in the National, including Time in 1964, who he felt was going 'really well' until making a mistake at second Becher's. Possibly an even bigger opportunity was missed in 1956, when Much Obliged fell at the fifth-last. He was another of those rides resulting from an unexpected phone call that could just as easily have gone to a different jockey.

MICHAEL

Coming back along past the Highwayman on the Cirencester Road, we went in to have a drink on the way home from racing. I rang home and Mary said, 'Neville Crump has been on the phone – will you ring him quickly?'

Crump had trained two National winners in the previous eight years, including Teal in 1952, when Michael had ridden Legal Joy to be second. He was promptly booked for Much Obliged, who had won the Mildmay Memorial at Sandown, and received advice from Crump's principal jockey, who ended up falling at the first on a more fancied runner.

MICHAEL

Arthur Thompson said to me, 'He'll be a hard ride: you'll be working hard on him all the way.' And I was going to Becher's the second time and I thought, 'Bloody hell, this is going nowhere.' And one or two fell, and for some reason or other he picked up the bridle. But I over-jumped five fences from home – he jumped it too well. ESB was probably in front of me, but I wasn't far behind him. Anyway, that was that.

Pathé footage shows Much Obliged looking like a hard ride as far as the second Canal Turn, after which he rocketed forward. Having been sixth moments before, he was on the point of taking the lead when he got too close to the 26th and turned over. Had he stayed upright, Devon Loch and Dick Francis might have been held in second place by the time of their famous belly flop on the run-in.

Above: Annual meeting of the Injured Jockeys Fund trustees, including the Queen Mother, at the Goring Hotel, London in December 2001.

Below: John Francome, Bob Champion and Peter approach a hurdle.

Above: Grand National glory for Derek Fox and One For Arthur in April 2017.

Below: A proud podium at Aintree. Peter's granddaughters, Margo and Myrtle get their hands on the trophies.

Above: Campbell Gillies celebrates Festival success aboard Brindisi Breeze in the Albert Bartlett Novices' Hurdle 2012. *Above right*: a delighted Campbell on the phone to his Mum on the way home from Cheltenham.

Below: One generation to the next. David Pipe, Martin Pipe, Tom and Peter at Pond House in Wellington, Somerset.

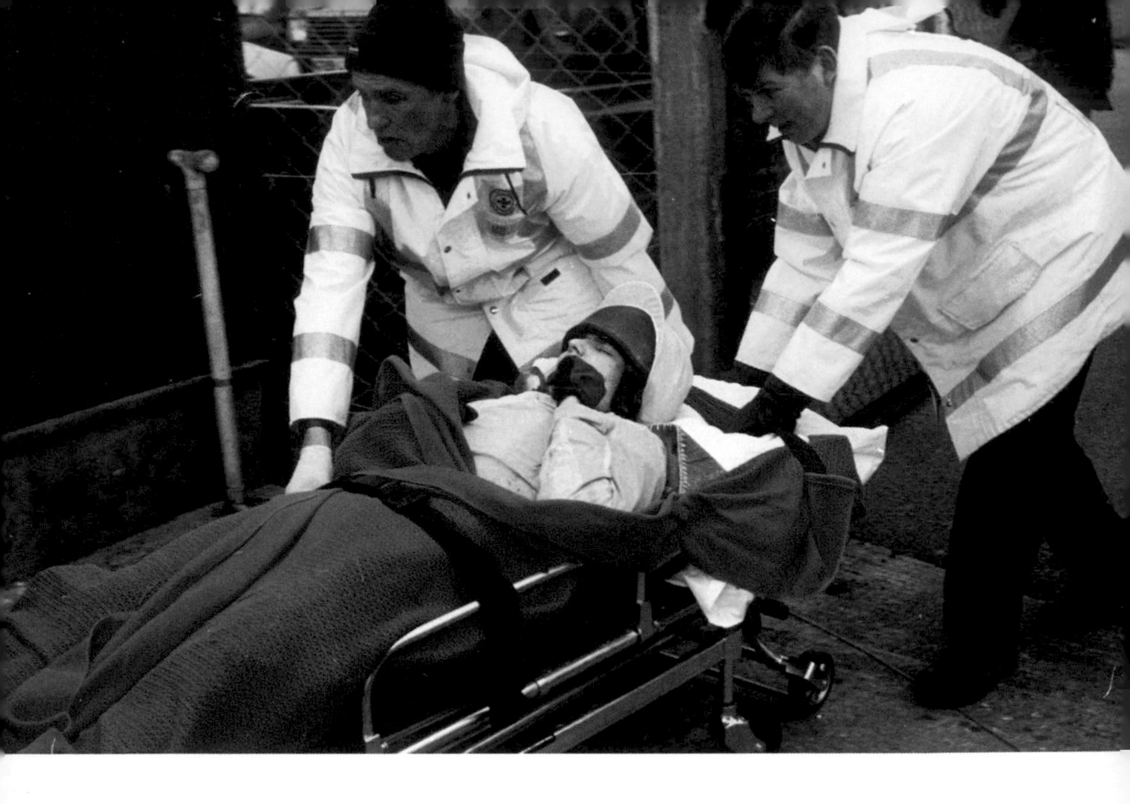

Above: Tom after his fall at Wincanton on Boxing Day in 2000.

Below: Tom and The Giant Bolster land in front over the last in the 2012 Cheltenham Gold Cup.

Above: Michael Jnr rides work on his stable star, Monbeg Dude, before the Welsh National.

Right: Tom holding the trophy for the 2016 John Bigg Oxo Handicap Chase run at Huntingdon in honour of Oxo and his owner.

Previous page: Paul Carberry gives a riding masterclass in the Welsh National as Monbeg Dude sees off AP McCoy and Teaforthree in a tight finish, January 2013.

This page top: Thistlecrack flies the last on his way to winning the 2016 King George VI Chase at Kempton.

This page bottom: Peter, flanked by sons Michael and Tom at Michael and Mary's funeral in July 2014.

Left: There was never a question of Tom not following in his father's footsteps.

Below: Michael, Tom, Michael Jnr and Peter. The Scudamores in 2004.

Towards the end of his career, Peter climbed aboard the hugely popular Docklands Express, a plucky little horse who repeatedly ran well in jump racing's marquee contests without quite being able to win them. Despite his lack of stature, he was sent off as the 15-2 favourite.

PETER

He'd fallen at the first the year before. He wasn't going to fall with me: I took that pride. I thought he was going to win. He was well in, wasn't he, at the weights, having been third in the Gold Cup? But in the race, he was never gonna win. Still gave me a fantastic ride. You get such admiration for those ones: a little horse, brave as a lion, didn't know he was little. Because he'd fallen, I was careful over Becher's with him, and he was just magic.

TOM

He was tiny, Docklands Express, and I think that was the problem: he had to use up so much energy just keeping in touch.

He finished fourth, a respectful distance behind Party Politics, the ride Peter might have had if he'd said 'Yes' far enough in advance.

Peter would have one more go at the race, on the strongly fancied Captain Dibble. Alas, they were lining up for The National That Never Was.

PETER

We had these animal welfare protesters. You don't see them, but sometimes at Aintree you could hear them banging their drums outside the course. I think there were protesters inside, waving their flags about.

We had a false start and were called back. Then, second time we start, there was no sign of a problem. And your level of concentration is: 'Becher's at the bottom of the straight here, I'm going to get over Becher's.' So you get over Becher's and you think, 'All right, where am I? Am I seventh, am I last? Let's get the Canal Turn right . . . OK, I can think about riding a race now. Oh . . . a few must have turned over.'

You can't look all round but I had a sense there weren't that many horses about. But in Nationals, they turn over. They could all have turned over at Becher's for all I knew.

And I was convinced he'd win, Captain Dibble. Absolutely convinced. He'd won a Scottish National, he could tap-dance in front of fences. Nigel trained him – there was just no weak point. And Nigel is totally positive: every horse he runs is going to win. So there was total belief. And I was just perhaps a little bit further back than I wanted to be. So you're thinking, 'Come on, I know you're going to stay.'

By the time I get to the Chair, I'm probably ten to 15 lengths off the leaders and there's bollards in front of it.

At that time, if there was a bollard in front of a fence, that meant there was a horse hurt on the other side: you couldn't jump it. But we hadn't jumped the Chair, so there couldn't be bollards in front of it. You think, 'This is clearly not an official bollard. It could be an animal rights bollard.' So I go past it, jump the fence, and when I land over the Chair, there's Martin Pipe waving me down. To me, Willie Stephenson and Martin Pipe are gods, and if they tell me to do something, then I do something. I pulled him up, and of course it turned out to have been another false start.

You would have had to be blind not to see everybody waving at you when you went round that bend, but a handful carried on. I do not blame those jockeys in any way. The officials at that time were so amateurish, we had no idea what was going on. So they carried on. If it hadn't been Martin Pipe, I might have carried on. It was typical of him to get himself in a position to intervene like that, typically professional.

Peter, John Francome and Jonjo O'Neill were admired jump jockeys from the same era, none of whom won a National. If Tom is to avoid ending up in that particular club, he will somehow have to get aboard a better National candidate than he has so far been offered.

TOM

To be fair, Soll had a chance, The Package had a little chance, Madison Du Berlais didn't jump well enough, obviously, but that year he then won the Hennessy, so maybe that was a chance of sorts. But all the others. . . Northern Starlight wasn't good enough, Smarty had gone, Blowing Wind had gone, Shardam couldn't jump, Iznogoud wasn't good enough, Puntal was gone by that stage, Battlecry wasn't good enough, Junior didn't jump well enough.

The Package didn't stay, but I had a good ride off him. Ballynagour was going all right, but he wouldn't have stayed. I had a good ride off Vieux Lion Rouge. He faded after coming back across the Melling Road, he just didn't stay. Dad and Grandad always said, 'There's very few that genuinely get four miles.'

But at least there still is a Grand National at Aintree every year, a continuity which seemed in great doubt in the early days of Peter's career, and might have been in serious question again had the course not made significant alterations to the fences in 2012 after four equine fatalities in the space of two years.

MICHAEL

I always say to these other jockeys, modern jockeys, 'You're not half the men we were! We had it tougher than you.' I think it's very sad. I mean, Becher's will be like any other fence, and the whole thing will turn out to be just a four-mile race. It's bowing to the people who don't know anything about it.

TOM

You used to jump round Liverpool and on the second circuit, where the spruce had been knocked off the top, you'd see bloody wooden stakes. That was wrong. I always felt that was wrong, and they had to change it. You'd hit them and it was like running into a brick wall: you'd just flip.

Whereas now, you'll hit them and they'll unseat you. All right, it might be, from your own point of view, embarrassing. I think there's probably more unseats over the National course than there were before. Ballynagour, when I rode him in the 2016 National – if he'd run in it four years earlier, he'd have cartwheeled. Instead, he dropped his hind legs in the ditch and all that happened was, I was sent up over the front. Before, you're watching those horses somersaulting.

I think they've got the balance and everything right now – of course they have, because the record speaks for itself. Andrew Tulloch, the clerk of the course, is always asking us, 'What do you think?' He works with us all the time, and he's sound as a pound.

Aintree, as a racecourse, has led the way in so many ways, in how they've managed to keep the race going. At the beginning of when Dad was riding, every year was going to be the last year of the National: they were going to sell it for a housing development. They've coped with everything that's been thrown at them in the past, and that gives you great confidence for the race in the future. What they've done recently, to get back on the front foot, they deserve an enormous amount of credit.

PETER

The National's changed, and I think it's a good thing. We don't want horses killed. It's never going to hold the place in respect that people had in Dad's generation but, from my experience of what One For Arthur's done, I'm surprised at the reverence people still have for the National. And I love the exposure: it's more than any other race that I've ever experienced. But it doesn't just stand alone because of 30 runners galloping down to what used to be Becher's: it stands alone because of the history of it.

Everything they've done at Aintree has been in the best interests of the race. When I jumped it, it was bigger and it took more jumping, but still . . . Three generations to win two Grand Nationals. That tells you it's quite difficult to do.

10

THE WHIP

'Good Lester, bad me.'

Peter has a theory about the way whip use in jump racing has changed over time. He reckons that the step forward in style which was made in the Fifties, when jockeys began to ride with shorter stirrup leathers, was a step backwards in terms of whip use. While jockeys were able to adopt a more aerodynamic position and be less of a burden to their mounts, they no longer had a length of leg that would allow them to encourage a horse forward. Many of them made up for it, Peter feels, by becoming more reliant on the whip. Meanwhile, the public's interest in animal welfare was on the rise. Racing officials found themselves having to intervene more and more to punish those who overused the whip and to deter others from doing the same.

PETER

My hero when I grew up was Lester Piggott. Everybody, including Peter O'Sullevan and John Oaksey, who were probably the most influential journalists in racing at the time, were waxing lyrical about Piggott. Therefore that influenced us as young men: 'This is how we have to use the stick.' While Peter and John were advocates of not using the stick, they were the ones saying how wonderful Piggott was. So I pull my leathers up, use my stick plenty, and then they say, 'Oh no! That's bad.' Good Lester, bad me.

At Haydock in 1984, I hit Bajan Sunshine 22 times from the last. O'Sullevan, in one of his books, quoted a letter sent to him by a racegoer describing that finish as 'the worst example of whip abuse' for years. I thought to myself, 'Hang on a minute . . .'

I was having a bad run and I landed over the last, the horse was holding its head back at me, and I thought, 'I am not going to get beat.' On one hand, though I shouldn't say it myself, it was a brilliant ride, and I won a neck. But I did use the stick too much. But it was a copying of what Piggott did, which Peter O'Sullevan and everybody was saying was brilliant. When he won the 1977 Derby on The Minstrel, I think he hit it 17 times in the last furlong. I found the contrast of attitudes hypocritical. You can't have, on the one hand, people saying Piggott is the greatest jockey and he's given The Minstrel ten in the last stride and that's great for him – but it's a welfare issue when you do it.

It wasn't just me copying Piggott. I remember Graham Thorner and a certain amount of jump jockeys would have long sticks because Piggott had one. Piggott thought, with a long stick, he could hit a horse round its tail end more.

The BHA has this idea that you're not supposed to win at all costs, but I don't think that's a helpful way of expressing the point. To the mind of a Piggott, myself, or a McCoy, or a Francome, if you're a champion, you do win at all costs, by which I mean, at all costs to yourself. You're sacrificing things to win. I'm not trying to say we're superhuman, but you have to use every advantage that you have.

When I used the stick, I certainly didn't imagine I was hurting the horse, and it would probably have been counter-productive if I had: pain isn't going to make him run faster. And then, we're horse lovers, after all. I go up to a horse, pat him and think, 'You look after me and I'll look after you. We're in this together.' I love the old line that says, 'Together a man and a horse can achieve things that neither could achieve alone.' And the stick is part of achieving that thing.

There's a mental side to it. Their attention has to be grabbed, and the stick is part of that: it's part of saying, 'This isn't a game – this is really, really serious that we win this race.' You can't get to the second-last in a three-and-a-half-mile handicap chase when the mud's up to your knees and say, 'Well, win if you like.' It has to be total commitment.

The stick in itself doesn't make horses go faster. It's the togetherness with the horse. I got much more enjoyment out of riding when I didn't use the stick so much: when you're extending the horse, when you're feeling really part of that horse, when you're feeling that you get every effort out of the horse without using the stick – because it's a better kind of horsemanship; it's more of a partnership. But that only works some of the time.

MICHAEL

I rode for Willie Stephenson, and d'you know what his orders were? Hitting was a last resort. And I've always stood by that: only hit him as a last resort. When you can't win otherwise, then give him a couple.

But Michael also remembers trainers from his day who were much more cavalier about how their horses were treated. Cheerily, they would tell him: 'When you've hit him as many times as you can and you can't find anywhere else, hit him between the ears.' Clearly, the jockey was not actually expected to poleaxe his horse. It was a jocular way of letting him know that mercy was not required.

PETER

A lot of responsibility for the use of the stick comes from owners and trainers. I think a lot of the cases where the jockey is done for the stick, the owner and the trainer should be done for the same thing. Because if you smack one and win the Group One, the owner benefits the trainer benefits and the jockey gets suspended. If the owner and trainer aren't happy with the way the whip's been used, why do they put the jockey up next time?

If you're hitting it five from home and you get it placed or you get it up and win, everybody says, 'That's a fantastic ride.' You're wishing to have praise, and people are giving you praise because you look to be working very hard on a horse. Then the owner of the fourth horse isn't very happy with his jockey, who's looked very pretty and hasn't been very busy on it. That owner looks at me, who's been very busy on it, and thinks, 'I want him on my horse next time.'

They used to say, when Piggott would ride a two-year-old and give it a few smacks, 'Oh, but when Piggott hit it, they always recovered quickly . . .' Absolute nonsense! The horse doesn't know whether it's been hit by Piggott or me. It's just a myth. We're full of so many myths in this sport.

TOM

Martin Pipe used to always go on about McCoy: 'Watch him, how he hits them.' He doesn't just hit them. He's pushed, he's kicked, he's cajoled. All right, he might have used it unusually early in a race, at the fourth-last or going away from the stands, but he's not hitting it for the sake of hitting it: it's for a reason. By the end of his career, he had a really good record with the whip, because he knew there was a right time and a wrong time. Years before that, he was getting into trouble over his whip use. It was just a case of technique rather than anything else, and as soon as he ironed that out . . .

Everyone goes through it. You feel like you're getting persecuted. You're just waiting for the stewards to say, 'Scudamore, we want to see you.' Unfortunately, the reason they're doing that is because you've broken the rules. And then you've broken them again. The transgressions that wouldn't have been noticed will now be seen. They're watching you in every race, and you have to change. You think you're getting persecuted, and you see someone else in the same race doing the same thing. But they're not the ones in trouble, if you're doing it day after day.

MICHAEL

I used to ride for Frenchie Nicholson, not under any retainer or anything, and at the same time I was riding for Fred Rimell, split between the two of them. They didn't get on very well. I think they'd had a fallout in their riding days. Frenchie's trained all these jockeys, but he's never told me a thing. The only thing he ever told me was: 'Use a short whip, for style.' Fred Rimell told me next day: 'You want to use a long whip, so you'll hit him harder.'

The authorities have, over the years, had a few goes at regulating whip use, without ever hitting on a formula that satisfies everyone in racing, let alone onlookers. However, Peter sees progress in the current regime, under which jockeys in jump races are allowed to use the whip, with their hand off the rein, eight times per race.

PETER

The Bajan Sunshine race was a real moment for me. For all that I've said about double standards, I respected Oaksey and O'Sullevan, and so I endeavoured to change in response to their criticism, to use the whip less. Though it had been acceptable to use the whip in that way, clearly times had changed.

I think a limited number of hits is a good thing. Having fewer hits makes you more aware. It's no use hitting it ten times on the run to the last and not being able to use it on the run-in. You've got to use it as an encouragement, not a punishment, and I think the whip rule makes you more conscious of that.

The first time I remember the stick being brought up was when Andy Turnell rode a horse at Cheltenham and hit it a lot from the last. I couldn't tell you how many times I hit a horse before then. Life was definitely a lot harder. I was living on a farm, and cows were hit with a stick. If I saw a cow hit with a stick now, I'd think, 'Oh, come on.' But back then . . . I never even considered that a stick hurt a horse. Stupidly, I thought, 'He's not gonna feel it.' I read somewhere that Tim Brookshaw said that 'the best treatment', as he called it, is one hit to take off, one in mid-air and one to land. That's manliness. It's what we were brought up with. It's only later that you thought about it.

But Peter also thinks more account should be taken of the way in which the whip is used. He recalls Stan Mellor, the champion jockey from 1960 to 1962, scribbling out a quick diagram during a conversation, breaking down the run-in of a jumps race into three sections, and asserting that the whip should only be used in the middle section.

PETER

Stan said he hated to see horses going to the last, been in front a long time, and then a jockey starts picking up his stick and flailing away at it. You've got to ride at the last to get over from one side to the other as fast as possible. And it's no use just picking up your stick as you land and hitting him. What you should do is pick up and drive – get that horse away from the fence as fast as you can.

Then you've got him running, and you can decide whether you're going to hit him or not. Now's the chance. Is he trying for you? Is he so tired that a smack is not going to help him? If you're in front and he's pulling up on you, well, you've got to use it a little bit more.

Then, when you get close to the line, Stan thinks you should probably put your stick down and drive to the line, because the stick's ineffective, and not going to make them go any quicker. Like Frankie Dettori does on the Flat: get him to stretch out his neck, put his head down and reach for the line.

I think it's wrong that Stan's never been used enough as an example of how to ride racing. To me, this is a pattern for whip use that would stick at all racecourses on all grounds. And then the punter would understand. It would be so much better if, instead of counting how many times you hit a horse, the stewards asked: 'Did you stick to that basic principle?' Then they might say to a jockey, 'Oh come on – you're clearly whacking it here when the horse is running for you. There's no thought in it: we're gonna do you.' Or: 'Actually, I can see the horse is pulling up, it's soft ground at Cheltenham, you've given it two extra but we'll allow it.'

TOM

I was watching racing from Worcester, and there were two instances of horses that were beaten, having harder races than they needed to. They were never going to win. One horse was beaten five or six lengths, finishing second. I think the jockey hit it seven times on the run-in, didn't miss it. And then another occasion, in the bumper, it looked like it was going to win for a little bit, but then it wasn't, and inside the final furlong he hit it three more times.

We can all be guilty of it, when you're young and you're trying. In a way, they're doing it because of the rules. You've got to be showing that you're trying.

If I'm in third place, and I'm on one that's had a little wander going to the last, you're giving a little hit to concentrate going into the last: no other reason – for your own and your horse's safety. But after the last, you don't need to hit it. If it's well beaten, you just push it to the line. You can achieve your best possible placing. If you're beaten a short head for third because you didn't hit it, you don't deserve days off for that.

I don't have an issue with a jockey who goes one or two hits over and he's won or been beaten a short head in an absolutely pulsating finish. I'd rather give a suspension to the jockey in fourth who's hit it eight times: hasn't gone over the limit, but he's never looked like winning.

PETER

I accept that John Francome has talked about a ban on whip use, and he could have a point. Take the stick away and then everyone's on level terms. But I've ridden in Norway, where you're not allowed to use the stick except for discipline, and I don't believe horses are any better treated there than here. In Norway, what used to happen in my day, their style of finishing changed, so, instead of pushing forward, you ride sideways with your hands.

Your hands don't leave the reins, but the whip in your right hand is slapping it all the time down the shoulder.

Improvements in the design of the whip have made a big difference. Since Michael's day, it has changed from a thing that may as well have been designed to inflict pain to a foam-padded device intended to avoid any pain. The theory behind the modern whip is that the horse will be impelled forward by the feeling and the noise of contact with its rear. Peter did what he could to assist in its development, spending a lot of time in the Nineties working with Jim Mahon, inventor of the air-cushioned whip.

PETER

You knew if you marked a horse it was wrong. I remember I bought an American stick, because it was flash, wasn't it? Use it twice and your horse has got great big weal marks on it. You think, 'Bloody hell, I can't use that!' We weren't callous: we were aware of things like that. You've got to be careful. Some sticks had wire in the middle. Obviously you didn't want those.

MICHAEL

I did get a bollocking from one trainer for marking a horse. I went to Towcester one day without a ride, and then arrived there with a ride, and said to the valet, 'Can you sort me out?' The valets, they had a lot of stuff of their own. If you didn't have anything, they'd find something for you that might be somebody else's. There was a bag of whips there as well.

The whip handed to Michael that day had wire down the middle, and it left a weal on his mount's rump. He recalls the trainer in question being unimpressed by his protestations that the equipment was not his own.

TOM

I think the only way they get hurt now is if you have a faulty stick – maybe it's got a thread showing that you haven't seen. The same as with any other gear: if you're going out there and the stick is in bad condition because you've had it eight months and you've ridden out with it 900 times and you just haven't looked after it very well, then it won't work as it should. They need to be checked: the padding still needs to be in good condition. They're pretty durable, and you don't change your whip as often as your helmet or your body protector, but you do have to change it.

It's the noise more than anything else, and the horses don't feel it much, but they are aware of it. I don't think I've seen any damage caused or any marks left by one of these sticks, like I did when I first started riding or when Dad was riding.

11

HOW THE JOB HAS CHANGED

'In what other walk of life do people touch their caps to their employers before doing the job?'

Compared with the sport we know now, in the immediate post-war years, horse racing was neither closely regulated nor well organised. It meant that jockeys could get away with a lot; it also meant they were thoroughly taken for granted. Safety does not seem to have been a priority for anyone.

TOM

When Grandad started, you look back now and think it was barbaric for jockeys, with concrete posts lining the course and little cork helmets, and at some tracks you could be falling on hard ground. But at the same time the people who were making up the rules and running the sport had fought in the trenches, probably, in the First World War. And the people he was riding with had been shot at in the Second World War. So it was a different level of fearlessness. They were just happy to get going.

MICHAEL

People look at our helmets now and say, 'Good God – fancy riding in that!' But they were bloody marvellous, I thought. 'Cos I remember in my father's day, before the war – I've seen photographs, and they never had any helmets at all. And if you look at pictures of Gordon Richards, they didn't wear helmets on the Flat till not so long ago. Just put the cloth cap over you and tied a knot in front.

Those old cork helmets, which fitted snugly onto the skull with no additional padding, did not come with a chinstrap. Michael describes how ad hoc efforts might be made to keep them in place, with bits of tape or trimmings from tyres that could be used as a kind of rubber band. Unsurprisingly, some jockeys found their helmet would hit the ground before they did, putting its usefulness in some question.

MICHAEL

I only ever lost one in a fall. It only ever came off once. In those days, you were weighed out with the helmet, so you had to make it as light as you could.

In 1957 or 1958 I went to America and had a ride. And they wouldn't let me ride in one of our helmets. They had a Caliente, they called them, and I borrowed one. They're quite heavy, the Calientes, and they'd got a buckle underneath. A friend of mine, who was a purser on the Queen Elizabeth, brought two back for me.

Eventually, the Jockey Club was persuaded of the sense of using the sturdier, better-quality helmets already in use in the US. Michael recalls that the Flat racing jockey Jimmy Lindley was particularly effective in pressing the case for them. Rules were changed so that helmets were no longer weighed as part of a jockey's equip-

ment before each race, meaning there was no incentive to cheat by using a lighter, more brittle version. But established jockeys were still not entirely convinced that such matters were something a real man should worry about.

MICHAEL

They made it mandatory. Up till then, we used to ride out and ride schooling with a cloth cap on, and turn it round to stop the wind getting under the peak. It was a bit embarrassing to walk into a yard with a helmet on, but once you got used to it . . . I mean, I wouldn't ride across a road without one now.

That's all we had, was a helmet – we didn't have any jackets [back protectors]. They didn't have jackets till long after I packed up, maybe ten years. I think they're probably all right, save for getting a kick, but if something happens with your spine, they just protect the kidneys. No, I think they're very good; I'm not knocking them at all.

PETER

Dad said it was seen as sissy to school in a helmet. They thought your bottle had gone if you schooled with a helmet on. The Flat race jockeys in Epsom were the first ones to be seen schooling in helmets: they were purely hurdle jockeys. The men I grew up around in Herefordshire were farmers, tough men, and they saw themselves as tough men. You didn't use Brylcreem, you wore a collar and tie, and fashion had nothing to do with it.

When I was first in racing, you didn't ride out with a helmet. I mean, I did, because Dad made me. But the stable lads didn't. You see pictures of Red Rum from the Seventies and he's cantering along; the man on top's wearing a cap.

And yet jockeys in the 1950s had an even more pressing need for safety equipment than those who do the job now, because field sizes were not closely regulated, and there could sometimes be an intimidating number of runners at a track that wasn't big enough to cope. If you happened to be at the front of one of those packed fields, falling became a really bad idea.

MICHAEL

I rode with 40 runners around Birmingham and 33 around Hereford, and it was nothing. I remember going to Chepstow one day and had eight rides and I don't think there was one race with less than 25 runners. I remember Buck Jones saying to me at Chepstow, going down the back side, 'Don't look behind.'

I said, 'Why not?'

He said, 'It'll frighten the bloody life out of you.'

There were 30 runners coming behind us. It was a worry.

PETER

Dad tells a funny story. There were too many runners at Hereford one day – they couldn't line them up across the course. So the starter said, 'Triers at the front, non-triers at the back' – and let them go. That's a story Dad repeated endlessly.

The modern jockey uses protective equipment that has been refined and improved over decades, with the encouragement of an enlightened regulator that recognises the importance of keeping competitors in one piece if at all possible.

TOM

We wear body protectors. It weighs 1.5lb: it's very light but sturdy. When Grandad was riding there was nothing like that, and when Dad started there was a back pad.

I can take a kicking. When Dad and Grandad were riding, that kicking would maybe knock them out for a few days. Now, I'll get up and walk away from it. It's not going to stop me from breaking collarbones or ribs or the serious injuries, but I can take a fall in the first race and then ride in the second.

PETER

We had back protectors as opposed to body protectors. They were a piece of foam that covered your kidneys and went up your back. We were so style-conscious. Amateurs had crooked backs and professionals had straight backs, or so the perception was. But these back protectors used to make your back look curved, so we didn't wear them. In those days there was no rule that you had to. So I remember a friend of mine, John Suthern, had a fall, and he's lying in the weighing room: 'Oooohhh.'

Francome comes up to him: 'You all right, John?'

'No,' he says, 'I've hurt me back.'

John says, 'Were you wearing a back protector?'

'No,' he says.

'Serves you fucking right, then.'

John got his mother to sew foam squares on a shirt: took the sleeves and the collar off it and put foam squares all over it, and those were the first body protectors. Wendy Cooper, who was my kids' nanny, she did a similar one for me. I say I invented it, but John says he did. John probably did invent it and I copied him.

Briefly, Peter considered taking out a patent and manufacturing his body protectors for sale.

PETER

But there's 300 jump jockeys in the world: there's not enough to make money out of this. So I never bothered, and of course I never thought for a minute that Flat race jockeys would start wearing them, the Pony Club would use them, and now of course it's an industry.

Mary Bromiley said the trouble with body protectors is, the better you make them, the more rigid they become, and you can't curl up properly. So there's a Catch-22 situation.

I went to a lecture on helmets, and they had a very clever man talking about what they use in the army. He said, 'The trouble is, the best helmet is a concrete block, but clearly you can't run around with a concrete block on.' But then, the bigger and better you make a helmet, the bigger the target you make. It's exactly the same with steeplechasing. The better your helmet becomes, the bigger it becomes, and the bigger the target is for a horse to kick it, which causes concussion.

TOM

The helmets are much thicker, much better. Put it this way: even the helmet I wore as a kid – I can't believe, now, that I rode in that compared to the helmets I use now. The helmets I wore then were so thin: they looked like they didn't offer any protection compared to the helmets we have now. There's plenty of padding, and you've got protection over the ears. A horse went under the stalls with Lester Piggott one day and nearly ripped his ear off. The way helmets are now, that wouldn't happen.

The other thing I use for concussion, which a lot of jockeys do now, is a gumshield. Dr Turner, who was the BHA's medical adviser for years, said to me they don't make any difference whatsoever, but I'm convinced that wearing a gumshield helps me with concussion. The reason I started wearing a gumshield is I remember McCoy had a fall at Cheltenham, lost some teeth, and then two days later they got infected and he missed three days because he was in hospital. I remember thinking that was needless. If you've seen the state of my teeth, you'll know the gumshield is not to protect my teeth: it's to stop me from having days off. And that sums up the mentality of jockeys.

To get another insight into the mentality of jockeys, ask Tom what the next step forward in protective equipment might be.

TOM

Look, there obviously is one, but I don't think about it. I don't go out thinking, 'How can we improve on this?' They tell me to wear it, so I wear it. If they told me to wear a swimming cap, I would. Of course, you should care very deeply about it, but I'm comfortable with the equipment we have, and I'm not stupid about it. I change my hat at least every six months, or I'll change it after a heavy fall, even if it's absolutely pristine. I wouldn't take any chances with that.

Jockeys in Michael's day were, on the whole, minded to put up with their conditions of work rather than challenge authority. As he pursued his career through the Fifties and Sixties, deference was beginning to collapse elsewhere in Britain, but it held up pretty well in the world of horse racing.

PETER

In what other walk of life do people touch their caps to their employers before doing the job? You were completely beholden to the trainer, and you called him 'Sir' or 'Guv'nor' or 'Boss'. I'd never have called Willie Stephenson anything else. I'd certainly never have called him Willie. He was like the Queen: he was of such magnificence and such complete control, you didn't even question it.

One of the first books I ever read was by Sir Gordon Richards. He rode for Fred Darling in the Thirties, and the owners used to come down on a Friday night from London by train, get picked up by the chauffeur, eat with him at night and watch their horses on the Saturday morning. The Duke of Portland comes down, eats with Fred Darling. At breakfast, Darling asked him to take his horses away because he didn't like his table manners. The world has changed.

For Peter, while his father embodied Fifties stoicism, Terry Biddlecombe was racing's personification of Sixties hedonism and the overthrow of restraint. Then he in his turn was superseded by the outright rebellion of John Francome.

PETER

I remember one day the steward came in at Newton Abbot and said, 'Francome! Francome!' and he never moved.

As the steward was walking out, John said quietly, 'It's *Mr* Francome to you.'

We were subservient. The stewards were country gentlemen, they were army people, so that's where you were. One time, John and I were hauled up to see the Jockey Club in London and treated like shit. Francome couldn't care less: his fingers are playing around on the end of the table, and Lord Manton says, 'Francome! What are you doing?' and we all sat up.

'Practising my piano, sir,' he says.

That was the beginning of the breakdown. Racing was so old-fashioned then. I did feel very much at times that the aristocracy, backed up by the army, ran it. I didn't just feel it: it was true. In certain circumstances, you were made to feel inferior. The professional sportsman was a pretty dirty word.

Ascot was terrible. I'd left the weighing room once and gone to see David Nicholson: I'd had my ride and changed. When I went back, they wouldn't let me in the weighing room because I didn't have any more rides to come that day.

When I was a kid, Nicholson used to tell me to get my hair cut. It was half a joke. Dad was friends with him, so we'd see him at the racecourse. 'Get your hair cut!' You were meant to conform in those days, and I felt it was exaggerated in racing. I remember seeing Andy Turnell turning up in jeans and trainers at Wincanton, and going out of the back door in case his father saw him. And he was a grown man of 35. I did think to myself, 'What's the point of putting them on if you're going out of the back door and nobody sees them?' But we're very old-fashioned in racing. Although we think we're enlightened, we're still very backward. You don't see very many long-haired jockeys even now, do you? You could get a helmet over long hair – women do. You don't see anybody with piercings.

Now I'm old-fashioned, I've become old-fashioned. I say to Blair Campbell, 'Look: you can no longer go racing in a pair of jeans. You have to dress in a way that lets people know you have some air of responsibility. If I've paid £250,000 for a horse, that's what I want to see from the man who's getting on it. You've got to show that you're responsible and you care about it.'

Thanks in part to Fifties deference, it was 1965 before jockeys banded together to form a trade body that could represent their interests. Michael was closely involved in the setting up of the Southern National Hunt Jockeys Committee, which eventually merged with its northern version and another body set up by Flat racing jockeys to become what is now the Professional Jockeys Association.

MICHAEL

We always used to go to a pub in Winchcombe. Was it the Angel? It could be the White Hart. Anyway, that's where we used to meet, and there was Stan Mellor, David Nicholson, myself and I think Johnny Lehane when we had the first meeting. That's how it started. Anything we wanted, we could have a meeting. There was nothing before that at all.

Michael brought in the Association's early driving force, Peter Smith, who united the three different groups and is now lauded by the PJA for his vision and energy in advancing the jockeys' cause.

MICHAEL

He was a major and he'd studied law. He jumped at it, and he was very, very good, 'cos he could put us right, and he loved a gin and tonic as well, the same as the rest of us. The trouble was, to keep everybody sober at the White Hart or whatever it was, we used to get a round of plates in, and that's how the meetings went. They did a lot of good. I mean, I don't think we ever went for more money from the Jockey Club or anything like that, but safety measures and so on. If we didn't like a certain fence or we thought it was in the wrong place, we could do that sort of thing.

There was one pompous inspector of courses one day: another horse had fallen at the water at Folkestone and we had a go at him, and he wasn't interested. That's the sort of thing we had to put up with until we had this association. I mean, we weren't troublemakers. That's the last thing we wanted. There were things that we thought we could improve.

It's changed a lot, the Jockey Club. It all used to be run by ex-soldiers, Major This and Major That. Some knew what they were doing, and some didn't. The ones that did were very, very good, and there were one or two who didn't have a clue, really.

PETER

Dad said they didn't want to be seen as a union, and I think Fred Winter definitely was not keen on coming into it, because it was going to be seen as a union. It's interesting how class-aware they were. They're riding for the lords and the country gentlemen, for whom anything union is Communist. Go to the Jockey Club Rooms in Newmarket and look at those old cartoons: there are lots of them where you see the very old, slightly bowed owner, obviously the lord or the steward with his cane, and he's looking down at the little jockey, who's about half his height, comically small. If that little man had dark skin, they'd have to take them all down.

Tom now serves on the board of the PJA and is strong in his support of the body his grandfather helped to establish.

TOM

I think it's a marvellous institution. It worries me and saddens me that some Flat jockeys are on about leaving, whether because it suits them or they've had bad advice. I think we're better as a union. They've made so many changes for the better. It looks after us all, and it doesn't matter whether you're Frankie Dettori or a 7lb claimer, it treats everyone the same.

We can't get insured individually, but because we're a group, we get Stobart written on our breeches and get insurance against career-ending injury along with it. Now, £100,000 isn't going to make any difference to the biggest earners on the Flat, but you have to think of the poor 5lb claimer that's just getting going and ends up in a wheelchair. That is a life-changing amount of money for somebody to have their house adapted, pay off their mortgage: the sort of things you can only get if you're all grouped together.

It's vitally important that we all come together. If we felt something at a racecourse needed changing, myself, Richard Johnson, Brian Hughes and the lads on the board could all go together to Richard Linley, the senior inspector of courses, and say, 'Look, this needs doing.' If we went individually, it would make no difference. If we go as a board, they have to listen.

Tom feels jockeys get something closer to appropriate levels of respect these days from officials, owners and trainers, though relations can still become strained from time to time.

TOM

I have a lot of respect for the stipendiary stewards, and I like to think they respect me. There are always going to be flare-ups and if something goes wrong, in my mind it's a massive miscarriage of justice. I can get quite wound up by them at times, and that's happened in the past when I've felt persecuted. But every single jockey will tell you that happens. The long and the short of it is, you've broken the rules, and you're not the unlucky one: you've been wrong.

The only thing that has really annoyed me is sometimes officials treat it as though we're only playing. One year I got concussed over Christmas and wanted to get back. Even though racing was going on, I couldn't get hold of anyone. I wanted to go and get concussion tests, go through all these procedures to get back, but the BHA had shut up shop for Christmas, so I couldn't. And I'm thinking, 'Well, if racing's on, there must be a way.' We're not on holiday, so I've got no sympathy for them to be on holiday.

Every now and again, you get that feeling that they think, 'Oh, it's OK, it's only a race.' There's that lack of respect for the fact that it's your livelihood. We're all self-employed, and if we don't ride, we don't earn.

And then the attitude of some leading officials . . . It's not the ones working at the racecourse that are the problem: it's the ones working in London. For instance, Jamie Stier, when he first got the job as Director of Regulation at the BHA: we had a seminar where he talked about corruption. And he gave us the big one about how he could stop people from stopping horses. And he said, 'You'll all say to me, "You've never ridden a horse." Well, I've never laid an egg, but I know when one's bad!' That attitude . . . there's a lack of respect and understanding they have, and you end up getting treated like schoolchildren. That makes my blood absolutely boil.

But I think in Grandad's time, those instances were plentiful. In Dad's time there were fewer, but it was still common. In my time, I can name you the occasions when it's happened; I can tell you who did it. And that's a good thing. My experiences are frustrating and annoying, but it doesn't happen very often.

In 1964, the year before the Jockeys Association came into being, the Injured Jockeys Fund was set up, a response to devastating injuries suffered by Tim Brookshaw and Paddy Farrell. The charity, which benefited so much from the drive of John Oaksey and the goodwill he attracted, has since provided invaluable support and necessary cash to those in need and built rest and rehabilitation centres in Lambourn and Malton. Peter serves as a vice-patron.

MICHAEL

It's A1: you can't say enough. Of course we've lost the president, John Oaksey. He was a lovely man. I think he did more good for jump racing than anyone in my time. He understood it.

They've been wonderful to me and they send an almoner down here once a month. They send me notes sometimes – would I go to Newbury or Haydock for this Injured Jockeys do? They just like to see you. It isn't just me, there's Mary as well: they're as worried about Mary as me. It's a wonderful set-up.

PETER

You felt the power of Oaksey and Brough Scott and Sir Edward Cazalet: it was their drive, their giving back to racing, that drove it. You felt almost in awe of Oaksey and what he put back into racing, although there was obviously no need for him to do so. I think his respect for his fellow riders came across massively.

The IJF now is as important as it's ever been. Jockeys have an insurance scheme as well, so if you fall and break your collarbone, you are looked after. If you fall down in later life, financially, mentally or physically, the Injured Jockeys Fund is there to pick you up.

While jockeys have, by degrees, won some influence over their working conditions, a still more gradual struggle has been going on among their own ranks. Female jockeys were not allowed to ride in races in Britain until 1972, by which time Michael had been retired from the saddle for six years. Almost half a century later, women are still enormously outnumbered in the jumps weighing room.

PETER

Clare Balding thinks I'm very sexist – she got quite cross with me. But you can't get away from it: a woman's pelvic shape is different. And that pelvic shape, in my opinion, gives a different projection, a different angle of a woman over a fence. They tend to sit forward more, and they do get fired into the ground more and get hurt more. Of course they can overcome that.

I have watched Nina Carberry and Katie Walsh: they're as good as I've ever seen among amateurs. Gee Armytage was fearless, absolutely fearless. Lorna Vincent and Gee were real pathfinders. Of course, there was a bit of a macho thing about it. 'Christ, I've been beaten by a girl there!' If I got beaten by Lorna or Gee, I shut up a bit.

Lucy Alexander is an exceptional rider, an exceptional thinker, but falls have hindered her, undoubtedly. Maybe she was unlucky. Maybe any male could have had those falls as well and suffered by them. I watched Bryony Frost the other day and thought, 'Christ, that is a good rider! Man or woman, that is a good rider.' And she's Jimmy's daughter, so she's brought up on the back of a horse. Maybe she's the right shape. I never thought I'd see a woman with the physicality to be champion jockey in this country. But watching somebody like Bryony makes me wonder if it's possible.

I'm not Floyd Mayweather, and I'm not a front-row forward for Saracens, but, for our size, what we do is physically demanding. I see Barry Geraghty's cracked his shoulder: he'll be back in three weeks and he's cheerful. I mean, nobody else is cheerful with a broken shoulder, are they? There's that type of robustness about it.

I've got a girl at our yard who rides very well. I've got a great big chaser that ran away across the fields with her the other day. What do I do after that? I put a man on it. Maybe I'm a dinosaur, stuck with a thought process from my father's time. If you asked him about women competing on equal terms with men in jump racing and doing as well as them, he definitely would have said, 'No way.' Maybe there is a way now. Lucy and Bryony have taken this professional thing to another level.

Michael was not entirely closed off to the idea of female success in the saddle. He mentioned the topic while criticising an aggressive approach adopted by some male jockeys, which he described as 'bullying'.

MICHAEL

Some horses reject that, you know. 'Wait till I'm ready: I'll do what you want me to, but don't you bloody start kicking and pushing and shouting.' I could be wrong, but I've seen horses like that. And that's why I think some of these girls ride so well. They ride a lot of bloody winners. They don't bully horses as much. Horses run for them.

Peter talks with a degree of reverence about meeting Julie Krone, the only woman to ride the winner of a Triple Crown race in US Flat racing. Between 1981 and 2004, she rode 3,704 winners, and her mounts won a total of over $90 million in prize money.

PETER

We went to Melbourne to ride in an old-timers' race, and she was an extraordinary human being, full of enthusiasm, energy, intelligence. You meet lots of people in this world who leave no mark on you, but once you'd met Julie Krone, you remembered Julie Krone. She told us stories: somebody bullied her and she gave them a right hand in the weighing room. She couldn't have been more than five foot two, but you wouldn't want a punch off her.

Can Peter imagine a woman achieving a Krone-like level of success in British jump racing?

PETER

Yes. But they're going to be an extraordinary person. It's harder for women, undoubtedly it's harder for them.

TOM

I'm old-fashioned. If my daughters said to me they want to race-ride, I'd be in Grandma's position: I'd want them to do anything other than race-ride. It's not because they can't do it. There are riders out there: Rachael Blackmore, Bryony – they have proved that they are very good jockeys. It's whether they can take the same punishment that a man can.

It's tough: you take those crunching falls and you've got to get up. One female jockey I know, she breaks: she has a fall, she breaks. You get blokes that have falls and break too. On the Flat, Josie Gordon and others have proved that it's not the riding that's the problem. But in jump racing, there are falls and, no matter how good you are, they're coming.

Tom can readily imagine a woman riding the winner of a Grand National or a Cheltenham Gold Cup.

TOM

They've come bloody close. Katie Walsh wasn't that far away in the National on Seabass. I'm sure it will happen. But the National is 40 runners, and if you get on a horse, you've got a chance. In a Gold Cup, it's obviously much harder to get on those horses. Owners and trainers are going to want an established name. And that's nothing to do with sexism.

Travelling to the races is an enormous chore for any jockey, involving hours spent behind the wheel each day. Driving was even more of a chore for Michael, who began his career at a time when petrol was still being rationed, and ended it years before the M4 was completed. And yet somehow he speaks as though the whole, tricky business was good fun.

MICHAEL

When I started off racing, I didn't have a car: too young to drive, so Alf Mullins used to take me racing. Then I became very friendly with Arthur Freeman. During the time of the petrol rationing, we used to get together – we'd be gone for weeks sometimes, saving petrol. Then when Arthur packed up, Terry Biddlecombe came on the scene, and we were great friends. So I was always lucky to have a good mate, share the journeys.

But going south of London in a car on the old A40, it was bad. So we used to get on the train at Gloucester or Evesham or Worcester. A lot of the jockeys came from Lambourn on another train: we all used to meet up and we used to play rummy for a penny a spot. Oh, we had tremendous arguments; it was great fun playing cards. The only problem was when Johnny Haine wanted to play for more money. I always remember being at Waterloo one day, and it came over the loudspeaker that 'Passengers are encouraged not to play cards with strangers.' We'd play cards down to Paddington, then go to Waterloo and play cards down as far as Folkestone, and do the same thing all the way back again. It was just fun.

We got back to Ashford to catch the train after Folkestone one day, and

John Oaksey was sitting there on a parcel-carrier with Johnny Haine and two others, with his trilby on the back of his head, playing cards. And I thought to myself, 'If only some of his newspaper readers could see him now, they might cancel their *Daily Telegraph*!'

PETER

I occasionally travelled down on the train, just 'cos Dad did. I remember going as an amateur, getting a ride at Folkestone, and thinking, 'You've made it, you've got a ride at Folkestone.' I got on the platform, brought up to believe in dieting and so on, and there's Francome tucking into a fried egg, bacon and sausage for breakfast. That was his way, all the way through. Of course I was too frightened to speak to him, and sat in a different carriage.

You had these punters on the train: they had the coats with the velvet collar and the trilby – they looked like something out of St Trinian's. It was lovely. It was just life. Dad talks about playing cards all the time for a penny a spot. We never played cards, but I loved those stories. Does it say life was a bit more relaxed? They'd play in the weighing room, and the doorman would wait to call them out because Dad had got a good hand.

Of course, then the M25 comes, and we can all drive there much faster. Do we enjoy it as much?

12

GETTING LOWER IN THE SADDLE

'It wasn't pretty to watch, and everyone thought it was wrong. He ended up being champion jockey'

From a spectator's perspective, perhaps the most obvious change in jump racing since the 1940s, when Michael's career began, is the way jockeys ride. The Scudamores have enlisted the help of some of their friends and rivals over decades gone by to explain those differences in style and the circumstances that caused them.

DAVID MOULD (RODE 1957–74)

The older jockeys were more upright: they rode long and sat upright. And the fences being so big, they used to lean all the way back. They'd be lying on their backs over fences. It was a survival style – it was staying on board.

STAN HAYHURST (1950–73)

If you look at photographs of the Thirties, we were roughly halfway between the styles there and what they do now. We obviously rode with longer stirrups than the present boys, but shorter than the older ones of the Thirties and

Forties. They were more hunting – National Hunt racing came from hunt riding. Round Liverpool in the old days, they sat well back at every fence, whether the horse made a mistake or not. We obviously improved on that, and the present boys have improved again.

GERRY SCOTT (1954–71)

I've got photographs of Liverpool, and back then there's no way you'd have sat up the neck over those fences like they do today. In my day, the Mildmay course was all miniature Grand National fences – there was no birch. They were smaller, but exactly the same in style and colour, and the idea was it was an introduction to the big fences. Aintree is more now a jockey's racecourse, whereas in our day it was a horseman's racecourse. I'm not saying it's wrong, but it's different. They go on, these days, about when a horse is in a good rhythm. Well, 'rhythm' was never in the vocabulary in our day. As far as we were concerned, the next object had to be jumped.

STAN HAYHURST

The fences were so different: they were straight up and down, like stone walls – no ground lines, no angles. George Milburn used to ride a horse at every fence as if he was riding showjumping: he wound it up with his legs, which you don't see now because they don't ride deep enough to do that. He was a fantastic jockey round Liverpool; he obviously doesn't get any credit because he didn't win anything, though he was placed in the National. But, a fantastic jockey round Liverpool, George. Horses jumped for him. He wound them up and he made them bold, which you had to be at Liverpool in those days.

If some jockeys of that era lacked style, that had something to do with lack of practice, because there might only be four race meetings a week, and even more to do with a shortage of examples to watch. There was no way to study a race after it had happened. If you didn't see it live, you didn't see it. And there were plenty of reasons why a 'survival style' seemed a very sensible idea.

GERRY SCOTT

Every racecourse was different. All the fences were different, not uniform like they are today. The head groundsman built every fence on his track. So they were all individual, and they were all definitely a lot stiffer than they are today.

It's not a case of me reminiscing, with me old walking stick, patting on the ground. It's a fact. You had to know each racecourse. Leicester's fences were among the stiffest, so much so that Fred Winter, our champion jockey, refused to ride round there. Kelso was really stiff. Many of them were.

I watch racing now, and – don't think I'm criticising in any respect, I fully admire the game altogether – but the difference . . . Even at Cheltenham, I see horses walking through the tops of those fences sometimes. In our day, you'd have turned six somersaults.

STAN MELLOR (1953–72)

They used to say the fences at Kempton were like brick shithouses. And Manchester had big black ones. I rode over them at 16 in a novice chase. There were four runners: two good ones and AP Thompson and me. AP said, 'Come on with me,' speaking to me like a little boy. 'We'll go around together, you and me, 'cos they're too good for us. We'll let them get on with their business. We'll jump round together.' And we did.

If you happened to take a fall in those days, the risk of injury was significantly greater than it would be now, because of the concrete posts that supported the rails alongside each track. They proved a remarkably durable part of racecourse furniture, considering the obvious danger.

JOHN FRANCOME (1970–85)

I hit a concrete post at Market Rasen when I was claiming 7lb and I was off for three months. My first ride back was at Southwell and they were just putting some new concrete posts in.

RON BARRY (1964–83)

You'd go to some courses and halfway through the winter there'd be no grass on it. And, with the concrete posts, the rails were never moved. You were on the same bit of ground all season, so you had to pick your own way round the course when the ground got heavy. No watering system either, and then if there was a shower of rain, they were slipping all over the shop.

And let's not forget that neither the safety equipment nor the medical assistance was all it might have been. Nor was it accepted that avoiding injury was something a jockey should care about. John Francome retells a Fred Winter story, of when the great man went to Epsom to school some horses.

JOHN FRANCOME

He put his helmet on and Ron Smyth said to him, 'What d'you think you're doing?'

'It's a helmet.'

'You're not schooling here with a helmet on, son.'

And Fred said, 'I was the idiot – I went and put it back.'

STAN MELLOR

I got married and then had a ride at Cheltenham. The horse fell. I was all right, but my helmet went rolling down the hill. And the missus was in the jockeys' stand. She said, 'Good God! His head's come off!'

DAVID MOULD

Michael Scudamore rode with broken collarbones – just strap 'em up: you'd see him with webbing on his shoulders. We never passed medicals. We just rode. You used to go into the doctor's, ask for a form, and he'd say, 'Are you all right?' And he'd hold up two fingers and say: 'Can you see them?' and that was the end of it.

We rode concussed. I rode half a season blind in one eye. I'd had a fall and I wouldn't tell my guv'nor I couldn't see, 'cos I would lose the rides. All you wanted to do was ride. You adjust to it. I got beat by a few that I didn't see coming on my blind side. You never even thought about it. We were war kids: we were never pampered or looked after.

On the track, the first aid was St John's Ambulance, which was old ladies and kids. They'd drag you off the course with a broken arm or a broken leg, to get you out of the way, 'cos they never dolled fences off in them days. You used to lie on the floor and say, 'Please, please don't touch me. I'll be all right.' Because they'd start pulling you about.

Josh Gifford, when he was courting Althea, he had two false teeth in front and he wouldn't tell her. If she went racing with him, he walked out to the paddock with his teeth in, so she didn't know he had false teeth. Then he fell and swallowed them. I rode with him one day at Kempton and we both fell. These two St John's Ambulance people said, 'Don't touch him! He's broken his neck!' I rolled him over, smacked him on the back of the neck. He coughed his teeth up.

'Thanks, Mouldy,' he said.

JONJO O'NEILL (1970–86)

Times have changed so much. Everybody has good facilities now. When we were riding, some stables didn't have hurdles or fences, and they'd never schooled them until they got to the racecourse. All the jockeys now, they go round to different yards and school horses: it's far more professional. It's improved so much, with the plastic rails instead of the timber rails and wings.

EDDIE HARTY (1953–71)

It was not an uncommon thing for a starter to make two lines at the start of a jump race. There'd be 30 runners. At Chepstow one day, the races were over, everyone's gone. The groundsmen were going round with the tractor, picking up the hammers and forks out on the track, and they came across a jockey, unconscious at the third-last. They put him on the back of the tractor and brought him in.

I remember as a boy, you'd hear about people having ridden a double and they couldn't remember it, because they were concussed from a fall the day before. That was common.

In such circumstances, a bit of self-preservation is not to be wondered at. All the same, riding styles did begin to change in the Fifties, becoming tidier, more in sympathy with the horse's movement.

DAVID MOULD

There was an era where a few of us came off the Flat, like Johnny Haine, Jeff King and me. Most of them came through the amateur way, like Michael Scu and Stan Mellor. They were point-to-point jockeys, rural jockeys. The Flat lads came in and it definitely changed. Flat jockeys were a lot tidier; they sat a lot lower. And the older jockeys rode long and sat upright.

I rode as I was taught to ride on the Flat. I sat up the neck and I didn't come up, over fences: I sat into the horse's neck and rode shorter than most of them, the old jockeys, Fred Winter and Scudamore. They rode with a lot deeper leg. I adapted a style so that I could stay on board and still sit low. It was just a different grip, a different style, a different way of racing.

NEALE DOUGHTY (1978–95)

He was brilliant, David Mould. Absolutely brilliant. One of my favourite riders. I can remember watching him on the TV when I was a kid. He was stylish in everything he did: the way he dressed, the way he rode. Just fantastic.

Josh Gifford was another ex-Flat jockey, forced over the sticks by increasing weight. Having been good enough to win the Chester Cup and the November Handicap on the Flat, he was champion jump jockey four times. Even so, it took him time to adapt to going over obstacles, and longer still to win the admiration of his new colleagues.

TOM

I remember Grandad saying, when Josh Gifford first started riding over hurdles and fences, everyone said he was too much of a Flat jockey. Grandad said he'd never seen anyone ride the last hurdle or fence like Josh – he said he couldn't work it out. He said he just used to ride it like it wasn't there and land running. It wasn't pretty to watch, and everyone thought it was wrong. He ended up that season being champion jockey. All of a sudden, they were like, 'He can't be wrong.'

JOHN FRANCOME

Josh used to ride with a loose rein nearly all the time. He'd go into a fence from ten strides away and basically let them do their own thing. And that worked.

Stan Mellor recalls that he and others used to call Gifford 'the piano player', because of the position he adopted when approaching the final obstacle at speed, leaning back with his arms extended in front of him and his fingers pointing down.

STAN MELLOR

He hadn't got an eye for the stride. He was hard to beat in a finish, if he got away with it.

DAVID MOULD

Josh was an amazing jockey. I mean, half the time he was pissed. If he'd been sober, there's no telling what he'd have done. We were piss artists, us kids – we just used to go out and have fun and get drunk, and that's how it was. These kids today, the jockeys, they're so disciplined. They don't drink, they train . . .

We had no racing on a Sunday, so wherever we were, we'd go out on Saturday night and have a real booze-up. And then we wouldn't race again until Monday or Tuesday. There was no testing – they never tested you. Some jockeys used to be pissed when they rode.

Terry Biddlecombe and Josh would have several beers under their bench, and if they had a fall and they're a bit shaken up, they used to get the valet to go and get them a large brandy before they rode again. No one thought anything of it.

Biddlecombe used to travel a lot with Josh, and they used to pull into a pub before racing, have a couple of stiffeners. I wasn't a good drinker – I used to get pissed, you see. I used to think, 'These lads, I don't know how they do it.'

The lads now wouldn't understand what the weighing room was; they really wouldn't. We had our arguments – you'd have a punch-up in the weighing room, but it wouldn't go outside. If the stewards had come in and someone would be fighting, they'd walk round and go out.

STAN MELLOR

Terry used to sit there with a couple of bottles of Guinness under his seat, have a couple of swigs and then he'd go out and ride in a novice chase. I don't know anybody else that did it.

JOHN FRANCOME

I knew Terry really well. He was an excellent jockey, as hard as nails. I saw him at Stratford one day; he got hung up. A horse fell and it galloped off and he had his foot stuck in the iron. It took him round the corner and his foot came out just in front of the open ditch away from the stands. He got up, hopped over the fence, came back in as though nothing had happened.

Considering the injuries he had, he was as brave as anyone you've ever seen. He'd broken every bone in his body. Most of the time he was riding he must have been in pain. He used to get changed next to me: he'd have a splint on both arms where he'd broken wrists, he'd have something else supporting this, something else supporting that. Even in the latter years when he was dying, he had terrible arthritis, he was in agony: never, ever heard him complain.

Drinking in the weighing room seems to have tapered off in the Seventies, but there were other places to have a swift half.

STEVE SMITH ECCLES (1973–94)

Jockeys are much more professional now. In my day, it was all a bit of a laugh. All right, once you're out there, it was every man for himself. You'd go and ride your two or three horses and then you'd have a bit of fun. Whereas now, you can't drink. Half the jockeys in my day, they'd get banned from riding.

We used to stop on the way to the races and have a quick snifter. I hate to say it, but I did it myself. Don't get me wrong: it wasn't to bolster your courage or anything like that – you'd stop off and have a chat about what was happening today at the races. 'D'you fancy that one? What are you gonna do with this.' You couldn't do it in a million years now.

One Monday afternoon in the middle of January, we'd ridden in the first race, it was freezing cold, sleeting with rain. Hugo Bevan, the clerk of the course, walks in and he put a bottle of whisky on my seat. He said, 'There you are, Steve: make sure the guys get warmed up for the next race.' Can you imagine that happening now?

In my day, if I rode in the first and didn't have a ride till the last, I would be expected to go into the owners' and trainers' bar and have a chat with my connections and also have a drink. And nobody gave it a second thought.

Clearly, jockeys faced a lot of problems, self-inflicted or otherwise. But there were riders in each generation who became an inspiration to the rest.

STAN HAYHURST

The one fella that I admired was Martin Molony. He was such a good horseman and jockey combined. He didn't knock horses about, he sat very still, they jumped for him and they'd run for him, he was excellent to watch. And so cool.

He rode a winner for us at Nottingham on Court Painter. He was a horse you had to give a slap between every fence, he was so idle. These days, you would be up in front of the stewards. Martin got after him in the finish, but during the race he was so quiet on him, and the horse jumped for fun for him.

Tim Molony was rough. I'm not taking anything away from him: he was good, but he was very, very rough. There was a lot of slap about Tim. He was very strong, built like a boxer, but no style at all.

Bryan Marshall was another fella who improved on our style. He was nearly to the modern style. He was very strong and didn't move over a fence. He was good to watch.

TOM

If you look at a picture of Bryan Marshall, the only difference between him and jockeys now is the length of stirrup. You see a still of him in a finish, he must have been a magician compared to a lot of the others at that stage – he's leagues in front of them. How tight he is on a horse in a finish – he looks like a Flat jockey.

EDDIE HARTY

Harry Sprague rode over hurdles for Ryan Price, who had a horse in the Whitbread called Done Up. Fred Winter couldn't do the weight on it, so Ryan Price told Harry Sprague he had to ride Done Up. It was the end of his career.

He said, 'I don't ride over fences.'

'You'll ride this one.'

And he won by a short head and retired.

He was, without a question, one of the best hurdles riders I've ever seen, maybe the best. He rode his horses through hurdles, not over them. To finish up as an elderly man – he'd have been pushing 40 then, I'm sure – and to win that race at Sandown, it was a thing that dreams are made of.

GERRY SCOTT

Michael Scudamore was the man I admired most of all. He was such a brilliant horseman. In those days, if you didn't have a ride in a race, we'd often walk down to the last fence, and you'd see him put a horse right ten strides from the fence. He was brilliant at it. He'd either take half a stride off a horse or add a half to it, so it would pick up at the right time.

RICHARD DUNWOODY (1982–99)

Francome was brilliant, and it was great to watch him on a horse, close up in a race. He laughed and joked about it, but at the same time he was deadly serious as well. For me, Francs was probably the most stylish jockey around at the time. That's what I was hoping to aspire to some day.

As an example of Francome's expertise, Hywel Davies tells a story about a novice chaser called Romany Nightshade.

HYWEL DAVIES (1977–94)

This horse was leggy, lean, tall and just hurdled fences. I said to myself, 'Jesus, I've got to get this horse to back off.' Every time I was schooling him, I'd try to get him to go short, and he'd try and take it off me. 'Fucking hell, this is going to kill me. When I ride this on the track, this is gonna muller me.' So I rode him and won on him, hurdling the fences.

Then I got injured and I was off for three or four days. John rode this horse. Captain Forster ran him at Newbury. I was thinking, 'This is not gonna get round in a bus. He's going to do three somersaults on this bloody thing.'

Do you know, John just jumped him off and that horse was brilliant. I wasn't gutted, I was just in awe, thinking, 'What am I doing wrong?' He just won half the track. Someone that didn't ride would say, 'He looks like he's not doing anything.' He'd just go with them, and if they needed something, you wouldn't see him doing it. Whenever John fell, it was always the horse's fault. 'Fucking thing,' he'd say.

I'm thinking, 'Why are you blaming the horse, John?'

'It's gotta get me over. That's his job.'

Less is more. And getting the horse to take responsibility as well.

JOHN FRANCOME

Jeff King: there has never been a better jockey since I began riding. He was lucky in that he was the right build. But he was a really good rider. He could have been a showjumper, an eventer. He was as strong as an ox in a finish. He could ride all sorts of races, he was balanced, he helped horses when they were getting tired.

Stan Mellor was a good jockey in many ways. He was a rider that helped horses a lot. Jeff was like Stan but more stylish. And it was only for the fact that he probably didn't get on with owners and trainers as well as he should have done . . . He was too blunt, voicing his opinion about horses. But if you ask me, did I ever see a better rider, I'd say definitely not. Not Ruby Walsh, not Tony McCoy, Richard Johnson or anybody.

STEVE SMITH ECCLES

Jeff was a hard man, gave everything a ride. You never messed around with him. I did actually model myself a little bit on him, because I'm the same shape and size, and I rode with him in his later years, my early days. And I rode for him when he started training. That was tough. I doubt there'd be anybody else in the weighing room could hold down that job, because I gave as good as I got, and I think in a funny sort of way he respected that.

He was never champion jockey, but there weren't many better people that rode a horse than Jeff King. But he wasn't diplomatic in any shape or form, and if a horse was no good, he'd come in and tell the owners it was no fucking good.

DAVID MOULD

Jeff was, I think, probably the most respected of them all in our era. He was a great jockey. He was just so tough, you couldn't beat him.

TOM

Grandad was great mates with Jeff King, and he would always say, when you bumped into him at the races, 'This was the best jockey never to be champion.' And Jeff would always counter with some swear word. Jeff used to scare the life out of me and my brother, because he was so rough and ready. The fact that kids were there didn't stop him from swearing. Wonderful man.

STAN MELLOR

Fred Winter was the really good rider: Fred Winter and Tim Molony in my day. Fred was very strong – they said he did a hundred press-ups a day. He kept it simple, didn't use the whip a lot. He just picked him up with his hands and he squeezed and he pushed, and that was pretty well it. And what he was doing to the horse was saying, 'I'm still here,' with his legs: 'I'm in charge, do what I say.' And he'd get in rhythm and he'd say, 'Let's go.'

JOHN FRANCOME

Fred was just like Jeff King, only he had the mindset of Tony McCoy. He was just absolutely driven. He said that the only jockey riding as strong as him in a finish was Harry Sprague. He wasn't the most stylish over an obstacle, but he was very effective. He was a completely different shape: he was much shorter, but in mindset and the way that he rode, he was more of a Tony McCoy than anybody else. Just absolutely driven as a rider.

STAN HAYHURST

Tony McCoy stands out, doesn't he? He was very, very good, brave; he could see a stride. Horses jumped for him because he obviously gave them confidence.

AP McCOY (1994–2015)

I analysed a lot of things Richard Dunwoody did. In terms of the perfect jump jockey, at that time, that's what he was. Very stylish, obviously very stubborn, physically and mentally very tough, which I think you had to be.

Obviously, Peter Scudamore had all those attributes beforehand, and there was a little point in my time when I was lucky enough to have had success, when I'd been champion jockey once or twice, I had to learn more about Peter Scudamore because he had all the records. I got this thing in my head that I had the opportunity to try and do what he did.

DAVID MOULD

The Scu boys have always been good. Peter was an amazing jockey. He was like his dad: he was as hard as nails. And so committed. He was champion and well deserved.

STEVE SMITH ECCLES

Scu was following in his father's footsteps – and obviously they were big boots to fill – and he was driven: he just lived, ate and drank racing. OK, we had a few good times when we switched off, but he couldn't get enough of it. He was lucky, I suppose, that Martin Pipe was around, because Martin Pipe was also driven, and when Scu teamed up with him they were just gonna be unbeatable. You'd think you had it won and they'd come past you. I can't tell you how many times that happened to me. Because Scu never gave up and the Pipe horses never gave up. Incredible partnership.

JOHN FRANCOME

Ruby Walsh is a lovely jockey to watch. He's a classic horseman. Like all sportsmen who are really good at what they do, he makes it look incredibly easy. And he rides a lot of good horses. By and large, he's the one who's done all the schooling on them, and if you put him on something else, he just makes horses look good. He makes it easy for them. Tom Scudamore, not because it's the book that we're writing, is a complete package. I'm sure if he'd been Irish, he'd have got the job that Barry Geraghty had when AP packed up.

Peter would have been successful, no matter what he did, because he was a thinker. He could work things out. He wasn't a natural jockey, but he made himself into a really good jockey. And incredibly strong and on the ball. He didn't make any mistakes because he had it all worked out: he'd know the form of the horses, and he'd probably have gone over it a thousand times more than anybody else riding.

If there's one word to describe the Scudamore family, it's honest. They're a really good, honest family that do the very best they can, all the time. His dad was a great role model for Peter, and also for Tom. Just a nice person who was as competitive as anybody you'd ever come across. Peter's the same, Tom's the same. You wouldn't want to have either of them upsides you in a finish, but you'd like to have any of them next to you if you were going out for a meal or something, because they're just genuinely good people.

JONJO O'NEILL

Pat Taaffe was a brilliant horseman. He'd be winning his races in the country. Brilliant at producing them at fences, and got the horse into a nice rhythm. He had a way of not taking a lot of energy out of the horse on the way round, so they had plenty of energy when he wanted them at the finish.

Tommy Carberry rode like a Flat jockey, knees up and let the horse do it naturally, never moved on 'em. He had a great pair of hands. Paul, his son, was the same, and Nina – the family are just totally natural on a horse, probably more natural on a horse than they were walking down the street. You couldn't teach people to do what they could do. And they were brilliant to watch; lovely to see them mould into a horse.

Ron Barry was a brilliant jockey and a marvellous help to me starting out. He was a great man to work a race out: suss out who was doing what and where they were going, what speed they were travelling at. He was a really good tactician. I learned an awful lot from Ron.

Andy Turnell also has plenty of admirers among his fellow jump jockeys, even if few were ever minded to copy him.

DAVID MOULD

Andy Turnell rode shorter than the Flat jockeys ride now. He was unbelievable. He never got unseated, he had amazing balance and strength. He rode with his feet on the flaps of the saddle. He rode as short as Lester Piggott.

His dad, Bob, who was the trainer, didn't stop him. Andy said to me one day, 'I keep chafing my legs on the saddle.'

I said, 'Wear pads' – we all used to wear pads on our shins to stop the chafing.

He said, 'No, I'll ride short.' It suited him. Lots of people wouldn't put him up 'cos he rode so short. But that didn't bother him: that's who he was.

Bob Turnell had four jockeys that were all good enough to be champion jockey: Bill Rees, Johnny Haine, Jeff King and Andy Turnell. And in the morning they didn't know what they were riding. Bob used to take Jeff off a horse he'd ridden and Johnny Haine'd get on it, or Bill Rees would.

I said, 'How do you stand for that?'

'Well, that's the way it is. What do you do? If your guv'nor says you're not riding it, you're not riding it.'

STEVE SMITH ECCLES

I was amazed at Andy's balance. To ride that short and not get unseated as much as a guy riding seven holes longer . . . They'd get unseated when a horse made a mistake. His horses made mistakes and, for whatever reason, he was still on board when it got to the other side. It worked for him: he was a one-off, a lovely chap. He looked good on a horse, and I think I did pull my jerks up a few holes [having been impressed by Turnell]. I hit the ground a couple of times, thinking, 'Fucking hell, I should have sat on that,' and I let them back down.

JOHN FRANCOME

Andy Turnell rode as short as anybody before or after. Tommy Carmody rode really short. I used to think they were very stylish in a finish but completely ineffective on a horse that wasn't jumping well, because they didn't have the use of their legs to get it going and compensate with the different positions that you'll get in when a horse is just backing off underneath you. Today, a lot of jockeys would ride with their toe in the iron. If I'm riding schooling, I can ride with my toe in the iron and I can equally ride with my foot right stuck in it. It's just a question of how you feel. It's like playing a backhand in tennis: some people have a different grip. It doesn't mean that it's better. But from a riding point of view, I think riding a bit shorter, you tend to be in a better position in terms of making it easier for the horse to carry you. It's the difference between having somebody on your shoulders and giving somebody a piggy-back. Ten times easier having them on your shoulders.

There's a happy medium. I never rode really short. If I rode a horse and I felt that I couldn't affect it with my legs, then I just didn't feel comfortable.

STAN MELLOR

I always rode for the horse. Today, I think they ride for the grandstand. I call it 'one-man-band riding', because what they're doing, in finishes, they're saying to the grandstand, 'Look at me! I'm doing everything I can.' They go riding short: toe in the iron, loose rein. Once you've got a sloppy rein, you've lost contact with the horse's mouth, and he's just going through the motions. And if you watch the head-on today when they're riding a finish and, worst of all, the kicking bit, you'll see they're not actually attached to the horse at all – they're about an inch and a half off it.

I think the best way is to get in rhythm with him, squeeze with your lower leg and get the hands so that you're in rhythm with the horse, and pick the horse up, squeezing his body and using your hands to connect to his brain.

I did showjumping, which is bound to leave you with good hands, and you're wasting that if you mess around with the whip. I've got a picture of me riding one-handed, jumping the last hurdle with the whip in one hand [raised], and that was the one and only time in over 6,000 rides that I ever did that. I didn't like it at all. Your hands should be doing the job there. When you land over the last, you really want to be in rhythm with them, push with your body and lift them with your hands. Get a nice hold of their head: 'I'm here – let's go.' Not, 'You're a naughty boy,' smack, smack. Bookmakers have changed the game a lot. If everybody's thrashing along, they love it, it's exciting. Go back and have another bet!

BOB DAVIES (1962–82)

As for just riding with your toe in the iron, it's bollocks, it's rubbish. If the horse makes a mistake, you're likely to lose it [your stirrup]. And it also puts more strain on your leg muscles: they're taking all the strain. If we'd have ridden with just our toe in the iron, all the old-school trainers would have gone ballistic. I think that's crept in from the Flat in America.

JONJO O'NEILL

If I did that, I'd fall off. I don't know why they do it, and I don't know how they can give a horse a proper kick in the belly like that. It works for them; I couldn't see it working for me. The first one I can remember doing it was Steve Cauthen, on the Flat. I think if you're riding in a jump race, I'd want my foot in the iron properly: then you've a proper grip on the horse and less chance of being unseated. But that's probably me being old-fashioned.

JOHN FRANCOME

The actual race-riding, nobody teaches you anything, and you have to learn it as you go along. You have to have a feeling for what the horse is doing. Some people can go down the road in a car with the window slightly ajar and will be completely oblivious that anything's wrong. Somebody's hardly got out of the drive and they'll say, 'Something's not quite right.' It's no different with jockeys or in all sorts of walks of life, whether it's a carpenter or a plumber: some people are more in tune with what they're doing.

From the second you get on, you want to be thinking about nothing else but the horse you're on. You want to be looking to see where it's putting its feet, so it's not standing on a stone, riding out. You want to make sure, in a race, that it's on the best possible part of the course, not cut-up ground or the softest part of the ground. You need to be making sure that it has a run through the race, that it's not getting bumped and buffeted, or where it's going to be stopping and starting.

There is nothing that tires a horse quicker than being knocked in a race, or where it's changing pace or changing direction. They are the things that use up your petrol more than anything. If you left the inside on one of Fred's horses and you didn't have a really absolute watertight reason for doing it, you wouldn't be riding for him very long. I see lads going round and I say, 'Fred Winter would make you give your riding fee back.' They just wander round in the middle of the field, and it's just shocking to watch 'em.

A big telltale sign, if you want to know how intelligent a jockey is, you just have a look, see which hand he's got his whip in. The number of jockeys that will go round with their whip in their right hand on a right-handed course and the open side is on the left . . . I'll tell you what's in your mind when you're doing that: absolutely nothing. Nothing has said to you, 'What is going to happen if this horse is going to run out? What is the point of me carrying this stick in my right hand when the open side is on the left and I'm on the inside and he's only actually going to go one way?' Nothing is going through your mind, and if nothing's going through your mind at that point, then there ain't much going through your mind at any other stage.

STEVE SMITH ECCLES

But at the end of the day, there's a hell of a lot of luck involved: being in the right place at the right time . . . You can be the best jockey in the world, but if you don't get a decent horse to ride, you just fall by the wayside.

NEALE DOUGHTY

My chance came at Bill Marshall's yard because of an old Grand National-winning jockey called Arthur Freeman. Arthur was down on his luck. Bill gave him a job as a yard man to help him out, 'cos Bill was aware of his past and his ability as a rider and a judge. Bill was like that.

Arthur went to Bill Marshall and he said, 'Guv'nor, you've got a kid in the yard that's an unpolished diamond.' And that's how I got my start. Talk about luck! I was thinking of quitting at that time. I was nearly 20 and I thought, 'I've only had three or four winners – this is no way to make a living.'

Bill said, 'Right, I've sent for your licence by courier. Get in the horsebox: you'll be riding three for me at Newton Abbot on the weekend.'

JOHN FRANCOME

There's good lads I like watching, like Callum Bewley, rides up north. He doesn't get many rides. James Reveley has done really well since he's been in France. Couldn't get going over here: he's too good for the trainers over here. He's got a brain in his head, he can ride a race, he drops one in, he's brilliant over an obstacle. Gone to France where people appreciate how to ride horses and how to get the best out of them, and he's thrived over there. It's not a good reflection on the trainers here.

Giving people a chance and starting them off on the right foot is not high on the agenda. It's a bit of a cut-throat business. If I was starting riding today, you'd never hear of me. I'd never have done any good at all. I got going at Fred Winter's because I used to service his car, take the kids to school, do every job in the yard, first in, last out, and he was a loyal man. If you worked hard, he gave you the opportunities. A lot of trainers don't give lads the opportunities, and if they win on a horse and it runs again and there's a more senior jockey available, they let him ride it. Fred Winter let me ride a horse that was second-favourite for the Grand National when I was claiming 5lb. Nigel Twiston's pretty good like that: he promotes from within, but by and large I don't think lads get given the opportunities, and a lot of that comes from the agents.

BOB DAVIES

There was a lot more loyalty. You hadn't got the massive yards then. The big yards then were 50, 60 horses. Those yards had a first jockey, probably had a second jockey, and somebody claiming. Now the agents are organising the rides. It used to be the top 20 jockeys always had the jam and the cream, but there was always a bit left. Now, the top 20 have got the bloody crusts as well. You've got no middle-tier jockeys, which is a problem for the sport. You've got the top 20, then you've got the conditionals and very few experienced jockeys in between.

Times are tough for inexperienced jump jockeys, evidently. Let's close with some words of advice for any interested youngsters from three men who fared reasonably well in the end.

AP McCOY

The one thing you need to do in a jumps race, as far as possible, is keep going forward at all times. Obviously, to win a race of any kind you have to keep going forward, but what I mean is, when you get to an obstacle, do not lose momentum or break stride. Always try and keep the momentum going forward, the revs up.

The thing about holding a horse up is there are some jockeys who people believe are better at it than others. But they don't ride the most winners, because when you do that you become very race-dependent. You can't win a race from the back when they go slowly. You have absolutely no control over what happens when you ride a race like that.

RICHARD DUNWOODY

Not being definite was something David Nicholson warned us against. One way or another, be definite at your obstacles. If you can't make your mind up, don't expect your horse to. That was a huge thing for the Duke. If I got a horse on the deck and he didn't think I'd been definite, I'd get a bollocking for it.

And ride each horse as an individual. Some jockeys say, 'Oh, I've got to go round the inside,' but if you're on a horse that needs a bit of space . . . You've got to adapt according to the race, the horse, and use your common sense. Be versatile. Be adaptable.

JONJO O'NEILL

Good jockeys make horses win by the encouragement and the confidence they have on them. They win races that they shouldn't win. It's motivating him and knowing how much petrol he has left, trying to humour him round, and get him running for you without him knowing that it's bloody hard work. That's the secret of good jockeys, really.

RON BARRY was champion jockey twice, and won the Cheltenham Gold Cup in 1973 on The Dikler. Limerick-born, he rode for the Cumbrian stable of Gordon Richards.

BOB DAVIES was outright champion jockey twice, and shared the title on one occasion with Terry Biddlecombe. He rode Lucius to win the 1978 Grand National.

HYWEL DAVIES was an outstanding rider of the 1980s, his career peaking with an unlikely success in the 1985 Grand National on Last Suspect.

NEALE DOUGHTY was another of Gordon Richards' jockeys, and a brilliant horseman whose biggest day came aboard Hallo Dandy in the 1984 Grand National.

RICHARD DUNWOODY was among the finest jump jockeys in racing history. champion jockey three times, he won Grand Nationals on West Tip and Miinnehoma, and also won the 1988 Cheltenham Gold Cup on Charter Party.

JOHN FRANCOME, the most gifted of riders, was outright champion jockey six times, and shared the title on one occasion with Peter Scudamore. He rode Midnight Court to win the Cheltenham Gold Cup in 1978.

EDDIE HARTY won the 1969 Grand National on Highland Wedding. He is also known as a shrewd spotter of equine talent, having found Killiney, Half Free and Captain Cee Bee among others.

STAN HAYHURST was a fixture for decades in the northern weighing room. He won the 1958 Cheltenham Gold Cup on Kerstin.

AP McCOY was arguably the greatest jump jockey there ever was. He rode a record 4,348 winners over jumps and was champion jockey 20 times in a row, also a record.

STAN MELLOR was champion jockey three times, and in 1971 became the first jump jockey to ride 1,000 winners. Possessed of an enviable 'racing brain', he thought the game through as well as anyone.

DAVID MOULD was a hero to many jump jockeys of the Seventies, and widely seen as the first to ride in the modern style. His notable successes included the 1970 Hennessy Gold Cup on Border Mask and the 1963 Imperial Cup on Antiar.

JONJO O'NEILL was a rider of astonishing resilience who was champion jockey twice, and rode two winners of the Cheltenham Gold Cup: Alverton in 1979 and, famously, Dawn Run in 1986.

GERRY SCOTT won the 1960 Grand National on Merryman II. He rode throughout his career for one of the great northern-based jumps trainers, Captain Neville Crump.

STEVE SMITH ECCLES won three Champion Hurdles aboard See You Then from 1985 to 1987. Because of his carefree approach, he was widely known as 'the last of the cavaliers'.

13

SCARS THAT DON'T FADE

'Look here. I think perhaps I shouldn't ride . . .'

If you suffer a serious injury, the normal, sensible, responsible approach is to get the medical help you need and follow the cautionary advice you're given, thus allowing your body the time and support it needs to mend. Jockeys, however, cannot always be relied upon for a normal, sensible, responsible approach.

You can't earn as an injured jockey. Insurance should stave off your immediate money worries, but then you have to sit on the sofa and watch other jockeys on your horses. If they win, you might never get the ride back. The weighing room cliché says, 'You're soon forgotten in this game,' and now each quiet day that passes proves the point to you. Racing ticks along fine in your absence and the phone doesn't ring.

No one wants that experience. So of course jockeys disguise the extent of their injuries and keep riding, even when they know they shouldn't.

PETER

I fell at Ascot and I had concussion, but you could hide concussion in those days. You never admitted you had concussion to the doctor, never. I remember falling and not having a clue where I was. Gone to sit in the car, have an hour's sleep, go and ride in the last.

They were worried about my arm. I went to the hospital and they said, 'You've broken the outside of it.' But I rode out next morning and it felt all right. I rode at Ascot the next week and, going to the second-last, I hit the horse and felt the bone in my arm move and break. Just stupidity, isn't it? Absolute stupidity. But that's the danger of seeing it as manly behaviour; seeing it as a badge of honour.

Another time, I got down to the start in a Champion Hurdle trial. Steve Smith Eccles is riding one that has to be held up, Celtic Ryde; I'm on Freight Forwarder. I got down to the start and I said to Steve, 'I haven't a clue where I am. Help me!'

He said: 'You're at Cheltenham, and you've been told to make the running,' so he'd just given himself a lead horse.

I had a fall at Hereford as a kid, when I was just getting going for David Nicholson. Niall Madden had been in the yard and, typical Duke, he was all over Niall. Voice Of Progress was expected to win a novice chase at Newbury the next day. And I've fallen at Hereford, put my hands to protect the back of my head, as you do, and a horse has kicked my hand and broken my finger. I knew if I didn't ride this horse, Niall would ride and I'd never get back on it. So you just strap it up and carry on.

TOM

I've done my right shoulder twice, dislocated and got reconstruction. I've done my left arm, not too bad, just cracked that. I've done ribs, I've punctured a lung, but it sounds worse than it was. It was just a slight tear – I didn't need to have it reinflated or anything like that.

PETER

When I broke my leg at Market Rasen, I was back riding in ten weeks.

TOM

Split my kidney. Again, only a little bit. Did three vertebrae, but didn't have to do anything for those: I got an injection for them last year. They were old injuries – I didn't know when I'd done it.

PETER

I'm partially deaf in my right ear. That was a cracked skull.

TOM

Collarbones, shoulder blades . . . Other than the shoulder, none of the other ones have stopped me riding for a long period of time. When I did my shoulder blade, ribs and lung, I think that was ten days. Maybe two weeks.

PETER

I had a fall at Chepstow one day and, Christ, it hurt. They X-rayed it and said there was nothing wrong. Weeks went by, and then I fell off one of Pipey's at Towcester and I'd clearly broken my collarbone. It moved: I couldn't lift the arm. I came back with the X-rays and was told, 'Well, you have broken your collarbone, but that was three weeks ago, and all you've done this time is move the callus.' So I just carried on riding.

TOM

Oh, my knee, that kept me off for a bit. I dislocated my kneecap and did my anterior ligament there, but luckily it didn't need an operation.

MICHAEL

I had a fall at Kempton one day and got kicked in the face. Not badly – kicked my chin. The doctors stitch it up, there and then, and say, 'All right, off you go, you're all right.' Which always baffles me: if you hit a boxer on the chin, you knock him out, but it didn't knock me out.

I went to London because it was Kempton the next day, and I went for a steak. I think it was Scott's Restaurant in Piccadilly. I'm having this steak and I thought, 'I ordered a medium-done steak – this is rare,' and it was getting rarer. But it was the bloody blood dripping from my chin! It was most embarrassing.

PETER

As an amateur, falling at Cheltenham, I thought, 'It's great to have a fall, that's part of the fun of it.' I got up, the adrenaline's going, and I'm walking back down the hill.

The ambulance man calls out, 'Come back, you're hurt!'

Nah, I'm not, I'm all right.

He said: 'Look at your shoulder!'

It had dropped about three inches.

It's hard for me, now, to lift my right arm above shoulder height. But I haven't really got much rheumatism. I imagine any sportsman has a bit of it. I never saw myself as a tough person, not in the way Dad was. Tom seems much more sensible about it, doesn't he?

MICHAEL

One Monday, I went to Wolverhampton and got a fall on one of Fulke Walwyn's. I got a kick and it just hurt a bit. When I got back to the weighing room, I felt funny and I went to the toilet. It had knocked all the shit out of me. It was a bit embarrassing, so I threw my pants away and cleaned myself up, and rode in the next race. The rest of the week, I think I rode two winners, but this kept hurting. It wasn't stopping me riding – it was just I thought I'd badly bruised the top of my hip. I got a fall at Kempton, was passed to ride in the next race, went to spend a penny, and it was blood. Frightened the life out of me. I went to the clerk of the scales, I said, 'Look here, I think perhaps I shouldn't ride.'

One would like to think, now, that a jockey with a similar complaint might be taken straight to hospital. Michael had to return home and call out his GP, who called for an ambulance, which broke down on arrival at his home. But there is a happy end to this story, which sheds a light on 1950s medical assistance.

MICHAEL

I was in hospital overnight, and the next afternoon the doctor came in and said, 'Come with me!'

I said, 'Oh bloody hell, there's something wrong.'

We went into the kitchen, he said: 'Michael, what are we gonna have? Drop of gin, or d'you wanna have a glass of whisky? You're going home tomorrow.'

Modern jockeys have free access to excellent rehabilitation facilities, thanks to the Injured Jockeys Fund, which has built Oaksey House in Lambourn and Jack Berry House in Malton. Plans are being laid for a similar building in Newmarket, to be named after Sir Peter O'Sullevan. The staff at Jack Berry House effected one of the miracles of modern racing when getting Derek Fox fit to ride One For Arthur in the National, just one month after he broke a wrist and a collarbone. But Peter, Michael and other jockeys of similar vintage had to sort out their own medical assistance. Michael came to rely on Bill Tucker, whose London clinic stayed open seven days a week and became popular with sportsmen who needed to get back in action as quickly as possible. Tucker had himself played rugby for England in the Twenties.

MICHAEL

You'd hit the ground and, before you finished rolling, you'd got Tucker's phone number in your head. He was wonderful. A lot of famous people went there – cricketers and footballers. He went on a cruise with the King.

A lot of 'rich old ladies' made up the bulk of Tucker's clientele but, Michael recalls, they would be waiting to see members of staff while he walked straight into Tucker's consulting room.

MICHAEL

He'd come in and sit down in his shirt sleeves. 'What won the 3.30? Oh. Well, what's the matter with you?'

He wanted to know when you wanted to ride. If you were rushing to get back for next Wednesday, well, why next Wednesday? And if you wanted to ride badly, he would have a few quid on himself. He would leave it to you when you rode; the only time he would stop you would be head and spinal injuries. The first collarbone I did, they took me up from Hurst Park. I was strapped up on the racecourse and went to Tucker and I rode in ten days. And fell.

At one time, he did actually say, 'I think you need a drop of brandy. It'll do you good!' He was a genius. He gave you so much confidence.

PETER

If you're in a football team or a rugby team, you have your own doctor. But the British Horseracing Authority doctor is not there to make you better. They're there to stop you suing the BHA for letting you ride when they shouldn't have done. All they're doing is stopping you riding. So you don't go near the BHA doctor. When you hurt yourself, you find someone like Tucker, who will get you back as quickly as he can.

They had no idea, in Dad's day. Him and Terry Biddlecombe are sitting in the sauna, drinking champagne cocktails: brown sugar, brandy and champagne, 'cos that makes your heart beat faster, makes you sweat more. They were taking piss pills, shit pills – they had no concept of their long-term future, absolutely none. And now it is better. Even since my day, it's streets and streets ahead.

Following a chance meeting, Peter came to rely on an orthopaedic surgeon called John Webb.

PETER

I broke my arm at Southwell and I was in Nottingham Hospital, sitting there with my breeches and boots on and a long plastic splint in my arm, and this man sitting opposite me said, 'Look, if you trust me, come and see me at the university hospital. I'll look at your arm and I'll get you back riding quicker. The reason I'm doing this is, my wife likes horses.'

He put a plate in it and he had me going again in no time. He said to me, in a Tucker-type way, 'You know you've got the plate in it. You can now go out and ride. The plate is as strong as the rest of your arm but, every time we operate on you, the chances of infection are increased.'

I fell and broke my leg at Market Rasen and ended up in Lincoln Hospital. They said, 'We're going to mend it.'

I said, 'No, no, no – just get me to Nottingham!' I had Webb's number, and when I got to the hospital, he was there in his dinner jacket.

'My wife's not so pleased with you now,' he said. 'I can put you in plaster for 16 weeks or, if you let me put a plate in it, I'll have you back riding in ten.'

And I was champion jockey again because he got me back riding.

TOM

If a footballer breaks his leg, within hours he's probably on the operating table. If he gets hurt in Birmingham, they'll know the best surgeon in that area that deals with broken legs. If I have a fall at Chepstow, I'll have to ring my mate who works for Bristol Rugby Club and find out who's the best surgeon. I'm lucky with the contacts I've made, knowing rugby players or cricketers, so I can get that kind of information. But it's word of mouth: there's no actual list for jockeys. And that hasn't changed since Dad's day.

One thing that has changed is there's a physiotherapist at every racecourse. You're always carrying a little knock here or a strain there. Your injury management is constant. It's very rare when you're riding without a bang. It's the nature of any professional sport. The only time you're playing completely without injury is when you've just come back from an injury. There are things you're constantly able to manage – it doesn't affect your performance in any way, but you might be limping, you might have broken your thumb or your finger. You can manage. Grit your teeth.

Don't you worry that some of those injuries will stay with you for years after you stop riding?

TOM

No, for some stupid reason you don't think like that. I know I'm going to have arthritis where I've broken bones. But Grandad just got on with it, and I've never seen Dad complain. If you're thinking about it and not willing to take those risks, you shouldn't do it. It's more, 'If I get hurt, have I got everything in place so that I can get back quickly?' I'm not thinking, 'Oh God, I don't want to break my leg.' I'm thinking, 'If I am in that position, how am I going to cope with it?'

Horses are also injured and, despite the advances made by veterinary science, cannot usually be saved if they suffer spinal injuries or broken legs. Nearly all jump jockeys know that experience of the willing partner, perhaps familiar from years of working together, who suddenly suffers what will prove a fatal injury, or perhaps even dies on the spot.

TOM

It's horrible. You try and brace yourself for it. You know it's around the corner, you know it'll happen at some point, and it's something you have to accept if you're gonna do it. The number of rides I have a season, it'll probably happen once or twice. It never gets easier. The horrible, empty feeling in your stomach . . .

Starchitect in a big race at Cheltenham: that was dreadful. But I had one the other day at Newton Abbot – jumped a hurdle, went one stride . . . The class of horse or where it's at doesn't make a difference: you still come away from there feeling horrible, helpless.

You talk about the mental toughness in dealing with your own injuries. But the hardest thing is when the horse gets injured. I remember the first time – it really shook me up – when a horse broke its pelvis between the last two. It's really, really upsetting; it's such a shock.

PETER

I remember as a child being at Ascot and seeing a dead horse under a canvas. I'm 14 or so. The fact that I'm this age and remember it, it obviously had some sort of emotional impact.

Obviously horses die, and you ask yourself, 'Why the bloody hell do I do this?' I do sometimes wonder if it's cruel. Maybe that's a lashing out. I do lash out. It's frustration, it's, 'Something has to be done! I need to do something! Maybe I should give up, then!' It's not a rational thought. And then your brain has the ability to forget it and move on.

They're not really pets, are they? But I do think that kindness to horses is important. I think Princess Anne put it better than anybody: the sport has given these horses a value. These horses are getting better medical treatment than some human beings.

Jockeys are also at risk of fatal injury on the racecourse. Thankfully, deaths are rare, the consequence of determined efforts over decades to make them so.

MICHAEL

I can remember two. A fellow called Ivor Beckinsale fell in front of me at Wolverhampton one Boxing Day, and I didn't take a lot of notice because you get so used to it. Picked up the paper the next morning and found he'd been killed. And Micky Lynn had a fall at Sandown, went out through the back door and landed head first. I didn't realise till the next day he was gone.

The main thing was, when you fell you didn't bloody move. The horse will try and miss you. You used to see some, what you thought were horrific falls, and you'd go back to the weighing room and the jockey was back there before you. Then you'd see an easy fall and you'd think, 'Oh, he's all right, he's got up and walked away' – and then you find he's got concussion or worse. You knew nine times out of ten they were all right. But the odd time . . . You might make enquiries when you got back to the weighing room, if so and so is all right, and, if he's a mate, you'd go and see him in the ambulance room.

Peter remembers being particularly affected by the death of Vivian Kennedy, a 21-year-old who suffered fatal head injuries in a fall at Huntingdon in 1988.

PETER

His poor parents – I remember being in a church in Lambourn . . . He was a very good rider, Viv. I suppose it's the way, you have to black it out. Motor racing drivers must have it. Someone gets killed, you can't stop.

In March 2012, Brindisi Breeze won the Albert Bartlett. For all sorts of reasons, this was a moment to cherish. It was a first training success at the Cheltenham Festival for Lucinda and Peter, and their first Grade One into the bargain. For the wider world, it was an introduction to the irrepressible winning jockey, Campbell Gillies.

Appallingly, both horse and jockey had died by midsummer.

PETER

He had a spaniel-like charm, Campbell. We love spaniels because they're always puppies. He had that charm that almost made him a surrogate son to us. You could never really get cross with Campbell. He was never infuriating. He knew his boundaries with his humour – it was just joy of life. He'd ride out in little short, pink wellingtons. Why? I never found out.

LESLEY GILLIES (CAMPBELL'S MOTHER)

He was quite quirky, really. It's wrong to say he didn't care what people thought, but he was so self-assured, it was like people would have to accept him the way he was. We always thought he was a bit unusual. He always had very unusual hobbies and interests when he was growing up.

Him and I were really close because he had that quirkiness about him. I always felt he needed that bit more of my attention than the other two. They seemed quite sorted and content with themselves. Campbell always seemed to be looking for something else.

But that something else was surely not a career as a jockey. He grew up in a horsey family and had riding lessons with his brother, Finlay, and sister, Rita, but didn't warm to it, and was 'terrified' of the pointers and ex-racehorses kept by his grandad in Hawick. 'The last thing anybody would have expected of Campbell would have been this,' says Lesley, gesturing at a giant print of her son and Brindisi Breeze bounding over the last at Cheltenham.

LESLEY

When Rita used to go up and ride the horses, Campbell decided he wanted to start this chicken business. He persuaded the farmer who had the horses that he'd keep chickens up there. He bought this run and bought chickens with his pocket money, and then had this wee business where he sold the eggs. He would probably be about nine, ten. He decided he could make better cookies than they sold in the school canteen, so every night he would bake cookies and sell them in the playground. He always had something up his sleeve. You just had to go with the flow with him. You couldn't say, 'That's ridiculous, Campbell – you can't be doing that.' You just had to let him and then support him at it.

What finally switched him on to riding was his sister's bad experience with an ex-racer, Breydon, who became unmanageable for Rita. When a more experienced rider tried to sort him out, Breydon reared over and broke her pelvis.

LESLEY

He was a horrible horse. I didn't know what to do with him. And one day, out of the blue, Campbell said he was going to have a go on him. Rita and I walked with him, till we got a mile out on the track, and then Breydon decided he was going back to the yard – just turned round and started galloping. We were like, 'Oh, my God, Campbell is going to be lying in a heap somewhere!'

We ran back to the yard, and Campbell's sitting on him, like, 'Is that the best you've got?' He was maybe 13.

From then on, it was like this love affair. Campbell could do anything with that horse. He would jump in the field, vault onto Breydon with no saddle or bridle and take him up to the yard. He would go up before school, even in the winter. And every night, him and his mate Zander Voy used to go up from school, because Zander kept his ex-racehorse up there as well, and the two of them would ride. He would come home and say things like: 'Are you allowed to just jump any hedge you see when you're out hacking?'

Four short years later, Campbell was a jockey based in the Borders with Willie Amos. In the yard was an unpromising beast called Lie Forrit, owned by Lesley in partnership with her brother, Crawford, and her father, John. Having cost £4,000 at auction, Lie Forrit was working like a horse who would struggle to win that much in prize money. His 17-year-old jockey, already with a winner to his name, was not impressed.

LUCINDA

I gather Campbell rode him in his last piece of work, then said to John, 'Look, Grandad, I know you love this horse, but it's very, very slow. It's not very good. But I'll ride it.'

LESLEY

Lie Forrit was so lazy at home, he never showed a thing, and that's why he was 100-1 first time out at Carlisle. I remember in the parade ring, he reared up and smacked Campbell in the nose, and Campbell was bleeding. We were saying: 'Campbell, just don't come last.' In the end, he couldn't pull him up.

LUCINDA

He got run away with. The whole way up the home straight, his head kept doing that [snapping back as Campbell struggled to regain control]. And it pissed up.

That autumn, Campbell started working for Lucinda and Peter, despite an inauspicious introduction.

LUCINDA

He came to his interview and managed to fall off about the easiest horse in the yard.

PETER

The first time he ever rode for us, she said, 'That's it. I'm never putting him up again!'

Two years later, Lie Forrit was a handicap hurdler, favourite for a race at Aintree.

LUCINDA

It hit the front going to the second-last, but it's flicking its ears around and it just jinks and Campbell pops off. But his big error was, he gets up and he starts running along the landing side of the hurdle. Wilson Renwick comes through on one of the other runners and just totally mullers him, straight over the top.

PETER

He's done everything wrong, just like a spaniel would.

LUCINDA

You should be cross with him. 'For fuck's sake, Campbell, you're gonna kill yourself!' But you can't, you just laugh at it.

Campbell's mother had watched the race, open-mouthed with horror, in a betting shop in Exeter, where she had been visiting a relative. She had to board a plane back to Scotland, still guessing how bad the consequences might be for her son, who had just been mown down by a racehorse.

LESLEY

He had a punctured lung, broken ribs, quite a lot of injuries, but three weeks later he was riding. It was crazy. He shouldn't have been able to do it. How he passed the doctor I'll never know, because you could see he was still in agony, just by his face.

But Campbell was determined to ride through the pain, so he could be on Lie Forrit at Cheltenham in November 2009.

LUCINDA

He came to ride out, do you remember? He went from white to grey to blue.

PETER

It was our responsibility to phone the doctors and say, 'Look, you've made a balls-up here . . .' But I couldn't . . .

LESLEY

Everybody was sworn to secrecy: nobody was allowed to tell me he was going to ride. I was saying, 'Peter Buchanan's going to ride at Cheltenham because Campbell's still not well.'

My niece phoned me, she said, 'They've jocked Campbell up!'

I said, 'That has to be a mistake . . .'

Campbell was well rewarded for his bravery, as he and Lie Forrit battled up the hill to hit the lead with about 30 yards to spare, pipping horses ridden by Ruby Walsh and Timmy Murphy. Davy Russell and AP McCoy were also in the race. It was a huge moment for a young rider.

Two years later, he was associated with another talented horse, this time in Lucinda's yard. Peter tells the story with a lot of pauses for throat-clearing and sighing.

PETER

I thought Brindisi was small and, when he went up the gallops, he was slow. We ran him in the worst bumper I could find, at Musselburgh, and he got beat. I thought, 'Oh Christ.' I took him to Carlisle to run. The ground was a bit frosty, and Tim Vaughan and Richard Johnson had come up, so I thought, 'We're going to get beaten again.' We were cowards and we didn't run him.

We got a message from the vendor: he jumps well. So we schooled him and ran him at Kelso. He was ever so lucky to win. Campbell rode, and the one that would have won made an awful mistake at the last and he won a neck.

I found a terrible race at Newcastle and he won. So we went to Haydock then. Nothing sums up Campbell better than this. I'm taking myself terribly seriously, and it's this good race, they're all going to go fast, and Brindisi's a front-runner.

I went into the weighing room beforehand to have a serious, fatherly chat. 'How should we ride this horse, Campbell? They're all going to take you on. What do you think?'

He said to me, 'Don't be worried. He'll win. He could have gone round again at Newcastle.' And that was his thing in life, he had a self-belief.

LESLEY

He was nervous about that race, more so than for Cheltenham. Peter Buchanan was stable jockey, and I suppose Campbell knew that if he didn't win that trial, Peter would get the ride. But he won.

Brindisi Breeze was therefore unbeaten over hurdles when he lined up at the Festival, presenting a familiar puzzle to punters: how seriously to take this horse from up north who's been winning by wide margins on bad ground against opposition of unknown quality? He had his backers, but Boston Bob was a predictably hot favourite at odds of 6-5, representing the formidable combination of trainer Willie Mullins and jockey Ruby Walsh.

PETER

I didn't think he'd win. The owner couldn't see him getting beat, which is obviously mad. You're taking on Mullins: he had the favourite, it was one of the bankers – he was just coming to the absolute height of his powers. Luce and I always try to stay realistic. I think that was the extra joy of it, because I didn't really expect to win, and it hits you, such a monumental achievement, to us. I don't care what anybody else thinks. I've had enough praise. It was just a private moment of our own satisfaction.

Ruby was challenging at the last, stayed on up the run-in, but he couldn't get there. To me, that's the heart of both of them, little lions. Brindisi wouldn't be passed on that day. And that's why we turn up at Cheltenham.

TOM

The way he won, flipping 'eck! I remember him coming past me at the top of the hill, still a long way from home, just running away. And he'd been up there all the way, jumping and galloping, and he bolted up in the end. They all came to him at the last and off he went again. He was a very good horse.

LESLEY

It was one of the best days of my life. It was the happiest I've seen him. There's a really nice photograph that Aidan Coleman took, when Campbell was in the back of Aidan's car. He's on the phone and his face is just shining. Aidan gave me it at the funeral. He said, 'That was him speaking to you that day.'

Two months after that glorious moment, a late-night phone call comes through to the yard at Arlary. 'There's a dead horse on the road.' Oh, God. One of the mares has obviously jumped out of the field and been hit by a tanker.

PETER

It's light, it's summer, so you drive up, look in the field. And Brindisi's not in his paddock.

Luce says to me, 'It's not a mare, it's fucking Brindisi.' The heart falls out of you. And then you see the dead body.

It becomes a very personal thing. Luce has got to ring the owner, Sandy Seymour, and tell him his horse has got out and got killed on the road. It's not our fault, but it's our responsibility. It makes you grow up in some ways: you've got to face things. You've got to dust yourself off and go on.

For no known reason, Brindisi Breeze jumped his way across two fields to get to the road. He evidently hurt himself doing so, because a trail of blood is found, leading into the driveway. Heartbreakingly, the trail stops at a pair of metal gates, only recently installed. Had he done the same thing six months earlier, he could have carried on up the drive to the stables. Instead, he turned back towards the road.

PETER

I felt more sorry for the owner and for Luce: it was awful for her. I didn't have time to feel sorry for myself; I didn't really mourn. There's a numbness. By the time you've dealt with all the detail, the sorrow and the emotions have moved on.

One month later, Campbell agreed to go on a hastily arranged holiday with some friends.

LESLEY

I had just negotiated to buy Campbell a house in Glenfarg. He's 21 and a real saver. He used his money from that race to help. I was at my friend's daughter's ballet performance and I got a phone call from Campbell, saying he was going to Kavos. I hadn't even heard of Kavos, to be honest. Why are you going to Kavos? – you've just bought a house!

'Oh, it'll be fine. I'll sign it all when I get back.'

It was very last-minute. I think it was because one of the boys had broken up with his girlfriend and had said, 'Let's go. I need some boy time.'

Mark Ellwood [Lucinda's head lad] told me as much as he could when he came back. He said, yes, they'd all been out for a drink, 'cos they arrived at something like three in the morning. They chucked their stuff in the room and went out. They came back about six o'clock in the morning and decided to go straight in the pool.

He said, 'Campbell, the most sensible of all of us, went up and put his swimming shorts on. The rest of us were just going in, wearing what we had on. And then Campbell said, "Let's have a race to see who can swim two lengths underwater the fastest. I'll go first."' Took a few deep breaths, got up one end, turned, got about halfway down. Mark was on the poolside and Harry Haynes was in the water – Mark was checking for cheating. And then he just went to the bottom.

They ignored him because he's always mucking about. Eventually, Mark's like, 'Harry, give him a kick, he's been down there too long.'

Having done some research, Lesley now believes Campbell was a victim of shallow-water blackout, a phenomenon that can particularly affect the physically fit. If the victim resists the urge to surface for long enough, oxygen levels in the body can drop low enough to cause a blackout, which would look just as Mark Ellwood described what happened to Campbell.

LESLEY

It's happened to loads of people and they just stop, go unconscious. He didn't hit his head, hadn't slipped and fallen into the pool, like a lot of people thought.

PETER

I still don't understand it. Sometimes when I swim, I think, 'How the fuck do you go down and not come up again?' It was numbing. I suppose that's the only way to deal with it. I remember when his agent rang, and what went through my brain was that he must have been killed in a car accident. But I remember thinking, 'This has got to be wrong.' He was so full of life.

Campbell's ashes were scattered over the gallops at Arlary. His helmet and body protector hang on display in the yard. Those who live and work there will not forget their Festival winners who disappeared almost as soon as they had arrived.

PETER

It was a James Dean thing, wasn't it? It really was going out in a blaze of glory. Brindisi had a heart of a lion. He wasn't fast, he was just braver than everything else, and that's why he won the race. Campbell was a fabulous talent. It was a privilege to be involved with him and his *joie de vivre*.

Campbell didn't get to see two familiar faces turning up at Arlary in 2013. First came his sister, Rita, who still works there. Then followed Lie Forrit, who had lost his way at his previous stable and seemed in need of a fresh start, with just one win in four years to his name. He was aimed at a handicap hurdle at Wetherby. Peter Buchanan, the long-serving stable jockey, was booked.

LUCINDA

Pete was a quiet man. Campbell had been coming and Pete could see it. Already, Campbell was getting some of Pete's rides. He spoke at the funeral and said, 'He wasn't just snapping at my heels: he'd bitten my leg off.' So it was nice that Pete then rode Lie Forrit.

PETER

Campbell definitely would have wanted that. Can you imagine the emotions that Pete must have been going through, to have Campbell coming up? Yet there was no animosity between them.

LESLEY

Lie Forrit doesn't look impressive. But what a heart. He only ever did enough, he never won by much, apart from that first race that Peter rode him in. He took off and we were like, 'What's he doing? He never goes out in front!'

To the delight of Lesley, her family and all those involved, Lie Forrit went straight into the lead at Wetherby and stayed there, sealing victory with a big jump at the last.

LESLEY

That was an amazing day. We all went and didn't really have huge expectations. We were very nervous and Peter was too. Everybody wanted it to be that dream that he would come back. Lucinda, everybody, desperately wanted him to win for us. It was very emotional.

LUCINDA

You kinda knew Campbell was there.

PETER

There was a joy rather than a sadness in it. If you can ever pick yourself up after losing someone, that was the sort of thing that would do it.

'We think about him all the time,' Lesley says of her lost son. But there is some consolation in the knowledge that, in the short time available to him, Campbell found exactly the right world for him to live in and enjoyed success there.

LESLEY

He was a thrill-seeker, a risk-taker, so racing suited him fine. He really enjoyed the close-knittedness of the jockeys and the camaraderie, and the whole bit about being totally absorbed – everybody works together, plays together, lives together.

Lie Forrit is happily retired in a field in Jedburgh, having eventually won five races for Lucinda and Peter. The colours of Campbell's family are to be carried by a newcomer to the yard, Prince Dundee. Racing is evidently a source of comfort to Lesley. Did she never feel like pulling away from the sport?

LESLEY

I wanted to, believe me. Even now when I'm watching, I still think, 'Do any of them look like Campbell?'

14

TRAINING: AN UPHILL STRUGGLE

'He had a Jag and she wore mink. I thought training was a pot of gold.'

While they may always be jockeys at heart, the Scudamores have done plenty of training, one way or another. Michael set up a yard as soon as it was clear that there could be no comeback from his Wolverhampton fall. Peter never took out a licence in his own name, but has been heavily involved in stables run by his father, his son and now his partner, Lucinda Russell, as well as in the yards of Denis Caro and Nigel Twiston-Davies. Michael Jnr has had his own licence for ten years.

PETER

People always say it's easier being a jockey than a trainer. It's a bit like people saying school's the best days of your life; just an annoying statement. When you're lying up at Leicester in a 17-runner novice chase, that grabs your attention far more than a bloody thing running badly on a Monday at Hereford.

I always think the difference between riding and training is basically this: if it wins, the jockey's a genius; if it runs badly, the trainer's an idiot. But, as Bob Turnell said, if there's ten horses in a race and you're on the best one, it takes a bloody idiot to get that horse beat.

As a jockey, it's never your fault. You come in, throw your tack down in the weighing room: 'I told him he should have gone to Leicester!' The horse wanted a left-handed track, a right-handed track, soft ground, good ground . . . it's just not your fault. Whereas, if you're the trainer, you made that decision to run. You could have gone to Plumpton, but you went to Hereford and got beat. And you'd told the owner to expect that it would run to a certain standard.

I get so frustrated. A horse is wrong and I think, 'There's got to be a reason for it! It's somebody's effing fault!' And while I try to contain that most of the time, I see why many trainers I've ridden for couldn't contain it. They explode, shout and scream, in a Basil Fawlty way. We're all Basil Fawltys.

I think I cope better with it now because Luce and I do it together. We say to ourselves, 'What's the level of expectation for this horse?' And then it can finish third and you're aware that, actually, it's run a good race. Sometimes you could have pulled them straight out of the field and they'd have run better. That's when you question your ability and why you're doing it.

MICHAEL JNR

For someone like myself, who's in a slightly different position to Dad, because you're driving the box to the races, you feel the highs and lows. It can be a very long drive home, with lots of thoughts going through your head, when it goes wrong. You're trying to sum up everything and work everything out.

Your first reaction is always, 'What did I do wrong?' You always blame yourself when one gets beat. You go through your head a thousand times to think, 'OK, what would you have done differently? What have you learned from it?' Sometimes you're hard on those around you, because you try to be happy and put a positive face on it for the owners, and then as soon as you're on your own, you let your real emotions out. You take the defeats very personally.

When you're riding, yes, you watch the replay with the owner and trainer, and then you drive home and you're away from it. When you're training, you drive home, wake up and see the same horse the next day and that annoyance, if you feel you've done something wrong, just doesn't leave you.

PETER

I've spoken to other trainers about it. You can take it very personally. Just because horses are running badly, it lessens you as a human being. Which is obviously a stupidity, but that's how you feel when they run badly.

Life becomes very false when you're champion jockey. You get told, 'Oh, you're wonderful,' and people invite you to places and speak to you who wouldn't normally speak to you, but there is that part of you that wants to know who your true friend is and who isn't. So when I packed up riding, I actually walked into a room as Peter Scudamore, rather than as champion jockey, and you notice how quickly people fall away from you. And I didn't mind that, but I think it's quite difficult for jockeys. Having had a big name as a jockey doesn't get you any more horses when you're a trainer. Fred Winter said to me, 'You've got to start again.'

You get to understand how difficult it is at the lower level. When you're dealing at that level, you tend to get badly behaved horses. I'd given up riding because I was trying to look after myself, and in the end I was riding out horses I might not have agreed to ride in a race. There was one, I had to get up on the old hunter alongside and climb across onto this horse, because it would rear over backwards otherwise.

In darker moments, Peter likes to recall a line of Sir Mark Prescott's about the hazards and frustrations of training.

PETER

'I've got 80 horses trying to kill themselves, and 20 stable lads trying to help them.'

MICHAEL

It's a funny game, riding and training: you do get down when it doesn't go right. You keep picking up the paper and seeing what other people are up to. And I think probably training is worse, 'cos there's nothing you can do about it. You know this bloody horse is useless: you can't give him a new engine.

I hadn't thought about training, because I'd got a farm. And then, when I woke up to the fact that all my friends were on the racecourse and anything I knew about life was racing, I kept the farm, but built some boxes and trained for the next 20-odd years.

PETER

The skills you needed to be a jockey are probably not that related to the skills you need to be a trainer. Julian Wilson said a trainer needs about 16 different skills. You need to be an accountant, you need to be a psychologist, you need to know how to handle staff, you need to know what a blacksmith does wrong . . .

If you're a good jockey, you never bandage a horse, you never plait a horse, you never see it getting shod, because you're racing all the time. The bad jockeys, they get the opportunity to be in the yard. I was lucky, because I worked in the yard with Dad when I was young, but once I was 18 or 19, I was gone. I was riding every day, so you never get the skills.

But Peter spent enough time around Martin Pipe to pick up a trick or two from the man who was British champion 15 times.

PETER

I copy everything from him. It's my Bible, it's Christ speaking to me. Martin taught me everything. Everything he said or did, he thought about. He was a very deeply thoughtful man: why a horse keeps breaking blood vessels, the size of horses – everything, he had a theory on. He studied horse weights, blood tests and the amount of work they did. He used to call it a jigsaw puzzle: if you can get the right track and a horse on the right weight, you can double your bet. That's how he looked at it.

His professionalism was the thing, which is what I've always admired in any sportsman. I think that's the reason we clicked more than anything, identifying in each other the professional attitude.

We keep in touch. I find it a little bit difficult, and I don't ring him every day because Tom's riding there. Often, when we go down to the West Country, I go to speak to him and we talk about old times, because I don't want to speak about how Thomas got beat on one the other day. If they have a big winner, I text and say, 'Well done, that's fantastic.' I might joke that it's not as good as we were, kind of thing.

Famously, Pipe took horses from other yards and achieved results that had seemed beyond them.

PETER

I rode a horse of Pipe's at Ludlow that I'd also ridden when it was with David Nicholson. It didn't get the trip at Nicholson's and I used to hold it up. I went to the paddock and said, 'I'll hold this up.'

He said, 'No, no, please make the running.' And it won.

He was definitely increasing their stamina and their speed. And there were other horses I'd ridden at Reg Hollinshead's, exactly the same, didn't get the trip with him, and they were fitter and faster with Pipe.

For all that Pipe was the upstart with limited facilities, Peter soon warmed to his approach.

PETER

I don't want to knock the Duke in any way, but I think we tried the pretension and the image more at one stage than we did getting down to train horses. And that's why I got on with Pipey so well, because it was completely the reverse. And my admiration for the Duke is that he got it right in the end, but I didn't feel he had it right while I was there.

When I went to Martin Pipe's, he was so different to anything else I'd ever seen. I'd go up his gallop, thinking: 'That's not very long.' Then he has us turn around and gallop back down again. I'd never, ever been back down the gallop. I was used to galloping a mile and a half, and suddenly I'm galloping over four furlongs.

Gradually, Philip Hobbs and Venetia Williams, Paul Nicholls, Nigel Twiston-Davies . . . that's enough, isn't it? They've followed similar methods. Whereas Nicky Henderson has kept to his methods, which is basically the Ryan Price, Fred Winter approach. I think they're still galloping over seven furlongs, probably galloping over a mile and a quarter, mile and a half.

I remember Pipey came to Nigel's to help us with the gallop. We were going to bring it across here and do this and that with it, and Pipey said, 'Just come straight up the hill.' Martin's convinced they should go in a straight line. If they're going round a bend all the time, each day is more pressure on one leg than the other.

With his gallop, I asked, 'Why d'you put it there?'

Because he had nowhere else to put it.

And it worked. He said you could train them out of pig sties, if you've got the right gallop. But if you've got pretty boxes and no gallop, you can't.

When I first went to David Nicholson, all his gallops had so many twists and turns in them, you couldn't actually gallop the bloody things. It's only looking back . . . I remember going there, thinking, 'Oh, these are wonderful gallops.' But there was one bend, if you went too fast, the horses would turn over on the shavings. And we had this long gallop, a mile and a half, with this short shoot up a bank, and because there was this turn, you couldn't let their heads go until they turned into the straight. It was completely different to what Pipe was doing, just letting them run up this four furlongs. Nicholson did do well at Condicote. But he only came to his strengths when he moved to Jackdaws Castle and had the gallops there, gallops you could run up.

And it's funny that it's changing again now, that Gordon Elliott and Olly Murphy are putting these round gallops in with deep sand. Dan Skelton's got one, and Colin Tizzard. I see Kim Bailey's put one in.

Vincent O'Brien took me round Ballydoyle towards the end of his career and he showed me all the gallops. He kept asking me about Pipe, and I said, 'He trains over three or four furlongs.'

'Do you know,' he said, 'he's right. I've got all these gallops and we did use them as Derby gallops. But up there's where I trained the majority of them.' Which was a three- or four-furlong gallop up a hill.

Vincent's God, isn't he? My memory was that he still had pictures on the wall of all those great jump horses he had in the Forties and Fifties: Cottage Rake, Hatton's Grace and the three Grand National winners. I was very proud of that – that he still held them in honour amongst those magnificent Flat horses he had after that. Heart still in your roots, type of thing.

As far as Peter can tell, horsemen have spent centuries rediscovering the benefits of short, sharp bits of exercise, repeated at intervals, as a means of getting the animal fit.

PETER

I looked at a history thing on television a year ago: they found some great chariot trainer, Kikkuli. All the other chariot trainers were galloping them over long distances. This one was sprinting them, and he was the best chariot trainer. So it's been there for thousands of years.

MICHAEL

At Fred Rimell's, when there was a freeze and you couldn't go on the gallops, they'd be sprinting horses up these banks to get some work into 'em. And then the thaw comes and we're racing again. Fred would tell me, 'Give this one a nice run round – it'll probably blow up.' And it would piss up.

But whatever your gallops look like, the message from the Scudamores is to get plenty of use out of them.

MICHAEL JNR

Just get them fit. Get them fit, the rest'll look after itself. And you've got to gallop them to get them fit.

I had ten or 12 horses when I started, and I was so worried about injuring them, I didn't work them as hard as I should have done. You're thinking, if you injure three of these, you're down to single figures, which is not a great business model. At the same time, if they're not fit, they're not going to win races and you're not going to get more horses.

When I started, I got a text from one of the girls who kept the whole thing going at Nigel's, 'Squeezy' Bagnell. She said, 'If in doubt, gallop it.' And it's quite right. They've got to be fit, and if you're not sure whether they are, send them up again.

PETER

In his book, Henry Cecil said he used to canter all these horses steady, early in his career. And Cecil Boyd-Rochfort, his stepfather, said, 'You'll never win races until you gallop them.' They have to go fast to win.

One trainer Peter has emphatically not tried to emulate is Willie Stephenson. While he sent out the winners of both the Derby and the Grand National from his Royston base, Stephenson was not easy to like.

PETER

He would have been hard on people, unbelievably hard. Today's modern society just wouldn't stand the way he treated apprentices and staff. There was no question of arguing. He had complete control: he was just a hard man. I don't think I've ever met anyone like him.

He had five or six daughters, lovely girls, but he wouldn't go to their weddings. He just wanted a son. He was very hard on the daughters. I think he must have come from a very tough school. He had a very high-pitched voice and a stutter. And yet he was terrifying.

He was a bull-in-a-china-shop type of person. They used to call him 'Perpetual Motion'. He would go down about six o'clock in the morning and watch his horses work, he would do some farming in the afternoon and then back to the stables in the evening. He started Doncaster Bloodstock Sales as well, with a couple of others.

In Peter's memory, it was not much fun to be in a car driven by Stephenson, who would carve up other drivers and never apologise. The experience was not much better if he let you drive, as Michael learned. He recalled Stephenson bringing 'a big packet of Rennies and the racing calendar' with him on long journeys to the races. The trainer would pore over future entries and, if he found something interesting, would lean over to lay the calendar, which was a broadsheet newspaper, across the steering wheel and ask his driver: 'Look, look, look, look! What do you think of that?'

MICHAEL

Then he'd go to sleep and you'd think, 'That's all right.' Then he'd start grinding his teeth and you'd think, 'Bloody hell, I don't know which I want!'

Then he'd wake up: 'Where are we? We'll never get there! Never get there! Go round him, go round him! Never mind about the lights – kick on, kick on! You'll never be a bloody jockey!'

Hopefully, Stephenson showed more regard for the rules of the road as a younger man, when he was a driving instructor in the army.

PETER

It's funny why people like that command such loyalty. People would do anything for him.

MICHAEL

I loved riding for Willie Stephenson, because if he got beat, he didn't blame you: he was a very good loser. If you won, he was exactly the same – you'd be lucky if he said 'Well done'. Whereas one or two others would nearly throw their arms round you, and then when you get beat, you get a kick up the tail-end.

I rode with more confidence for him than anybody. The only pressures were the ones you made for yourself, knowing you just wanted to do well for him. I had great faith in Willie, because he knew the format. He's the one man that, if he said the horse would win, it bloody won.

A prolific winner for Stephenson was Sir Ken, the hero of three Champion Hurdles, who once went unbeaten for 16 consecutive races, a record in jump racing that stood for 60 years. Then, at the age of nine, he won over fences at the Festival, in the race we now know as the Arkle. Stephenson told Peter what he did on one occasion to ensure immediate payment of a bill by the horse's owner Maurice Kingsley.

PETER

Sir Ken was a really, really nasty horse and attacked other horses; he killed one in a field. Willie told the owner, 'You'd better send the money down here now, 'cos I've turned Sir Ken out in a paddock with all your other horses and he's kicking hell out of them.' He said, 'The Rolls-Royce came from Manchester with the money.'

He told me how they couldn't get the saddle on Sir Ken close to the Champion Hurdle one year, and they had to poultice his back because he'd got this big lump, and he still won.

It took till Big Buck's came along to beat Sir Ken's record, yet we don't ever give Willie the credit. I Googled him: there's nothing there on him. He's trained a Derby winner, a National winner, an Eclipse winner. He was a major character immediately after the war, but it's slightly lost.

Willie would tell me about the old times – he almost wanted to get it off his chest. Frenchie Nicholson did the same: he was a lovely old boy, he trained for Dorothy Paget, he rode Golden Miller, Dad rode for him, and he'd produced all these wonderful apprentices – Pat Eddery, Walter Swinburn, Paul Cook, Tony Murray and others. Frenchie would pull me to the side when I was young – he wouldn't want to talk with the adults at the bar – he'd give me lessons in life, about when he'd ridden for the Rimells and fallen out with them.

I said, 'Frenchie, you should write a book.'

He said, 'That's a good idea; but no, no, I'd have to tell the truth.'

They're products of the time when it was all about gambling, when it was a bad sport, when the only way you lived was by stopping some and backing others. And then it's gradually become unacceptable, and now we are where we are. These were our wicked old devils, but they had to be to survive.

Plenty of other formidable trainers have crossed Peter's path, including Stephenson's cousin, Arthur, based near Durham.

PETER

Arthur Stephenson dominated, numbers-wise. He trained 2,988 winners, a record until Martin beat it. Graham Bradley says in his book how rough it was at his place in Bishop Auckland. I went up there once or twice. You had to be tough. Ridley Lamb and Chris Grant were tough people riding for Arthur, and I was not his type of jockey. He helped me be champion one year, because I think Ridley had been hurt and I stepped in for a whole lot of rides. And then I fell off one, and he said I made too much use of Fortina's Express. I clicked for three weeks, a month for him.

Fulke Walwyn had an air about him. He dressed properly, had a deep voice, trained for the Queen Mother. I don't think he'd wipe you off his shoe if he stepped on you. It shows you how much he meant to me: when I had a pee next to him at Sandown, I was thinking: 'I've had a pee next to him!'

I spent a summer with Jim Bolger in the late Seventies. His number one jockey, John Harty, invited me across to come and spend time there as an amateur. I learned more about the importance of professionalism and attention to detail in my short time there than I had in my previous 19 years. The conditions were tough. He'd got a yard just outside Dublin that he was renting, a few years before he moved on down to where he is now. They knew it was going to be built on, so there was no money spent on it.

He ruled the yard with a rod of iron. Aidan O'Brien and AP McCoy learnt their trades with him, years after I passed through. When you deal with people like Jim, although they're very, very hard on you, their hardness is a kindness, because it prepares you for life in a way nothing else can.

Monica Dickinson was immensely powerful. She wouldn't speak to you. I remember at Southwell one day, there were all the Dickinson jockeys, and it was like a mother hen with a brood of chicks. 'If I say, go and pick up that bit of paper over there, they will go and do it.' There was no question.

Mercy Rimell was like that, but she dressed in mink. I remember going there to ride out and you had breakfast on a silver tray. She was a proper lady. Fred Rimell was a nice man: he had been champion jockey, he had trained all those winners, won four Grand Nationals, he was a hero to us. I went there to ride out and he was very kind to me, drove me round and showed me his land. He said, 'I've bought cattle and a bit of farmland and I've made more money out of that than I ever have from horses.' He drove a Jag and she wore mink and they lived in a smart house. I thought training was a pot of gold.

Peter was soon disabused of that idea by his early experiences with Earth Summit, at about the time he started as assistant trainer to Nigel Twiston-Davies. This was one of several youngsters acquired by Peter with the aim of making a quick profit through the sales ring, but no buyers liked the look of Earth Summit, so back he came to see if the new partnership could find a race for him. Ownership was passed on to a six-man syndicate including Nigel Payne, a PR man who worked for Aintree, and Ricky George, scorer of a famous FA Cup goal for Hereford in 1972. The others involved were Peter Earl, Gordon Perry, Bob Sims and Mike Bailey.

PETER

Earth Summit was so slow up the gallops. If he set off in front, he'd have to pull over and let the others by. He was useless. I retired about the time he won his novice hurdle. I think he was one of the first horses I saddled as assistant trainer.

He jumped fences absolutely fantastically at home. We sent him to Perth for a novice chase: wouldn't go a yard. He didn't like going right-handed. We were so disappointed with him at Perth, we put blinkers on, and then he ends up winning the Scottish National as a novice.

A couple of years later, he broke down at Haydock, and I remember the vet coming and saying, 'I'm going to shoot him.' I was always bad, always bad when they were being shot. I would always say no, and sometimes I would take them home when they should have been shot. I remember Cathy Twiston-Davies giving me a bollocking about it.

Anyway, I said, 'No, we don't want him shot.' Took him home and basically stuck him in a field for 18 months. And I remember seeing him in the winter, he was just bare, just a common thing. If I'd taken a picture and said, 'This'll win the National in a year's time,' you'd have said, 'Don't be stupid.'

The next autumn, we had a terrible time. Nigel put nappies on the horses to save bedding. They stank, they were heavy, and of course the dampness of them . . . They did save the bedding, but the lads hated them. By the time we got to about Christmas, we'd had very few winners and we were suicidal. And it was a type of unspoken rebellion, is how I remember it. Everybody just said, 'Fuck it,' took these nappies off. They were £250 apiece. Nigel must have approved it. Anyway, we took the nappies off, changed the food and, within days, we won the Christmas Hurdle with Kerawi and Earth Summit won the Welsh National.

Just over three months after that, Earth Summit was 7-1 favourite for the Grand National, having been granted the soft going that suited him so well.

PETER

I remember being on television, watching the race, working with Richard Pitman for the BBC. I was terrible on television: I never concentrated, because we've got runners and I'm watching them.

They're just dropping like flies around him. By the time he's jumped the third-last, there's only two horses that can possibly win. I get emotional about it now. There's Suny Bay, who's cantering, and Earth Summit. He's going to be second, Suny Bay's a class horse. And then of course the weight has told: Suny Bay's got almost two stone more. Earth Summit went up the run-in as if he'd just joined in.

I remember with Nige, sitting down in the pub after, and getting absolutely plastered, drinking three port and brandies and falling over. Just pure relief, pure celebration: two scruffy little kids from Herefordshire, we've trained a Grand National winner together. I would argue Nigel is as good a trainer as there is in the country.

Tom, just 15 at the time, has since had plenty of experience of riding for Twiston-Davies, and shares his father's admiration.

TOM

Nigel's very, very misunderstood in that, from a distance, he looks great fun, which he is, but he's also extremely shy. He's the most loyal. When you ride for him, you're his man, but if you fall out with him, it's over. He is black and white.

I love riding for him. He knows his horses inside out, he is a brilliant trainer, brilliant horseman, brilliant stockman, but if he says to you, 'Make the running,' make the running. In fairness, if something goes wrong, there's never anything done in public. He'll be like, 'I'll stick up for the boy, the boy was only doing what I said.'

I remember one day at Cheltenham: I was 17, on a horse called Moorish, and he told me to make the running. Somebody else wanted to as well – it was Jamie Goldstein, and he worked for Nige, too. I was still at school, and Jamie probably got the hump that he wasn't riding Moorish. He took me on and we ended up going too quick. I came back in, I knew I'd done something wrong and I was expecting a bollocking. Nigel was like, 'I told you to make the running. I should have explained it, it's my fault.' And for a young rider, when the trainer has that much faith and belief in you, it's brilliant.

But then there's also been times when I haven't done what I'm told or something, and he will go red in the face, absolutely apoplectic, completely bananas at you. And then it's forgotten within two minutes. Not a problem. The point is made, move on.

If something goes wrong schooling, he'll absolutely make the arse fall out of your trousers. He has delivered some of the biggest bollockings I have ever seen and gone absolutely all out. He can make people cry – I've seen him do it. But you would walk through a brick wall for him, he's the most loyal. And bloody stubborn.

He's as good as anyone I've ever ridden for. I don't know how he does it. Some people thought Dad was running it in Nigel's name, but Dad left and nothing changed. That became, 'Oh, Carl Llewellyn must have a massive input . . .' Carl left, nothing changed. Then it was Fergal O'Brien, but he goes, and Nige just keeps on going. He does it in his own way, and it might look chaotic, but the one thing that's consistent is that Nigel Twiston-Davies is in the top five. Him and Henderson have been the most consistent for 30 years. It's phenomenal.

MICHAEL JNR

Grandad could never get his head round somewhere like Nigel's. He'd say, 'It can't work, but it does.' He always used to say the hill at Nigel's was a magic hill, because that stable was probably not the most organised place in the world, but it works. Somehow, everything comes together for Nigel to be able to be one of the best trainers there is.

These days, Peter is putting into practice all he has learned at the base he shares with Lucinda near Perth on Scotland's east coast.

PETER

I've moved from one idyllic rural situation to another. I also find that, while they might speak with a slightly different accent at Kelso, you could take them out of Kelso and put them in Wincanton and it's exactly the same: they're country people having a day's racing. And the city tracks are the same: Nottingham, when it was jumping, was always a city track, I felt, and they would be the same kind of people at Musselburgh.

I enjoy the stable side of it. It's an idyllic life, sitting on the gallops watching horses going up and down. But just 'cos you enjoy it, doesn't mean it hasn't got to be done.

Luce works tremendously hard – harder than I do, really. I get older and more tired. She's a workaholic. She'll study every catalogue, she'll have watched every point-to-point online. We're too old to lie on the beach now; we enjoy going to the point-to-points, we go to most sales, even if we don't buy.

I tend to attend to the training. I go and watch the horses on the gallops, she'll do all the lists; I do the entries, she does the bills. In the morning, before declarations, we'll have an argument as to whether one should run. She's very good on form, probably better than me. She has a good, analytical brain; she takes in information well.

Luce did some eventing, and eventers tend to spend all their time plaiting and brushing and bandaging them, so her level of stablemanship far exceeds mine. She's bandaged and patted and kissed and mucked out horses all her life. I think that's one of the reasons it works.

She was doing well before I got here. I couldn't come straight in and say, 'Change everything.' I might look to change something, and she will argue that she does it for a reason. There's things I've argued for and we've changed and I've been right. And there's other things that she's been right. I feel it's very much a partnership.

She had staff that had been here a long time and it was very friendly. Peter Buchanan was here, but after that it was very female-oriented. And I came along and we've made it a bit nastier, I suppose. We've doubled the number of horses. That's one of the reasons the Grand National was so gratifying: we felt it was a reward for the hard work we'd put in for the last ten years.

LUCINDA

I couldn't train this many horses without him. We definitely work as a team. When you get to my age, you decide that you want to do things you want to do, and there are some things you like doing that you're good at. And what's brilliant is, I'm good at doing the veterinary side, I'm good at the horse welfare side, and Scu is very good with the jockeys, Scu's very good at watching the work, and that's what we do. We're both quite good at seeing if a horse looks ready or not, just by watching it walk past us. We're only doing what we're good at, which makes it a happy day.

Peter and Lucinda have reached a stage where they can cheerily discuss their differences and finish each other's thoughts.

PETER

The tension is the drive for success. When things are going wrong, she's very good at dealing with me. But I suppose you can't have the ambition to be a champion jockey and then just lose that. I have that drive, which possibly doesn't make you a happy person. But she is much more rounded than me, and she controls me, in that sense.

LUCINDA

I'm probably a bit more optimistic.

PETER

Yes, you are. You're more level-headed than me.

LUCINDA

Everyone's got a bit of emotion, so sometimes you have to take the emotion out of an issue. Racing for me is: I can't believe I can spend my whole life doing what I always wanted to do, which is look at horses every day.

PETER

That's the difference between you and me. I love horses, but you would happily go to a show ring. I would have no interest in that. My dad was a professional jockey, and professionalism was subconsciously drummed into me all the time. I can face failure, I can handle failure, but I can't handle failure –

LUCINDA

– without preparation.

PETER

Exactly. That was the satisfaction of Arthur. He wasn't a lucky winner.

When Luce and I got in the car after we bought him at an auction at Cheltenham, in December 2013, I remember saying, 'We paid too much money for that.' Because he'd had five runs. It was the owners that really picked him. There was a horse we wanted, coming a few lots afterwards, but we thought he might be beyond our budget. It's no use saying, 'I want Horse B,' miss out on Horse A, and end up with neither. So we rather threw our lot in with Arthur, and in fact Arthur made more. In the end, we paid ten grand more for Arthur than the other horse went for.

He ran in bumpers and ran OK. We always thought, as you do when you buy a horse, 'Oh, this is it! This is a nice big horse, forget its point-to-point form.' It gets beat in a bumper and it shatters the illusion a little bit. But we've still decided it's the best horse we've got in the yard. It runs again, over hurdles at Kelso, twice, and gets beaten both times. I said to Luce, 'If that's the best fucking horse in the yard, we may as well give up.' Then we ran him at Hexham and he got beat. So we're still trying to deal with our disappointment, and keep everyone's spirits up.

We took him to Haydock because, with a horse like this, the answer to all your problems is fences. He's still a hurdler at this point, but this race is over those brush hurdles, a bit more fence-like. Pete Buchanan rode a brilliant race on him. I think you could run that race ten times and he'd get beat five of them. But Pete kicked, and the other horse never got to him. That was the start of him winning three in a row.

One For Arthur ended his spring campaign in 2015 with a tilt at a Grade One novice hurdle at Aintree, for which he was 40-1. It was a moment in which bits of Scudamore history collided, because this was the race in which Tom first rode Thistlecrack and ended up winning at 25-1, the start of a partnership that would eventually carry them to King George glory the following year. One For Arthur couldn't live with Thistlecrack's class that day and was pulled up, along with more than half the field. His owners were disappointed, and their patience was tested again the following season, when he made only a steady start to his steeplechasing career.

PETER

We hadn't got our horses right. We did a few things, we changed food. We had an assistant come in, a chap called Jamie Turnbull, who's been very, very helpful. I think the structure of the yard got a bit tighter.

One of Arthur's owners, Fraser McClung, noticed that Timeform kept putting a 'P' by his rating, to say they expected improvement. And then we went to the Becher Chase. I don't know why, really. There was nothing great before, but if he's gonna improve, it's going to be over those Grand National fences. And he ran ever so well.

We could have run him in the Welsh National, but I always felt that the Warwick race is probably the worst of that type of race you can go for, and if he doesn't win that, he ain't gonna win the Welsh National. So he's won it, wearing a tongue tie for the first time, which is Derek Fox's doing. That definitely had a bearing on it.

I think there was a consensus that we'd got him wrong the year before, and therefore we were going to give him plenty of time between his races. Derek said, 'Let's go straight to Aintree with him.' So we did. And the fun was, I remember Fraser, myself and Luce each went and had £100 each-way on him at 33-1.

Part of the annual build-up to the Grand National is the Jockey Club's construction, in Lambourn, in Yorkshire and in the West Country, of Aintree-type fences. The idea is that intended runners can be schooled over them, so that the different look of the big, green obstacles is not a shock on the day. But it's a long way from Perthshire to Yorkshire, so Peter and Lucinda went for the home-made option.

LUCINDA

We were really excited about making these Grand National fences. Scu got all this plastic grass, like you get in greengrocers. We took ages and put it over the tyres and made this lovely, big Grand National fence. We brought Badger Foot, the point-to-pointer, who jumped up here beautifully; Imjoeking, who was running in the Topham, jumped up them beautifully; and One For Arthur, who jumped absolutely terribly, terrified himself, cramped behind and was just awful. And I had it all videoed for Facebook. I thought, 'We won't be showing that to any public.'

Scu says, 'Go again, go again,' brightly. So he went again.

And I thought, 'I'll take a still photograph this time.' It was terrible. Just awful. This was about ten days before the National. So we didn't mention it, we didn't do anything. We had a nice photograph of Arthur, cantering, on the website and no photographs of him jumping.

Ten days later, the Aintree race produced rather more in the way of publishable pictures.

PETER

I think Luce would say the same: that result gives you confidence. Of course, you're always trying to move forward. Tom rings me the other day: 'Send your assistant down to Olly Murphy. They've got the new Wexford sand gallop – that's the way to train,' after Murphy had had a few winners. And you think, 'Hang on – I've just trained a Grand National winner! We've trained 70 winners in a season!' I can tinker with it, which we all continue to do. But you know your methods are correct, and it gives you that confidence to keep doing what you do, while watching what other people are doing.

We're racing against science all the time. There's a new machine, or there's a new boot with ice in it; there's a new vitamin injection. It's difficult, because if you don't try to improve, you can lose an edge to your rivals. Luce said we mustn't get too taken up in fads and lose the concentration. We had heart-rate monitors one year, and she feels that studying the heart rates all the time possibly took our attention off other things. We weigh them, which we'd never have done in Dad's time. We blood-test them, we do trachea washes, looking for infection or inflammation.

We're trying to prevent injuries. Luce is like Martin in many ways. She studies a veterinary book. She wanted to be a vet – I don't know why she wasn't. She'll go to a trainer and the first thing she'll ask is, 'What's your most common injury?' Then she tries to work out how to prevent that.

But the training of horses is hardly an exact science, and some in the industry appear quite content, at times, to wander off into the realm of pseudo-science. Lucinda is entertained by the idea of radionics, in which the practitioner attempts to use a black box to send out healing waves to the afflicted client.

LUCINDA

You get a bit of hair and you put it into a box, and you put different crystals into the box . . . and at that point, I get lost. It's for humans as well, but horse people love it because the message is, 'Give me a piece of your horse's hair and I'll make it sound.' We had people after the National writing to us, saying, 'Could we have a bit of Arthur's mane?' because presumably they want to say they've had a Grand National winner in their black box.

PETER

Even in my day, you had a witch doctor who would take a hair out of the horse's mane and put it in a black box, and this was meant to change the character of the horse. The black box was something I grew up with but it's clearly voodoo. Supposedly, Arthur Stephenson used to tie a tight shoelace in a horse's tail to stop it bursting a blood vessel.

There's always been this combination of the latest science with the old ways of doing things. When I was a young man, we used to pick comfrey, dandelions and dandelion roots; Martin Pipe was big into dandelions, always picking them to feed to the horses. We gave them Epsom salts, they had cider vinegar, they had potassium permanganate in their water. Diviners say they can tell if the horse is ill: they'll come out to the stable looking for energy fields. There are magnetic field therapists – they come out and put all their magnetic lines in the right order. We still cling to these myths of how to treat horses, but no vet has ever said to me, 'Get diviners round it, send its hair off in a black box.' There's a tendency in humanity to have this belief almost in witchcraft. It was prevalent in the horse world and still is.

Peter and Lucinda's alliance has worked. Down in Herefordshire, Peter's sons might one day agree to a similar division of labour, once Tom's riding career is over.

TOM

I'm not going to train racehorses. I'd like to stay involved, and I'd probably enjoy being a jockeys' coach, and I'd enjoy helping Michael. I'd be very happy doing declarations, speaking to owners, that kind of thing. I'd like to do it how Dad did it with Nigel: I'd leave Michael to train them, move back up to Hereford, but work in media as my bread and butter, for one of the racing channels.

Tom is smiling now, building up to another moment of Scudamore ruthlessness.

TOM

Basically do what Dad did on TV. Just better.

15

LOOKING FOR LINWELL

'You silly bugger, you're in front in the Gold Cup – kick on!'

Two years before Oxo did his thing around Aintree, the Cheltenham Gold Cup had fallen to a Scudamore for the first time when Michael rode Linwell to victory in the 1957 race. At the time of writing, it has been the family's only success in jump racing's most prestigious contest. A follow-up is certainly due. But how to achieve it?

PETER

Any time a horse wins a race, you say, 'Is this good enough to go to Cheltenham?' Everything leads to the Gold Cup. Of course, the Grand National is wonderful, but the Gold Cup is really about elite athleticism, something that we cherish. You realise how great these horses are, and how difficult it is to go and buy them.

As a jockey, you can win any other Festival race on the Friday, but you know the headline is the Gold Cup, and you have to go to page five of the *Racing Post* to see if someone noticed you winning the Grand Annual. The Gold Cup takes it to another level.

Watching some of those racehorses of Dickinson's, say Wayward Lad, you cannot believe that a horse can jump like that, and even he couldn't quite win a Gold Cup. Denman, if a fence came in his way, he just kept galloping. I remember standing there in awe of Dawn Run. And I grew up knowing Pat Taaffe, who was Arkle, and Dad was Linwell. So every time I go to the sales, I flick over a page and then I think, 'Hold on. That might be the one. That might be the Gold Cup winner, the Linwell I've been looking for.' He's out there, somewhere.

MICHAEL

Did I tell you how I got the ride on him?

I wasn't going racing at Kempton one day, and Rex Hamey rang me up and said, 'Come to the races!'

I said, 'I'm not going. I don't wanna go – it's too far without a ride.'

Anyway, he said, 'Oh, come on,' and he talked me into it.

So we got there and Tommy Cusack came to me; he said, 'Look, I'm in trouble – I've taken two rides in the same race!'

In those days, before the legalisation of betting shops created a pressing need for race entries to be sorted out a day in advance, horses were only committed to a race on the day itself. Jockey bookings were often made at a similarly late stage. This was why Michael could travel to the races without a booked ride and reasonably expect to pick up work.

MICHAEL

Tommy said, 'Will you ride one?'

I said, 'Not bloody likely. I'm not gonna ride around Kempton on a novice chaser, first time over fences.' I mean, you don't do that at Kempton – they were a bit big at Kempton. Anyway, he talked me round.

I went to canter to post and he wasn't a very impressive horse. I thought, 'Look after number one and see how you go.' Off we went, and he was giving me a lovely ride. This is quite clever, this horse: he could tap-dance in front of a fence.

Going to the second-last, I thought, 'I'll see if we've got anything left in the tank, see what happens.' I was about fourth or fifth at the time, looking after number one. And the next thing I remember is waking up in the ambulance room and Rex Hamey standing over me: 'Are you bloody coming home or not?' Everybody was very pleased, 'cos he was flying when he fell. I could remember that much.

The partnership was cemented when Michael won on Linwell at Warwick soon after. The horse was trained by Ivor Herbert, who was also a journalist and therefore barred by the Jockey Club from holding a trainer's licence, presumably on the grounds that it could give rise to a conflict of interest. However, there seems to have been no objection to the polite fiction that the licence for Herbert's yard was held by Charlie Mallon, who was in reality his assistant. Linwell was owned by the industrialist David Brown, whose initials had become famous over the previous decade through their attachment to the latest Aston Martin models, a business he owned.

MICHAEL

You always had to settle Linwell, drop him out. Of course, if he got beaten, Ivor and one or two people, they used to get the needle; they used to say I'd dropped him out too far. So they said, 'Ride him handy.' One time, Tim Molony gave me a bollocking: he said, 'You should know how to ride him by now – don't listen to them!'

Molony was well placed to comment, having been champion jockey five times. Michael did not enjoy one effort to comply with instructions to ride Linwell prominently, at Kempton, describing how the horse raced like 'a lunatic' and tried to bank some fences, meaning he used his feet to push off from the top of the fence instead of jumping it cleanly.

MICHAEL

He won three or four races at Cheltenham, and I learned a lot about him there because, coming down the hill, you could change gear: he was like a car. You could change gear and he'd go, and the faster you went, the further off the fence he would stand.

Linwell was allowed to start at odds of 100-9 in the Gold Cup. Michael had done his best to let punters know about the horse's chance, judging by a front-page preview in that day's Sporting Life. *'Linwell has several pounds to find,' wrote Man On The Spot, the* nom de guerre *used for decades by the* Life*'s chief tipster, 'though I should not be surprised to see him placed, for Scudamore, who will ride him, told me that he never settled at all in that last race at Kempton and we know that normally he races comfortably on the bit till asked to provide that usually devastating finishing run. He might spring a big surprise and Scudamore is confident he will.'*

MICHAEL

I was coming down the hill at a million miles an hour; there were about six horses in front of me. Well, he bloody took off at the second-last, and he landed in front. Somebody said, 'You silly bugger, you're in front in the Gold Cup – kick on!' That was wonderful.

'Michael Scudamore rode a copybook race,' reported the Life*'s Tom Nickalls, 'for he was content to lie last but three in the early stages of what must have been one of the fastest-run Gold Cups for several years.' George Milburn, who finished*

second on Kerstin, told Nickalls the winner had sealed it with a 'brilliant leap' at the second-last. But when he lined up as second-favourite the following year, Linwell ran out of luck.

MICHAEL

Mandarin fell in front of me. I hit him up the tail-end, and that buggered that up. He beat Kerstin on two occasions, and she won that Gold Cup.

He was a very underrated Gold Cup winner. Fred rode him once, in another Gold Cup, and he got hampered at the last. He would have gone very, very close. And then I think he got a bit of a problem. Charlie Mallon rang up one day, and he said would I like to ride him at Hurst Park. 'Yeah, love to!' He dropped his hind legs in the water and he had no chance, so I coasted home on him.

The press played hell: they said, 'Gold Cup winner tailed off, shouldn't have run . . .' Anyway, David Brown rang me one night, and he said, 'I was away when he ran at Hurst Park. What did you make of him?'

I said, 'He ran very, very well. I'm not at all worried about him.'

He said, 'Well, can you ride him at Lingfield next week?'

We won half a length, and we sat there in the members' bar, drinking champagne. He was a very nice man, David Brown. He said: 'That's good. I'll retire him now.' He just wanted to stuff it up everyone.

He wasn't a great horse to look at: he wasn't very big, he was a plain little thing. There wasn't much of him. He wasn't a Kauto Star.

If Peter was able to revise his career so as to have ridden a Gold Cup winner, the simplest thing to do would be to stay with David Nicholson rather than moving to Fred Winter in the spring of 1986. He would then have been on Charter Party when he won the great race two years later, a race in which Peter was in fact third on Beau Ranger, a 33-1 shot trained by Martin Pipe. 'Charter Party, when I rode him, he was a bad jumper with a wind problem,' Peter recalls, but the horse had a wind operation in the summer after Peter left the yard.

A year before his retirement, Peter had what seemed a golden opportunity to win the Cheltenham race. His Gold Cup mount in 1992 was unbeaten in three runs since joining Pipe from Jim Dreaper. He had cuffed Party Politics by 20 lengths in the Welsh National, giving him 19lbs. He had won the Irish Gold Cup by almost as far. Who could doubt the claims of Carvill's Hill?

TOM

When Carvill's was running, we all of us felt the pressure. I couldn't watch him. I went up to Chepstow when he won the Welsh National: I remember not watching it until he turned into the straight.

The Gold Cup made for gripping viewing throughout. In contrast to his previous races, Carvill's Hill was never given a moment's peace, being joined for most of the first circuit by the free-going Golden Freeze. Peter was happy to settle behind that rival but, when Michael Bowlby steadied Golden Freeze after the second fence, Peter steered around him. Bowlby then made a visible effort to urge Golden Freeze forward to stay with the favourite. Describing the race live for the BBC, Sir Peter O'Sullevan said Golden Freeze was 'clearly trying to bustle him'.

PETER

In a race, you think, 'Well, for fuck's sake, go on or stop.' But I'm happy, I don't care. Even if he's doing it on purpose, I'm on such a good horse that it makes no difference anyway.

Carvill's Hill made three significant errors on that first circuit while racing alongside Golden Freeze, but moved into a clear lead on the final lap and still looked the likely winner at various points, despite the earlier mistakes.

TOM

Coming down the hill, he takes off again. One by one, he's got them at it. I remember thinking, 'He can still win this,' especially being such a relentless galloper. You'd think he'd outstay them all. He changes his legs turning in, going to the second-last. He's trying, he's really, really trying, but he's only on two legs by now. Dad straightens up, and now the writing's on the wall. Poor old boy. And he'd given Dad absolutely everything. But his body was always fragile – that's how Martin came to have him. If he didn't have a fragile body, Jim Dreaper would have won three Gold Cups with him.

Carvill's Hill came home a tired last of the five finishers, and was found to have pulled muscles in his chest and suffered a tendon injury. Jenny Pitman, trainer of Golden Freeze, found herself accused of having run the horse as a spoiler, to unsettle the favourite and thereby improve the chance of her more fancied runner, Toby Tobias. She denied it furiously. Peter said Bowlby had apologised to him in mid-race, saying: 'I didn't want to do this. I hope you win.' Pitman said Bowlby denied saying any such thing, when she pressed him on the subject. Resentment between the two camps ran very high.

PETER

Where people got me wrong with the Jenny thing is, I don't think Golden Freeze had any bearing on the result. If Carvill's couldn't stand up to that, then he didn't deserve to win a Gold Cup. If Michael hadn't apologised to me, I wouldn't have thought a thing about it.

TOM

Look, Carvill's Hill probably wouldn't have won the Gold Cup anyway, however it was run. He never ran again after this; he came back with his injuries and things. But I just think the way in which it was done was wrong.

PETER

To put the Carvill's Hill incident in perspective, I was told to go fast on Beau Ranger in the 1987 King George, to take on Desert Orchid. But I didn't keep reining back or anything: I just went very fast on him. Unfortunately, I didn't realise that Cybrandian would be doing something similar. So there were three of us going flat out. Somebody said we went quicker for the first two furlongs than they did in the Guineas . . .

Twenty years after Carvill's Hill, it was Tom's turn to brush up against Gold Cup glory, thanks to a 50-1 shot.

TOM

I knew The Giant Bolster was a good horse, but I thought he had a fair bit to find. He had bolted up at Cheltenham in a handicap two months before, in a manner you very rarely see a horse win any race. He was off a low weight, but he killed them, and they were good horses. They hadn't entered him in the Ryanair, so it was the Gold Cup or nothing, really.

David Bridgwater sent The Giant Bolster for a Gold Cup trial, the Denman Chase at Newbury a month before the Festival. Tom tried to repeat the tactics which had worked so well in the Cheltenham handicap and 'run them ragged', but three of his four rivals went past him pretty easily in the last half-mile.

TOM

So I thought, 'He's got no chance in the Gold Cup, he's gonna struggle to beat that lot.'

But Dad rang me on my way home and said, 'If he's going to run in the Gold Cup, you can't ride him like that. You have to show a bit more panache. Those good horses, you'll just end up giving them a lead. You can't do that, you'll have to do something differently on him.'

So in the Gold Cup, we just took our time a bit, and I rode him with loads of confidence. He was a funny horse around Cheltenham – stones better round there than anywhere else. Eventually, I learned with him that if you jumped the water jump down the back the last time in touch, he'd win or go very, very close. The hard bit was getting him to the water jump in touch, because he was a bad jumper, he was slow. You couldn't afford to make any mistakes. You were nearly better off allowing him to take his time over one than being really aggressive over a jump and missing it. If you gave him a kick in the belly and tried to make him jump one, you'd lose more ground than if you just let him do his own thing. If you warmed him up, his jumping then got a bit better towards the end, though it still wasn't great.

I remember basically being flat out all the way, and then, all of a sudden, from the water jump to the top of the hill, he started going better and better and better. When I jumped the third-last, he wasn't running away or anything, but all of a sudden he was going better than anything else in the race.

We turned in, straightened up, and I remember it going through my mind: 'This is what you've been waiting for, practising for.' It was that moment when people talk about visualising where they are. Like Neil Jenkins says: when he's taking a kick for the Lions, he's in his back garden, practising at home, he's not in front of 80,000 people in Johannesburg. It was really weird: suddenly this thing came over me, going to the second-last. As a kid on my ponies, I'd gone round and round and round at home, building show jumps and going over them, for just this moment: I'd been practising riding in Gold Cups. I remembered that vividly, going to the second-last. It was suddenly as clear as daylight in my mind: *this is what you've been working towards for your 29 years.*

I'd ridden in big races and had good chances: Monkerhostin had been beaten a neck in a King George; Grands Crus went close in a Stayers'; Osana had run well in a Champion Hurdle – but none of those at any point had really looked like winning. Whereas this one is going to the second-last, in front, and he's not stopping. At that moment, you're not thinking, 'Bloody hell, this is a Gold Cup and this horse can't jump!' It's, 'Don't make any mistakes!'

He jumped the last two fine, but McCoy collared us at the last on Synchronised. Long Run came past us, then we came back past Long Run and finished second.

I just remember that deflation afterwards. Not, 'I wish I'd done this differently,' or 'What a fuck-up that was,' or anything like that. It was, 'Is that my only chance?'

It was hard to take, because it was an unbelievable ride on the winner. That was where I learned a lot from watching AP. All he concentrated on was Synchronised. He wasn't bothered how far back he was, he wasn't bothered about any of those things. It was just, 'I have to get this horse jumping and then try and get him to run well.' I don't think he thought he was ever going to win the race until jumping the second-last, and then all of a sudden he'd got Synchronised up and going and he knew he'd gallop all the way up the hill.

Sometimes in those races, you're trying to make the horse go faster than it's capable of; you're worried about your position in the race and everything going on around you. You need to take a step back and think, 'Right, I've got to get this horse jumping, and if it's outclassed, just allow it to work its way into the race if it can.' He did that, and it's a phenomenal ride.

Gold Cup chances don't come along that often. Kauto Star, that year, was pulled up. Synchronised had gone from being a high-class handicapper to suddenly being a Grade One horse – he'd won a Welsh National and a Midlands National, but never did you say, 'Christ, that's gonna win a Gold Cup,' until he'd won at Leopardstown the time before. They weren't even going to run him in the Gold Cup. They chucked him at Leopardstown over Christmas because they had nothing else for him, and he won that, and all of a sudden he was a Gold Cup horse.

It was a winnable Gold Cup. Coming back in front of the stands, you're thinking that next year, Bobs Worth is going to be in the race, Silviniaco Conti's going to be there, Grands Crus might be in the race. Is that the only chance I have of it? That was where the deflation came from.

The Giant Bolster ran a distant fourth to Bobs Worth the following year, on ground that was far too soft for him. But in 2014, the Gold Cup was once more run on good ground, and his latest run had been a highly encouraging seven-length success at Cheltenham in January.

TOM

It was very similar to the first Gold Cup: flat out all the way, keeping in touch and then suddenly, from the last water jump, I knew we were going to go very close. Going to the second-last, I thought we'd win it, but On His Own wiped us out, jumped very badly right at it. That cost us. We still jumped the last upsides with everyone. But it's not ideal to get a thump in the ribs at any point, especially not at the second-last in the Gold Cup. It had to make a difference. We were beaten three-quarters of a length, and he'd taken an absolute broadside.

The thing that probably cost him was his size and scope. He wasn't big enough to really stand off his fences and, however tough he was, he could get bullied by the bigger ones. On His Own was twice the size of him, has knocked into the side of him and I've noticed it, I've felt it, whereas it didn't make the slightest bit of difference to On His Own.

If he could jump like Dynaste, he'd have won a Gold Cup. If you could throw him at his fences and he'd come up for you and you could gain a length here, gain a length there, he'd have won a Gold Cup. But he couldn't do that.

Grandad told me this: watch horses run through the line. Some of them take a bit of time to pull up. The Giant Bolster after that Gold Cup, as soon as I stood up on him, in three strides he was walking. I remember thinking he'd given absolutely everything. He'd been to a place he'd never been before and he never wanted to go back. Everything else was cantering up to the top. He hasn't even got to the end of the rail and he's walking, head down. You see it every now and again. You watch one and think, 'That was impressive.' And then, three strides after the line, they take no pulling up and they don't want to do it again.

While The Giant Bolster put up a couple of big efforts in defeat after that, he didn't win again. He and Tom had one final tilt at the Gold Cup, in the 2015 race won by Coneygree, but pulled up on unhelpfully soft ground. As chance would have it, Tom was just a month away from his first ride on another horse with 'Gold Cup' written all over him.

TOM

I don't think anything Dad rode would have held a candle to Thistlecrack. To make your debut over fences in October and win a King George two months later . . . You don't appreciate it at the time but, thinking back, he won the King George. Christ! That makes him pretty special.

A latecomer to chasing, which he started at the age of eight, the Colin Tizzard-trained Thistlecrack went to Kempton as the easy winner of three pushover novice chases. On Boxing Day, he was facing Cue Card and Silviniaco Conti, who, between them, had won the King George for the previous three years. The sudden step up into a top-quality race had Tom worried.

TOM

What I didn't want was Paddy Brennan on Cue Card coming to me, going to the third-last at the top of the home straight. It's a tricky fence, and I thought his lack of experience of jumping at that pace could be the thing that might beat him. It's a big ask on your fourth start over fences, whether you'll be able to do it at that speed.

So when Paddy took me on down the back, I was delighted for two reasons. Either he'd fucked up and taken me on at the wrong time, or he had no other option. Looking back, I think he felt he had no other option. I don't think he realised how good Thistlecrack was, and how much he'd put them under pressure without doing anything at all. Paddy must have thought, 'I'd better go and put his jumping under pressure here.'

I thought all my Christmases had come at once when he did that. When he eyeballed me down the back, I thought, 'Here we go – we'll see what you're made of now.' Thistlecrack jumped all those fences fine. I just gave him a little squeeze off the bend and, as soon as he took off like that, I was delighted, because it meant I could jump the third-last on my terms and I wouldn't have to be rushed.

The home straight turned into a procession that day, and Tom was able to ease Thistlecrack down to score by a comfortable three lengths. He was immediately a hot favourite to follow up in the 2017 Gold Cup. It was a huge moment in Tom's life, with the promise of better to come. Alas, at the time of writing, the King George remains Thistlecrack's most recent victory. He was beaten a head by Many Clouds in a slog at Cheltenham the following month, and was soon found to have torn a tendon. An encouraging fourth in the next year's King George, which was just his second race after that injury, Thistlecrack was then sidelined again by a stress fracture in a leg. He is now ten. Perhaps there is still time for a last hurrah.

He had provided the Scudamore clan with a second success in the King George. Sixty years earlier, Michael's main concern on Boxing Day morning had been getting to the London track from his home in Herefordshire.

MICHAEL

We were snowed in. My brother towed me about four miles onto a main road with a tractor, a little Ferguson T20, and when we got to the main road my radio told me the racing was off. So he towed me back again. And then I moaned about it all day: 'Bloody hell, if they race tomorrow, I'm not going to get there.'

So I took a train from Hereford that night and went up to London. Stayed the night in the Savoy Baths on Jermyn Street, where we always did. You could stay there for 30 bob – you could bloody near live there. 'Cos you could go and have a drink and a meal and come back and sweat it off. And you always met somebody there, some of the jockeys or rugby players.

The following day, Kempton was able to race, and Michael got the leg-up on Rose Park, the least fancied of three runners saddled by Peter Cazalet. The others were Lochroe, who would win the race two years later, and the Queen Mother's Devon Loch, trying to atone for his extraordinary bellyflop in the Grand National nine months earlier.

MICHAEL

Rose Park was a top-class two-miler, and I remember seeing one or two jockeys run away with him going to post – he took off with them. He'd won some decent two-mile chases, and I suppose he got older, but he could still pull.

Cazalet said to me in the paddock,'If you can, hold him, 'cos he won't get the trip. But if you can't hold him, don't fight him.'

Well, my theory was not to fight a front-runner: just drop your hands on their neck and, if they're going to settle, they will. If they're not, the harder you pull against them, the harder they pull against you.

Rose Park duly settled into a rhythm at the front of the small field. Early on the second circuit, Michael sensed an opportunity.

MICHAEL

Going down the back, I suddenly thought to myself, 'I bet these buggers are talking to themselves because they know I won't get the trip.' So I slap him down the shoulder and give him a back-hander round the bottom, and went for my life. I think by the time they looked up, I was gone.

What I think was going through their minds, they all knew this Rose Park. They saw me go down the back in front and thought, 'Well, he won't get the trip.' So they rode it as if I didn't exist.

But I often think, from Cazalet's point of view, it wasn't the best result, because Devon Loch was second. He would probably rather he had won.

Great sporting drama is born of athletes like Linwell and Carvill's Hill, Thistlecrack and Rose Park. Sturdy yet vulnerable, they gave everything they had, again and again, and it was often good enough.

PETER

Gold Cup horses are heroes, aren't they? To a small group of people daft enough to stand on a hill on a Friday in March and worship their tenacity and bravery. There's something in us that still appreciates those horses. The reception the Gold Cup winner gets, you could put Royal Ascot, the Derby and all the Guineas together and not match it. And I think 75 per cent of it is for the horse.

Peter is not the only one who knows exactly how hard it is to lay hands on one of those horses. He puts on his most upright, respectable voice as he rehearses the cautionary advice he passes on to new owners with big ambitions.

PETER

When somebody comes to me and says, 'I wanna pay £100,000 for a horse' – which is nothing, really – you have to say, 'Well, look, you realise this is not an investment, you know . . .'

And £100,000 is just the beginning. Who can afford it? A football team, most of the time, in the end, you can sell them. You accept a boat's going to cost you, but at least it's got some residual value. Jumps horses have got no residual value. Owners are spending all this money just to win at Cheltenham. Financially, it's hopeless. But also, it's worth it.

The rewards include the chance to shine on the same stage that has made stars out of racing's leading players.

PETER

But, while we're celebrating AP McCoy and Willie Mullins and Gordon Elliott and Gigginstown, we've got to remember that, without Paddy Mullins or Willie Stephenson, or Fred Winter, Michael Scudamore, Tim Brookshaw and the Queen Mother, we wouldn't have this. And this is what I wanted to put on record: to thank those people, a long, long list of them, whose admiration of the horse made the Gold Cup what it is.

Of course it all costs money, but there is a purity to the sport that goes beyond that at times. Native River's people don't jump up and down at

Cheltenham because they've won a third of a million. They jump up and down because their horse is the best steeplechaser in Britain and Ireland.

That's the legacy. That's what we have to hand on.

INDEX

PHOTO ACKNOWLEDGEMENTS

Plates section 1

Page 2 (top) The Illustrated London News, (bottom) PA Images

Page 3 (top) PA Images

Page 4 (top) PA Images, (middle) The Dowdeswell Family

Page 5 (top) PA Images

Page 7 (bottom) Alex Livesey/Getty Images

Page 8 (top) Steven Cargill/Racingfotos.com,

Plates section 2

Page 2 (top) Edward Whitaker, (bottom) Peter Haygarth/Action Plus via Getty Images

Page 3 (top left) John Grossick, (bottom) Edward Whitaker

Page 4 (top) John Beasley, (bottom) Patrick McCann

Page 5 (top) Edward Whitaker

Page 6 Alan Crowhurst/Getty Images

Page 7 (top) Andy Watts/Racingfotos.com, (bottom) Steve Davies

Page 8 (bottom) Trevor Jones/Racingfotos.com